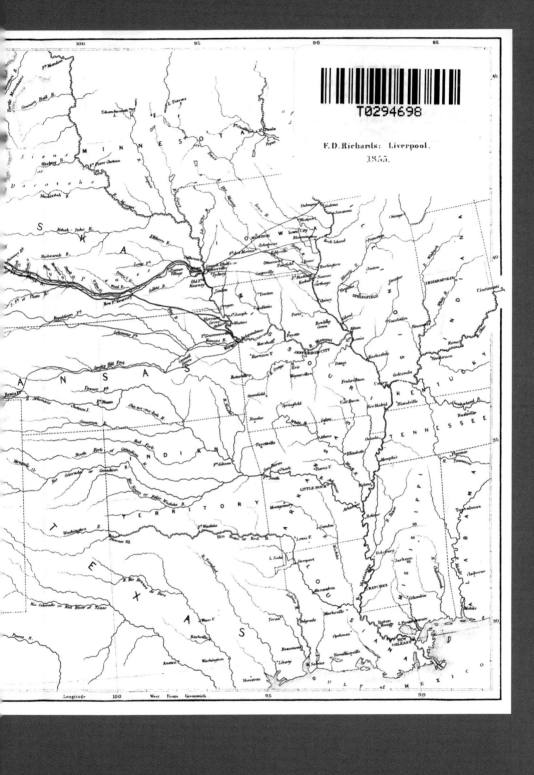

F.D. Richards: Liverpool.
1855.

Confessions
OF A
Revisionist Historian

✤

At one of the first meetings of the Utah Westerners in November 1969, A. R. Mortensen, David L. Bigler, and Everett L. Cooley presented an American Association for State and Local History award to Charles Kelly, noted curmudgeon, printer, artist, author, historian, and the first superintendent of Capitol Reef National Park. COURTESY OF THE UTAH STATE HISTORICAL SOCIETY.

Confessions
OF A
Revisionist Historian
☙
David L. Bigler
on the Mormons and the West

With an Appreciation by
POLLY AIRD

Edited by
WILL BAGLEY

NUMBER SIXTEEN IN THE SERIES
UTAH, THE MORMONS, AND THE WEST
Tanner Trust Fund and J. Willard Marriott Library

LIBRARY OF CONGRESS CATALOGING-IN-PUBLICATION DATA
Bigler, David L., 1927–
    Confessions of a Revisionist Historian: David L. Bigler on the Mormons and the
West; appreciation by Polly Aird; edited by Will Bagley.
        p. cm. — (Utah, the Mormons, and the West; v. 16)
    Includes index, maps, bibliography.
    ISBN 0692371206
    ISBN-13 978-0-692-37120-6 — (hardcover : alk. paper)
1. Bigler, David L. 2. Historians—Utah. 3. Pioneers—Utah. 4. Mormonism—
History—19th century. 4. Mountain Meadows Massacre, Utah, 1857. 5. Utah—
Description and travel. 6. Utah—History—19th century. I. Bigler, David L. and
Aird, Polly. II. Title. III. Series
2015
979.2'02—dc23   2015–16876

The paper in this book meets the guidelines for permanence and durability of
the Committee on Production Guidelines for Book Longevity of the
Council on Library Resources, Inc. ∞

Contents

❧

Illustrations

An Appreciation of
David L. Bigler

POLLY AIRD

THE FIRST BOOK I READ WHEN BEGINNING MY OWN JOURNEY
into Mormon history was Wallace Stegner's *The Gathering of Zion: The
Story of the Mormon Trail*. First published in 1964, it includes a final section, "A Word on Bibliography." Here Stegner speaks to the problem of
finding balance in telling the Mormon story:

> The literature on the Mormons is enormous, repetitious, contradictory, and
> embattled. . . . The more one wades into this morass the deeper he is mired,
> and the farther from firm ground. There *is* no firm ground here; there is only
> Mormon opinion, Gentile opinion, and the necessarily tentative opinion of
> historians trying to take account of all the facts and allow for all the delusion,
> hatred, passion, paranoia, lying, bad faith, concealment, and distortion of
> evidence that were contributed by both the Mormons and their enemies.[1]

Nevertheless, into this morass stepped David L. Bigler, newly retired
director of public affairs for U.S. Steel. David is descended from a number
of notable Mormon ancestors, including George D. Watt, the secretary to
Brigham Young who recorded in shorthand a great many of the leader's
sermons; and Jacob G. Bigler, bishop of Nephi in the 1850s who was
implicated in the Aiken Party murders. He is related to Henry William
Bigler and Azariah Smith, both Mormon Battalion veterans who were
on the spot when gold was discovered in California and whose diaries
established the event's correct date. No longer a Mormon himself, David

---

1   Wallace Stegner, *The Gathering of Zion: The Story of the Mormon Trail* (Salt Lake City:
     Westwater Press, 1981), 313.

did not take Stegner's "Gentile opinion" approach as had many before him. Instead, as he loves to say, he followed the facts and took Yogi Berra's advice, "It's amazing what you can see by just looking." David went on, "I looked . . . and, Shazzam!" He found firm ground.

I was present in a plenary session at the Mormon History Association's 2007 conference when a noted professor from Brigham Young University disparagingly called David, along with a few others, "revisionist historians." Another BYU professor sitting next to me whispered, "It's probably because they don't have PhD's!" More likely the label was aimed at any historian who appears to criticize Brigham Young. But whatever the reason or intent of the speaker, David took up the label in his good-humored and gentle way and made it a badge. In 2011 he proudly proclaimed his title as revisionist to the Utah Westerners. He concluded that talk with, "If ever there was a revisionist historian, I'm it. And if ever a chapter of our nation's history needed revising, it is this one. . . . This history [of mid-nineteenth-century Mormonism] must be more than a counterfeit rendition that encourages complacency and false pride. It must reflect the aims of all who lived it. And it must be as balanced and, above all, as honest, which means factual, as admittedly flawed historians can make it." As a revisionist, David has succeeded admirably, and we are the fortunate recipients of his fair and perceptive accounts.

David never hesitates to take on the most controversial subjects—the ones most in need of revising—often in the company of Will Bagley. The Mountain Meadows massacre is with little doubt the most difficult, complex, and emotional event in the early days of the Utah Mormons. In their comprehensive volume of documents related to the massacre, *Innocent Blood: Essential Narratives of the Mountain Meadows Massacre,* Bigler and Bagley suggest that the ideas of the early church are key to understanding the massacre:

> The bones [of the slain Arkansas emigrants] tell of forgotten doctrines and beliefs that no longer energize true believers: the Kingdom of God as an earthly state—the imminent coming of the Son of Man—oaths to avenge the blood of the prophets—American Indians as instruments of divine justice—the shedding of human blood for the remission of sins not forgiven by Christ's sacrifice—divine land ownership—unthinking obedience to higher authority—revealed justice—the sealing up against all crimes save

shedding innocent blood—the law of adoption—and others. All can be found at Mountain Meadows.[2]

David maintains that knowing Mormonism's founding beliefs and doctrines is the only way to fully comprehend Utah Territory in the 1850s. The biblical Book of Daniel was often quoted in convert diaries and was linked to the advent of Mormonism in Parley P. Pratt's 1837 highly successful missionary pamphlet, *The Voice of Warning*. It tells how the prophet Daniel interpreted the king's dream to mean that a stone "cut out of the mountain without hands" would break all man-made kingdoms into pieces and fill the whole earth.[3]

Reiterating these ideas after the death of Joseph Smith, Jr., the Twelve Apostles issued a proclamation to all the world: "Know ye that the kingdom of God has come, as has been predicted by ancient prophets... even that kingdom which shall fill the whole earth, and shall stand for ever." Further on it declared that this kingdom would "reduce all nations and creeds to one political and religious standard" and prepare the way for the "coming of the Lord."[4]

Such religious ideas led Brigham Young, if not the whole Mormon people, to relentlessly pursue divine sovereignty. The beliefs had both immediate and long-lasting consequences, for it was impossible for a theocracy to exist peacefully within a democratic nation. The thrust for theocratic sovereignty becomes the meta-theme in David's articles and talks. The theme appears, repeats, and grows more complex:

THE MORMON BATTALION. The Mormon contribution to the Mexican-American War moved five hundred church members to the West Coast. In addition, their government payroll enabled the main body of the Mormons to purchase wagons and oxen and all things needed to move west from what was then the United States to a place where they could establish an independent and godly kingdom.

---

2   David L. Bigler and Will Bagley, *Innocent Blood: Essential Narratives of the Mountain Meadows Massacre* (Norman, Okla.: Arthur H. Clark Co., 2008), 473.

3   See Daniel 2:34–45.

4   *Proclamation of the Twelve Apostles of the Church of Jesus Christ of Latter-day Saints to All the Kings of the World, to the President of the United States of America; to the Governors of the Several States, and to the Rulers and People of All Nations* (New York: Pratt and Brannan, 1845), 1, 6.

THE GOLD RUSH AND THE MORMON KINGDOM. Here we find the earliest conflicts between the church leaders and Gold Rushers who by circumstances had to spend a winter in Utah. Much of what being a U.S. citizen meant was denied to these winter residents, and instead they were subjected to theocratic law, denial of free speech, and little economic freedom. It was the start of the collision between the American republic and the Utah theocracy.

GARLAND HURT AND THE MORMON INDIAN POLICY. This article examines Brigham Young's view of the Lamanites as fellow latter-day sons of Israel with a major role to play in the Last Days. Indian agent Garland Hurt's experiences illuminate one of the main causes of the conflict between the Mormons and the federal government—reports that the Mormons had been influencing the Indians to take their side in any coming fight.

THE MORMON REFORMATION. To sanctify and prepare his people for the Second Coming and ready them to separate from the United States, Brigham Young instituted the Reformation. Beyond purifying the members and their homes, Young hoped to flush federal officials, apostates, gentile merchants, and any other non-Mormons out of Utah. The Reformation was the spiritual side of severing the connection with the rest of America and becoming a sovereign nation, or at least a state with officials of their own choosing. As such it is an integral part of the Utah War, even though the esteemed historian Leonard J. Arrington only mentioned it in passing in his biography of Brigham Young.[5]

THE GENESIS OF THE UTAH WAR. Millennialist beliefs were the basis of the Mormon conflicts in Missouri and Illinois, which in turn led to the rebellion against the U.S. government in 1857–1858. The Mormons viewed confrontation with the federal government as a necessary step before God's kingdom could "fill the whole earth," but it also underscored the impossibility of a theocracy ruled from the top down existing within a democracy, which governs from the bottom up.

THE MOUNTAIN MEADOWS MASSACRE. This heinous crime cannot be separated from the Utah War, as it arose in part from Young's plan to establish God's kingdom with the help of the Lamanites, in part from

5   Leonard J. Arrington, *Brigham Young: American Moses* (Urbana and Chicago: University of Illinois Press, 1986), 300.

war fever, and in part from religious fanaticism. This massacre, as well as other murders in 1857–1858, refute the idea that the Utah War was bloodless. Sadly, this violence continues to distract from the real accomplishments and good character of the majority of the nineteenth-century Mormon people. In David's words, it is "a black hole that swallows up and distorts much that is praiseworthy in early Utah history."

THE AIKEN PARTY MURDERS. Along with the Mountain Meadows massacre, these murders were among the crimes committed before, during, and after the Utah War under the justification of purifying God's land and hastening the day of his rule on earth. Ordered by church leaders, the Aiken Party murders in central Utah are a reminder of the absolute power of Brigham Young over all who entered Mormon territory.

THE ATTACK ON FORT LIMHI. This event dramatically changed Brigham Young's view of the impending conflict with the U.S. Army, which was camped in today's Wyoming but within Utah Territory's border. No longer could Young count on the full support of the Lamanites in a fight with the U.S. government—and so he backed down from a confrontation.

David found that each of the above events was directly related to Mormon ideas of how the Lord wanted his people to live and prepare for the millennium. But he also found that the early Mormon settlers were truly remarkable. Describing them in Brigham Young's Pioneer Camp of the Saints—a description that could apply to most Mormons in the first decades in Utah—David wrote:

> They were mostly farmers, but the band included architects, blacksmiths, carpenters, mathematicians, musicians, former Indian agents, politicians, potters, printers, slaves, and wagonwrights. They came from England, Scotland, Ireland, Germany, Denmark, Norway, and virtually every state in the Union. Men of such caliber were responsible for the success of the Latter-day Saints in settling the Great Basin, where they founded and built more than three hundred villages, towns, and cities.[6]

These hardened pioneers had gained leadership skills from leading companies overland to the Salt Lake Valley and creating and managing the settlements they established in Utah.[7]

6   David L. Bigler and Will Bagley, *The Mormon Rebellion: America's First Civil War, 1857–1858* (Norman: University of Oklahoma Press, 2011), 26.
7   Ibid., 192.

If the BYU professor at the Mormon History Association conference in 2007 berated David because of his presumed criticism of Brigham Young, did he have a case? Here David would no doubt reply with another quotation from Yogi Berra: "I never said most of the things I said." In his writings and talks, David does not criticize Young. Instead, he focuses on what actually happened. Young inevitably is there, the larger-than-life autocrat tightly in control of what went on. But rather than make character judgments, David focuses simply on the facts—and especially on the motivating beliefs—in as honest a way as the sources and his skills allow, and in so doing, he lets readers make up their own minds.

Thus we come to David's commitment to honesty in writing history. David was born into a Latter-day Saint family in Utah but some years later left his birth faith and eventually became an evangelical Christian. Some former LDS members and many evangelicals take up the banner of anti-Mormonism, but not David. Instead, his faith in Christ has led him to honesty in his life and work. Eschewing historical myths, familiar Sunday School or Institute accounts, and works by faith-promoting historians, he stands back and takes a wide view of all the facts. He then searches for consistency among primary sources and looks for fresh understandings. He is not one to worry about what church leaders or other historians might say—he simply stands by what he sees "by just looking." This quest for truth is related to his drive for justice for those who can no longer speak for themselves. Wanting to know what really happened, as far as any historian can decipher, takes him down paths that others are wary to tread on and often leads to tangled, difficult subjects. But David keeps moving forward, heartened by the biblical injunction to "Be not afraid."

Be not afraid, plus integrity. He sees these traits first in the Protestant missionary teachers who came to Utah after the completion of the transcontinental railroad and who then opened schools. He sees these in Sandra and Jerald Tanner and their work in the Utah Lighthouse Ministry. He sees these in the life and work of his friend Harold Schindler. And finally, he sees them in the bravery of one John Hawley, who voiced opposition to the Cedar City leaders' plan to massacre the Arkansas emigrants then surrounded in Mountain Meadows, as explained in his last chapter, "A Few More Good Men."

We also must never forget David's great love of trails. President in his day of both the Utah Westerners and the Oregon-California Trails Association, he gives voice to this interest in two of the last chapters included in this volume. First are the exploratory trips through the Great Basin made by James Hervey Simpson, which resulted in the route chosen for the Pony Express and the telegraph wires across today's Nevada. And secondly, David writes of the Lincoln Highway and the changing plans for its possible route through Utah in more modern times.

If I were asked to pick one quotation that best epitomizes David and his work, it would be from the biblical prophet Micah: "What doth the Lord require of thee, but to do justly, and to love mercy, and to walk humbly with thy God?"[8] Justice, mercy, and humbleness—these are the characteristics that best define David L. Bigler. With this volume, presented in his spirited and clear writing style, he leaves us a legacy of path-breaking research, honesty, and historical integrity.

---

8   Micah 6:8.

✤

David L. Bigler:
A Brief Biography

THE DISTINGUISHED AUTHOR OF THIS COLLECTION WROTE A "Biographical Brief" in 2014 that is just that—brief. Born on May 9, 1927, David L. Bigler is a native of Provo, Utah, a veteran of World War II and the Korean War, and a University of Utah graduate. He holds an Honorary Doctor of Letters degree from Southern Utah State College, now Southern Utah University, where he served as a member of the Institutional Council, 1969–1977. He retired as director of public affairs for U.S. Steel in 1986 to devote himself full time to the study of the overland emigration and the history of early Mormons in the West. He is a Fellow and Honorary Life Member, Utah State Historical Society; a former director, Utah Board of State History and Friends of the Marriott Library at the University of Utah; a charter member and first president, Utah Westerners; and past president of the Oregon-California Trails Association. His seven books and articles on early Utah, California, and Western history have won awards from the Utah State Historical Society, Westerners International, the Mormon History Association, the John Whitmer Historical Association, and Western Writers of America.

Mr. Bigler's typically modest biographical brief failed to mention significant accomplishments of a life dedicated to public and private service, beginning with serving as editor-in-chief of the University of Utah's daily newspaper, *The Chronicle*, and his years as a member of the Mormon Tabernacle Choir. He served as director of Public Relations, Mountain States District, U.S. Steel, where he worked with the corporation's most progressive leaders to improve the competitive position of Geneva Steel. The integrated mill near Provo, Utah, at that time produced much of the hot-rolled steel sheet, plate, and structural steel used in the western United States. This cooperative effort inspired Utah Valley steelmakers to help save thousands of high-quality jobs. Not a prideful but a profoundly religious man, Mr. Bigler does take satisfaction in the role he played in providing productive employment to thousands of workers throughout the Intermountain West and for his service as an elder in three Christian churches.

At the peak of his career in the 1980s, when U.S. Steel was one of the world's largest steel-making firms, he served as director of public affairs. Among community activities, Mr. Bigler served as chairman of Utah County's first United Way campaign, as a founder of Utah Heritage Foundation, as chairman of Utah's first Equal Opportunity Conference, and as vice president of the Utah Advisory Council for Vocational Education.

David L. Bigler writes "about people, not dates or events." He celebrates the ordinary, forgotten folks who made this colorful history happen, not the better-known characters who made it so violent and controversial. Captivating prose and thoughtful analysis shows how much affection and sympathy he has for Saints and sinners alike. David and his wife, Evah, reside in Roseville, California.

✤

Editorial Notes

WRITING, DAVID BIGLER ONCE SAID, IS ORGANIZATION. HIS crisp, lively prose, with its sprightly transitions and wry asides, offers much for any writer to admire, while his spare, direct style reflects his training as a journalist. This collection of the historian's shorter works seeks to accentuate his gifts. "How I Became a Revisionist Historian" provides the author's own introduction to his work. Articles then proceed in chronological order. Subjects include the Mormon Battalion, the California Gold Rush, and the conflicts between the United States and Brigham Young's "theodemocracy" that led to the Reformation and the Utah War, with its two most brutal acts of violence, the Mountain Meadows massacre and the Aiken Party murders. Two selections and a remarkable love story cover aspects of the Mormon mission to the Indians at Fort Limhi, a central theme of Mr. Bigler's work. Articles follow on the U.S. Army's exploration of the Great Basin, the forgotten role of Christian educators in Utah Territory, and the first "coast-to-coast rock road." After two tributes and a concluding essay that calls on us to "be not afraid" and, when needed, to stand with "A Few More Good Men," the volume ends with a bibliography of Mr. Bigler's books, articles, and selected book reviews.

A few editorial housekeeping details: We have edited and updated these articles and presentations for clarity and comprehension, occasionally adding material that reflects recent discoveries and the expanding historical record. We use [sic] sparingly. In manuscript transcriptions, Mr. Bigler has capitalized the first word of sentences and added punctuation at their end. Brackets enclose letters or missing words added to original sources. Otherwise manuscript documents are presented as written. Newspaper citations seek to provide all the information needed to locate them, and when obtainable, include page and column information: 2/3. The book identifies the Church of Jesus Christ of Latter-day Saints and members of the faith using the popular terms: Mormons, Latter-day Saints, or LDS.

Since these essays initially appeared in noted journals with varying editorial standards, I edited the footnotes for consistency and simplicity but did not add annotations to selections that did not originally use them. We gratefully acknowledge the permission of the editors of the *Utah Historical Quarterly, Montana The Magazine of Western History,* and the *Western Historical Quarterly* to republish articles that first appeared in their pages. Most of these articles stand as published, but we occasionally incorporated evidence recovered after the initial publication—for example, the fate of Aiken Party member John Chapman is no longer a mystery. There is some repetition, which I have tried to minimize but not entirely eliminate, since it can reveal how a masterful historian's perspective and interpretation evolves and deepens over time. Source information on the original publication or presentation appears below the title of the entry, except for "More Than a Beacon: A Tribute to Jerald and Sandra Tanner," an unpublished original.

Our age of labels and intellectual ferment in historiography begs the question, "What sort of historian is David L. Bigler?" His investigative and interpretative techniques reflect Jack Webb's famous "Just the facts, ma'am" style of crime fighting. In a post-modern world, which calls into question whether facts, let alone truth, exist, this approach has fallen on hard times. University of Texas historian Randolph B. Campbell has characterized much modern historical writing as belonging to the "post-factual school," so our colleague Gustav Seligmann might identify Mr. Bigler as a "pre-post-factual historian."

Mr. Bigler has little time for post-colonialism, post-structuralism, or post-modernism. Except for being certifiably post-Marxist, he is neither pre nor post anything. He comes from the simpler school of history known as historicism, which Dorothy Ross explained as the idea "that all events in historical time can be explained by prior events in historical time." As Dale L. Morgan, Utah's most gifted Western historian, wrote in 1965, he has long been "more interested in practical questions, straightening out the enormous distortions of the record that I have found on every hand; and beyond that, being continuously interested in the causes that produce certain effects, and the effects that are produced by certain causes. Historians seem to have trouble enough with all these fundamentals, to say nothing of wrestling with large abstractions." Mr. Bigler's distinctive talent is his ability to examine the facts surrounding a historical event, evaluate the circumstances in an entirely new light, and step outside the box of the venerated interpretation to offer perceptive new insights into what happened and why.

On a personal note, I was delighted when Gregory C. Thompson, director of Special Collections at the University of Utah's Marriott Library and general editor of the Utah, The Mormons, and the West series, asked me to act as managing editor of the series' sixteenth volume. A number of possible objections sprang to mind, beginning with a long friendship and collaboration, credited or not, on so many books that critical wags sometimes refer to us as "Bigley" or "Bagler." We have adapted to such compliments and prize our great affection and enduring respect for our many friends and historians among the Latter-day Saints.

Dr. Thompson's request was an honor. People from all walks of life often tell me how much Dave Bigler's work has meant to them. Reading his first book in 1990 was a galvanizing experience for his historical apprentice, for he often delivered more insight and information in a hundred-word footnote than many historians could fit into a hundred pages. His example and advice have inspired all my subsequent work. It is a privilege to edit someone who is a better writer and historian, not to mention a better person, than oneself, and David L. Bigler is all three. This gentleman-scholar's heartfelt Christianity, unwavering integrity, generosity, consideration, and good humor have informed every aspect of his long life. In every way, David L. Bigler has set a high standard for historians of the American West.

WILL BAGLEY

❧

Abbreviations

FOOTNOTES USE THE FOLLOWING ARCHIVAL ABBREVIATIONS:

Beinecke Library	Western Americana Collection, Beinecke Rare Book and Manuscript Library, Yale University.
BYU Library	L. Tom Perry Special Collections, Harold B. Lee Library, Brigham Young University, Provo, Utah.
California State Library	California History Room, California State Library, Sacramento, California.
Huntington Library	The Henry E. Huntington Library, San Marino, California.
Journal History	Journal History of the Church of Jesus Christ of Latter-day Saints, Typescript, Church Library and Archives, Salt Lake City, Utah.
LDS Archives	Church Library and Archives, The Church of Jesus Christ of Latter-day Saints, Salt Lake City, Utah.
Marriott Library	Special Collections, J. Willard Marriott Library, University of Utah, Salt Lake City, Utah.
National Archives	National Archives and Records Administration, Washington, D.C.
Sherratt Library	Special Collections, Gerald R. Sherratt Library, Southern Utah University, Cedar City, Utah.
USHS Library	Utah State Historical Society Research Center and Library, Salt Lake City, Utah.

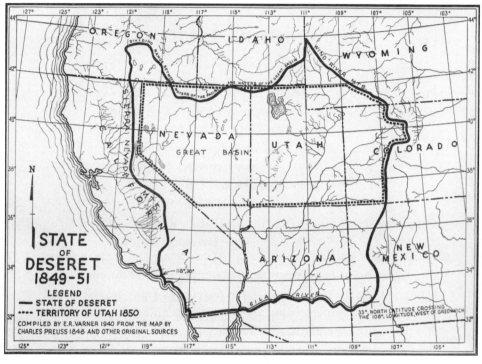

THE STATE OF DESERET AND UTAH TERRITORY, 1849–1850
Created in 1940 to accompany Dale M. Morgan's groundbreaking study, this map
shows the extent of frontier Mormonism's ambitions and the original borders of
Utah Territory. COURTESY OF THE UTAH STATE HISTORICAL SOCIETY.

❧

How I Became
a Revisionist Historian

Presentation to the Utah Westerners,
Salt Lake City, Utah, September 20, 2011. Since their
first meeting in December 1967, the Utah Westerners have gathered
monthly at the Alta Club. Carl T. Woolsey, M.D.,
is the club's other living founder.

As one of the last two surviving charter members of this august body, I appreciate your invitation to clear my conscience before joining the many dear friends now in our Celestial Division. I come tonight to confess: I am a revisionist historian. I didn't realize how far I'd come until a noted Mormon scholar, whom I respect, named me as such. Then it hit me. I had taken too seriously the teaching of Yogi Berra, who said, "You can see a lot by just looking." What I had overlooked, however, was that Berra also said, "I never said most of the things I said."

Either way, it got me thinking how I became a revisionist historian. It all began over forty years ago. During the ten years I served as president of this motley body, I always opened our meetings with a report titled "Tomorrow's History in Today's News." In it, I revised current events to make fun of politicians, environmentalists, and others who take themselves too seriously. From such practice, I rose—or fell, if you prefer—to become what I now am.

My late friend Harold Schindler unintentionally led me to my first Utah War revision. For over a week in 1858, Thomas Kane tried to get Brigham Young to allow him to offer food to the snowbound Utah

Expedition at Fort Bridger as an inducement to make peace.[1] He failed. On March 8, 1858, as Kane prepared to head for the U.S. Army camp, Young received shocking news. Indians had attacked Fort Limhi, the northernmost Mormon settlement, then in Oregon, killing two missionaries. On the very next day, Young dispatched his son with an offer to give hungry American troops two hundred cattle and ten tons of flour, at no cost. Joseph A. Young rode all night to give Kane the offer before he reached Fort Bridger.

I looked, as Yogi said, and, Shazzam! The over-sized Bannock chief known as "The Big Rogue" who led the attack on Fort Limhi had more to do with Young's sudden change of heart than Thomas Kane did.

Even greater temptations to revise outdated versions of the Mormon Rebellion of 1857–1858 have proved irresistible to Will Bagley, my esteemed partner, and me. If we had set out to write a history of the Civil War, we might have assumed that most readers would know something about its roots, such as slavery, and not dwelled on them. But when it came to our first civil war, we found it necessary to spend early chapters on actual causes because so few, including some here tonight, have a clue on how it began and why. And if they do, they won't say so.

Accordingly, the picture our latest book presents is strikingly different from the one advocated by most historians.[2] We looked and saw history repeat itself at three consecutive locations within a twenty-year period. There was the Mormon War in Missouri in 1838, the Illinois Mormon War of 1845–1846, and the 1857–1858 Utah War. We saw that the actions of a revolutionary millennial movement provoked conflict again and again—and again—with the same result each time. In our early chapters, we offer selected examples.

Underlying all of these causes was the issue that Thomas Kane put his finger on in 1849 that made confrontation predictable: the question of sovereignty. As Kane explained, an independent city, or territory, ruled

---

1   Son of a powerful federal judge and an influential political operative in his own right, Thomas Leiper Kane became renowned as an ally and defender of the Mormons. He was instrumental in the creation of the Mormon Battalion in 1846 and helped Brigham Young win his appointment as the first governor of Utah Territory in 1850.

2   The University of Oklahoma Press had published the Bigler-Bagley collaboration, *The Mormon Rebellion: America's First Civil War, 1857–1858,* earlier in 2011.

by the Almighty, could not co-exist within a democratic republic, ruled by its people, without conflict. Only as a sovereign state of the Union (as state jurisdiction was then recognized) or as a standalone nation would God's Kingdom be positioned to fulfill its destiny to supersede its parent, the United States, and go on to universal dominion within the lifespan of its followers at that time.

The failure to meet this condition in 1850 introduced a forty-year struggle to gain sovereignty, not just statehood. Brigham Young himself said statehood was simply desired "for the independent sovereignty which the act of admission carries with it."[3] The Mormon Rebellion of 1857–1858 is exceptional, for it represents the only attempt to free God's Kingdom from the bonds of territorial rule, a form of colonialism, by force of arms and win the sovereign standing of nationhood, not just statehood. It witnessed declarations of independence and a stunning assertion of sovereignty that Washington could never allow to stand. More on this shortly.

In the meantime, the singular nature of this conflict and its outcome gave many opportunities to revise this story to make it more honest, which means factual and internally consistent. Like the Bannock raid on Fort Limhi, we discovered that the most significant events were those fictionalized or ignored by revisionists before our time and faithfully followed by later revision-keepers, as if copying holy writ, to create a spurious past. Thanks to both, in time, the bogus became the real thing.

We begin some illustrations with an episode that receives little or no coverage in Utah's history—Brigham Young's 1857 trip to Fort Limhi at the zenith of the great Reformation to sanctify his people prior to taking an independent position from the United States. He announced his decision to go there less than a week after couriers from the Mormon colony delivered a description and map of Bitterroot Valley and the Upper Missouri country. A party from Fort Limhi had explored this region and concluded that it would become the future abode of the Saints.

Young would see for himself. He would evaluate the potential of the northern region as a future home in the event that latter-day Israel lost its bid for sovereignty. A favorable assessment would largely rest on an

---

3   Young to Smith, Bernhisel, and Taylor, August 30, 1856, Brigham Young Papers, LDS Archives.

all-Israel partnership of the House of Joseph between white Mormons with Ephraim's blood in their veins, and powerful northern Indian tribes, or Lamanites, believed to be progeny of Jacob's other grandson, Manasseh. Accordingly, Young came bearing presents for Native leaders in Oregon Territory, far outside his jurisdiction as head of Utah Indian Affairs. Also traveling with him was Ute chief Arapeen and a picked party of settlement, military, and religious leaders whose makeup reveals the trip's importance. To go both ways, southern Utah's Nauvoo Legion commander, William H. Dame, had to go as far as from Nauvoo on the Mississippi to Salt Lake Valley.

Later, Young refused to say where his people would go in the event that the United States sent an overpowering force against them. Said he, "I will leave it for you to read in the Book of Mormon and guess at."[4] A good guess would be the Mormon scripture's story of the good Nephite king, named Limhi.[5]

The Indian attack on the Oregon colony that liquidated this option apparently claimed another unidentified casualty. This was the bizarre military outfit known as the Standing Army of Israel, a full-time force of a thousand mounted riflemen or bowmen being organized and equipped in early 1858. Its purpose is unknown, but my guess is that it was to defend the borders of Deseret at various trail entries in alliance with the Native cousins of the Mormons, the Lamanites.

Compared with this example, it is hardly worth mentioning that Young had known for a month that U.S. soldiers were coming before the announcement was staged at Brighton on July 24, 1857, to fulfill his professed prophecy ten years before. But largely unreported was the arrival of Orrin Porter Rockwell's mail wagon the previous evening with Eleanor McLean Pratt, Parley P.'s emotionally unhinged widow, crying vengeance for the Mormon apostle's blood. Ten days later, a train of emigrants reached Salt Lake Valley from the same part of Arkansas in which Pratt was slain. Mostly women and children, the Baker-Fancher Party was just passing through on the way to California. God willing.

---

4   Brigham Young, Unpublished Discourse, August 16, 1857, Brigham Young Papers, LDS Archives.

5   See The Book of Mormon, Ether 13:1–10.

If Deseret had won independence, the question of Brigham Young's role in the massacre of all but seventeen of the party's youngest children would have been as dead as their still-unburied remains on the headwaters of the Santa Clara River. It did *not* win, however. And historians have been hard put ever since to clear him.

Will and I looked at the facts, just what is known for sure. We found that the atrocity at Mountain Meadows was not an anomaly unrelated to other events of the time. Instead, it was an intrinsic part of the Utah rebellion and fully consistent with Young's design to win the sovereignty of God's Kingdom, which rested decisively on alliances with the Lamanites. As the Fancher train headed south from Salt Lake, he instructed a trusted deputy on Loup Fork to tell the Indians, "If they permit our enemies to kill us they will kill them also." Make them our friends, he said, for *"all Isreal [sic] will be needed to carry on the work of the last days."*[6] "All Israel" meant a partnership of Mormons and Indians, with both the blood of Jacob and the House of Joseph in their veins.

One episode caught our eye. It took place during a week of unexpected visitors at Salt Lake. On September 8, 1857, U.S. Army captain Stewart Van Vliet arrived to line up supplies and winter quarters for the oncoming Utah Expedition. He was still there on September 10 when James Haslam delivered a now-vanished message from the Cedar City militia commander. The Indians have the emigrants corralled at the Mountain Meadows, it said. What should we do? Haslam left that day with Young's answer: in effect, do not interfere with the emigrants; the Indians will do what they please, but keep them on our side. Van Vliet would be at Salt Lake for three more days.

Question: Would the governor of an American territory inform an officer of the U.S. Army that a train filled with women and children was in deadly peril and seek his help? Would he show him the message from a local militia officer and his reply as commander of the territorial militia? Would he seize the moment to demonstrate his loyalty to the United States? Or, would he cover up what had happened and not allow Van Vliet to know that he had ordered territorial soldiers under his command not to interfere? The answer, we think, is consistent with his letter to the underling on Loup Fork and bares his culpability in the crime.

---

6   Young to Cunningham, August 4, 1857, LDS Archives.

Some historians might argue that he was no longer governor. Fair enough. But on September 12, two days after Haslam had headed south and while Stewart Van Vliet was still in town, Young submitted vouchers to U.S. Indian Affairs commissioner James W. Denver. Among other statements, he also told him that he had "learned by report that many of the lives of the emigrants . . . have been taken." But he failed to report the danger facing a wagon company in his jurisdiction and what he had done about it. He signed his letter, "Governor, and ex-officio Superintendent of Indian Affairs, Utah Territory." Even more revealing was what he did after Van Vliet left. Sparing the officer's feelings, he at least waited until the next day to declare the U.S. Army "an armed mercenary mob" and order territorial forces to repel their invasion. Historians typically refer only in passing, if at all, to the significant part of his September 15 proclamation. It came in the martial-law decree that "no person shall be allowed to pass or repass into or through or from the territory without a permit," which meant a passport.[7]

Now, behold, as Yogi said. In two dozen words, the appointed governor of an American territory, whose term had expired three years before, sealed off an area of the western United States large enough to enclose New England, New York, Pennsylvania, and Ohio that lay athwart major lines of travel and communication between the eastern and western sections of the American republic. A territory of about forty thousand inhabitants virtually cut in half a nation of some thirty million. Note, too, that what had already taken place at Mountain Meadows served notice of what could happen to anyone who invaded the Mormon-Indian domain without permission.

This astonishing assertion of divine sovereignty produced consequences both immediate and long lasting, but you would never know it from the standard Utah histories. California governor John B. Weller soon after demanded federal action to protect immigrants to his state. As he spoke, volunteer companies were forming in mining towns along the Sierra Nevada, ready to invade Utah from the west.[8] In the nation's capital, Secretary of War John B. Floyd said the government could no longer

7   "The Utah Expedition," House Exec. Doc. 71 (35-1), 1858, 184, 34–35.
8   John B. Weller, Inaugural Address, January 8, 1858, California State Library.

avoid a collision with the Mormon community. Young's border closure made bloodshed certain if he did not back down or get out of the way.

That he chose to back squarely down still isn't clear to many Utah historians. As a result, a misled *Deseret News* reporter wrote last May that a "tenuous peace had been negotiated."[9] No negotiations were held. To avoid bloodshed, President James Buchanan sent Lazarus Powell of Kentucky and Texan Ben McCulloch to deliver a final take-it-or-suffer-the-consequences offer of a pardon in return for a pledge to obey federal law. They had no authority to negotiate or settle past differences. As they presented Buchanan's ultimatum, Albert Sidney Johnston menacingly advanced his army, now reinforced to over five thousand men, toward the entry of Echo Canyon. Brigham Young saw the light. The only error Buchanan's agents made was to allow Young to prepare the minutes of their meeting. When McCulloch read them, the straight-shooting Texas Ranger fired back, "there isn't a sentence correct." He and Powell then wrote a record of what was said and sent it to "ex-governor" Young with a request that he certify it, which he did.

This is the only factual account of the commissioners' responsibilities and how they carried them out, as approved by them *and* Brigham Young. In it, they make clear that they had no power to negotiate, settle past grievances, real or imagined, or investigate alleged wrongdoings. Their sole duty was to give Mormon leaders a last chance to submit peaceably to the jurisdiction of the United States or suffer the alternative. There has never been any justification whatever to revise or play word games with their account of what took place.[10]

Meanwhile, our book also revises one of the better-known revisions of Utah War history, which holds that Brigham Young ordered Mormon troops to repel the U.S. Army, but not to shed any blood. He violated this claim so many times the miracle is that nobody I know of got killed in combat. How about this one: "Pick off their guards and sentries & fire into their camps by night, and pick off officers and as many men as

9   R. Scott Lloyd, "Buchanan's Secret Plan," *Deseret News*, May 29, 2011.
10 Powell and McCulloch to Floyd, August 24, 1858, in John B. Floyd, "Report of the Secretary of War," 1858, Sen. Exec. Doc. 1 (35-2), Vol. 2, Serial 975. See also Hafen and Hafen, *The Utah Expedition, 1857–1858* (Glendale, Calif.: The Arthur H. Clark Co., 1958), 355–359.

possible by day." But the order that stands out on this subject is the one he sent to Daniel H. Wells after learning that Johnston would winter at Fort Bridger and not try to enter Salt Lake that fall. But if they did try it, he said, "they could at once be surrounded with an overwhelming force and be used up or compelled to surrender."[11]

Those who seek the Almighty's hand in Utah history must look elsewhere. For the record shows that the credit for preserving the respect, growth, and acceptance, which the LDS Church rightly enjoys today, belongs in fact to James Buchanan and three West Point graduates named Captain Stewart Van Vliet, Colonel Albert Sidney Johnston, and Colonel Edmund Brooke Alexander.

Meanwhile, the new governor, Alfred Cumming, found out what Young meant in 1850 on learning that Deseret would be a territory with the unwanted name of Utah. Said he: "I am the governor of the state of Deseret. If they send a governor here, he will be glad to black my boots for me."[12] Eight years later, Brigham Young never meant to honor his pledge to obey federal law. Life went on as before. He was governor in fact. His replacement was governor in name. But as the nation divided between North and South, where do you think Lincoln might send troops to keep it stitched together, east to west? He could not suffer a repeat of Young's 1857 trails closure.

So it came to pass that more American soldiers arrived in 1862, only this time they came from the West. With them came an unacknowledged consequence of Young's shutdown of Utah's borders just five years before. They were the Third California Volunteer Infantry, recruited in Sierra Nevada gold mining towns, led by their Irish immigrant colonel, P. Edward Connor, whose company of Texas Volunteers won General Zachary Taylor's commendation at Buena Vista during the Mexican-American War.

Outnumbered nearly ten to one, they marched straight up today's Main Street, 750 strong, bands playing and flags snapping in the wind,

---

11   Young to Wells, Rich, and Grant, November 18, 1857, quoted in Bigler and Bagley, *The Mormon Rebellion*, 222.

12   David L. Bigler, *A Winter with the Mormons: The 1852 Letters of Jotham Goodell*, Volume 15 of Utah, the Mormons, and the West Series (Salt Lake City: Tanner Trust Fund, J. Willard Marriott Library, University of Utah, 2001), 50.

with the mounted color guard and Connor in front, followed by infantry, cavalry, artillery, and an infantry company guarding the rear. "Not a cheer nor a jeer greeted us," Chaplain John A. Anderson, former pastor of Stockton's Presbyterian Church and second president of Kansas State University, reported. A little boy, running alongside, said, "You are coming, are you?" to which it was replied that we thought we were, he said. "There was none of those manifestations of loyalty any other city in a loyal territory would have made."[13]

At First South, the column turned right and marched onto the bench overlooking the city, where Connor established Camp Douglas. His cannon on the high ground served notice that the time for sovereignty, either as a state or independent nation, was not yet. Utah, one of the first places settled west of the Missouri River, would instead be one of the last to enter the American Union as a sovereign state, at least as state sovereignty was then respected.

Equally hurtful were Congress's actions to dismember the Mormon dominion. In 1861, it created Nevada Territory. Some say it was a normal practice to make small states out of large territories. But a leader of the drive to create Nevada was Judge John Cradlebaugh, who tried to investigate Mountain Meadows and found himself exiled to Carson Valley. Another was California governor John Weller, who had called for federal action to protect emigrants from Mormons and Indians. The president who signed the bill as one of his last acts before Lincoln took his seat was James Buchanan. Later bites made Nevada a state larger than Utah, with a border at Wendover, thirty-six years ahead of our own state.

You've now heard my confession, which I make before this select body, as a condition of joining our many friends in the Celestial Division of Utah Westerners. If ever there was a revisionist historian, I'm it. And if ever a chapter of our nation's history needed revising, it is this one. For there is much we should learn from this teapot struggle between freedom and theocratic rule, beyond the faith and courage of our ancestors, as our country today faces similar challenges on a world scale.

---

13   *San Francisco Evening Bulletin*, November 1, 1862, 1–3, quoted in Edward W. Tullidge, *The History of Salt Lake City and Its Founders* (Salt Lake City: Star Printing Company, 1886), 281.

To identify and benefit from such lessons, however, this history must be more than a counterfeit rendition that encourages complacency and false pride. It must reflect the aims of all who lived it. And it must be as balanced and, above all, as honest, which means factual, as admittedly flawed historians can make it. At this critical time in our history, there can be no purpose that justifies any exception to this rigorous and righteous standard.

⚜

"Sword of Jehovah": The March of the Mormon Battalion

Remarks before the Sacramento Book Collectors Club,
November 12, 1999.

Note: This essay incorporates material
from Mr. Bigler's Foreword to Norma B. Ricketts,
The Mormon Battalion: U.S. Army of the West, 1846–1848
(Logan: Utah State University Press, 1996). The article concludes with
an appreciation of Norma Baldwin Ricketts,
late historian and our friend.

"HISTORY MAY BE SEARCHED IN VAIN FOR AN EQUAL MARCH of infantry," said Lieutenant Colonel Philip St. George Cooke on the completion of the two-thousand-mile march of the Mormon Battalion in 1846 from Council Bluffs, Iowa, to San Diego during the Mexican-American War to claim California for the United States. The battalion's commanding officer might have added that history could be searched in vain for a company of soldiers anything like this distinctive corps. For it holds a unique place, not only in U.S. military annals, but in the history of California and the story of America's move west during the nineteenth century as well.

Unlike other military outfits, the members of the battalion, with fewer than ten exceptions, were recruited from the same religious body. They made up a homogenous corps whose members marched to a radically different drummer than any other military unit that ever served in the American armed forces. Almost all belonged to the Church of Jesus Christ of Latter-day Saints, popularly known as the Mormons, a militant and highly controversial millennial movement founded in 1830 at Manchester, New York, by Joseph Smith, Jr., who claimed to be an American prophet.

Few if any of these so-called "volunteers" really wanted to enlist in the first place. Having been driven from their theocratic city-state on the Mississippi River, they were on their way to California or the Great Basin, both then in Mexico, to establish the Kingdom of God as an earthly state, ruled by God through inspired men as a condition of Christ's return to inaugurate His millennial reign. They believed that the American Constitution had been inspired for just this purpose and deeply resented being asked to serve a nation that had failed to protect them or preserve their religious freedom. Thirty-seven-year-old New Yorker Albert Smith voiced such feeling: "For government to make Such a demand when we ware driven from our homes & Possesions & were scattred upon the plains from Nauvoo to the [Missouri] river was more cruel than the Grave."

In contrast to the thousands of other young Americans who flooded recruiting stations in 1846, Mormon Battalion members answered a church call, not the voice of patriotism. They volunteered out of obedience to the leaders of their faith. Throughout their service, the majority gave their first loyalty to their church and the authorities it placed over them, not to the U.S. Army or its officers. Most of them served for only twelve months. While other Americans, usually outnumbered and long-since forgotten, fought desperate battles deep in Mexico, the battalion never fired a shot in combat with an enemy of their country.

Even the battalion's enlistment in July 1846 at Council Bluffs, Iowa, appears to have been the result of a bureaucratic snafu. Traditional accounts hold that, despite years of persecution, its members left their families in the wilderness to serve the nation in its hour of need. To Brigham Young goes the credit for a bizarre earlier version. He claimed the government's offer to enroll Mormon soldiers was all part of a conspiracy, hatched by Missouri senator Thomas Benton, to exterminate the troublesome faith as it headed west. Under this scenario, Benton figured that Young would reject the so-called "requisition," at which signal President

James Knox Polk would call on governors of Iowa, Missouri, and Illinois for troops "to march against us and massacre us all," Young said. But he had seen through this plot and foiled it with a ringing display of loyalty.

Both versions are inspirational, but less interesting than the real story.

Early in 1846, after years of conflict in Missouri and Illinois, the Mormons began their exodus from the United States. That same year, one of the nation's most important, if least recognized presidents, James Knox Polk, deliberately or not, goaded Mexico into firing the first shot of the Mexican-American War when he stationed a small American army on a disputed strip of sand, sagebrush, and swampland at the mouth of the Rio Grande. This provocation was the first step in his goal to annex New Mexico and the land he coveted most, California, to make the United States a continental nation.

Now, when it came to California, the president feared Mexico much less than he worried about Great Britain and the designs this old adversary had on the Pacific region. With one eye on the British, Polk was about to decide how large a force it would take to occupy New Mexico and move on to claim the isolated land of Alta California when on June 2, 1846, he received a letter from one Jesse C. Little, who said he was an "Agent of the Church of Jesus Christ of Latter-day Saints in the Eastern States." Little's appeal was not the first time the young religion had looked to the national government for help.

Just before his murder in 1844, Joseph Smith, Mormonism's founding prophet, had proposed federal legislation authorizing him to build military posts along the Oregon Trail and to raise a force of a hundred thousand volunteers, apart from the U.S. Army, to defend American interests on the frontier. Although he possessed no military training, Smith commanded the Nauvoo Legion, a private army of some four thousand followers, as a lieutenant general, a grade last held in the American army by George Washington. Not surprisingly his proposal, which was apparently linked to Mormon plans to create a sovereign state in the West, found few supporters in Congress.

Amid growing strife in western Illinois, Smith's successors looked to Washington for assistance to move their people to the Far West. On Brigham Young's orders, Samuel Brannan, a Mormon newspaper editor at New York, had gone to the nation's capital to seek federal contracts to finance a journey by sea of the faith's eastern seaboard members to the West Coast. Instead he became involved in a questionable land deal before sailing in February 1846 for San Francisco with some 230 Mormons on the ship *Brooklyn*—the only shipload of American emigrants ever to round Cape Horn and reach the Mexican province of Alta California.

In the meantime, as the first Mormon wagon companies prepared to evacuate the city of Nauvoo and cross the Mississippi River, the Quorum of the Twelve Apostles had named Jesse C. Little to head up the church's eastern operations, replacing the departed Brannan. With time running out, they handed the thirty-year-old New Englander an urgent mission: embrace any help Washington might offer in moving west. And Little, acting, he said, "promptly upon my own judgment," succeeded where others had failed.

The key to his success came in the form of a five-foot-four but feisty new friend, who took up the Mormon cause after hearing Little preach in Philadelphia. Twenty-four-year-old Thomas Kane was the son of an influential Democratic judge and a disciple of Auguste Comte, father of so-called "scientific socialism." A self-appointed humanitarian, Kane was also a gifted political operative. It was undoubtedly he who advised his new Mormon friend to play on Polk's fears of a British plot to take over California. When all else failed, Little wisely decided to take Kane's advice. He wrote a respectfully worded but not so subtle threat to the president of the United States.

Little opened his letter with an emotional account of how the Mormons had been persecuted for their religious beliefs. They had been driven into the "howling wilderness," he said, to make new homes in the very place Polk wanted to annex to the United States: California. He said that as many as fifteen thousand Mormons were already on their way there, that thousands more were preparing to go, and that another forty thousand from Great Britain planned to settle there. These numbers, outrageously exaggerated, added up to at least four times the known population of Alta California in 1846, not counting Indians.

Despite the injustices they had suffered, Little went on, the Mormons were "true-hearted Americans." They would never seek help from a foreign power, he said, unless their own government "will not help us, but compel us to be foreigners." He might have said British, but Polk got the point. On the very day Polk received this coercive letter, he decided to allow a "few hundred of the Mormons" to serve with the occupation forces in California. The reason, he said, was "to prevent this singular sect from becoming hostile to the U.S."

While Polk yielded to Little's thinly veiled threat, he nevertheless insisted that no members of the faith should be enrolled in the army *before* they reached the West Coast. His policy was clearly stated, but it was unintentionally nullified by a carelessly drafted order from the secretary of war that appeared to authorize Colonel Stephen Watts Kearny to enlist *on receipt* a battalion of Mormon infantry to serve in his little Army of the West.

So, contrary to the president's expressed intention, which was that no Mormons be enrolled before reaching California, an officer from Fort Leavenworth appeared in June 1846 at Mormon emigration camps in Iowa. First Dragoons captain James Allen would have little trouble signing up the five hundred recruits he was authorized to enlist. With Brigham Young himself acting as recruiting sergeant, Allen soon had plenty of so-called "volunteers" to fill the muster rolls of five companies, even if many of them did fail to come within the age limits of eighteen and forty-five.

To the young religious body, the enlistment returned many benefits, including urgently needed approval to settle temporarily on Indian lands along the Missouri River and time to make ready for the larger move west. It opened a way to relocate five hundred followers to California at government cost. And it provided cash dividends in soldiers' pay and clothing allowances to finance the Mormon emigration to Salt Lake Valley the following year.

What the nation received, in return, bore little resemblance to the new regiments that sprang up that summer, filled with young men eager for adventure and bursting with patriotism. Instead, it was a rough slice of the refugees who flooded Mormon emigration camps that year across Iowa. In age they ranged from fourteen to sixty-eight. Some rode in wagons, too sick to walk; and one died on the short march from Council

PHILIP ST. GEORGE COOKE
This image from the June 12, 1858, issue of
Harper's Weekly captured this striking and
capable officer more than a decade after
he led the Mormon Battalion from
New Mexico to California in 1846.

Bluffs to Fort Leavenworth. According to battalion historian Norma
Baldwin Ricketts, more than thirty brought their wives with them
(senior captain Jefferson Hunt took two), plus more than forty children.
Including family members and assorted camp followers, they added up
to over six hundred. Seldom, if ever, would Fort Leavenworth see the
likes of the aspiring soldiers who arrived at the Missouri River post on
August 1, 1846. From such singular and unpromising beginnings would
come a unique corps, one whose members would take part in events of
such magnitude from 1846 to 1848 that they shape the lives of Americans
in our own time.

WHEN CAPTAIN PHILIP ST. GEORGE COOKE OF THE FIRST
Dragoons, a superb field officer and a stern disciplinarian, took command
of the Mormon Battalion at Santa Fe in October 1846, he was deeply dis-
appointed with his "extraordinary assignment." The thirty-seven-year-
old professional soldier had hoped to win glory and advancement at the

seat of conflict in the war with Mexico. Instead he had been handed the most remarkable body of volunteers ever to report at Fort Leavenworth for duty in the U.S. Army.

It hardly took eighteen years of service on the American frontier for the six-foot-four officer to see that some of the men assigned to his command were too old, others too young, and that the whole outfit was "embarrassed by many women." Cooke thought his untrained soldiers often showed "great heedlessness and ignorance, and some obstinacy." It was certainly true that these men usually marched to a different drummer than the one to which a West Point graduate was accustomed.

The newly breveted lieutenant colonel trimmed the collection of refugees into an efficient, if untrained, body of some 336 muskets. It was hardly a crack outfit, but it was now equal to the task of opening a new wagon road to southern California. Cooke would change his mind about his Mormon footmen by the time the battalion reached the Pacific, completing one of the longest marches in the annals of military history. Of all the apocryphal stories about the battalion, the one that rings most true is that Cooke bared his head in tribute to his former comrades when in 1858 he rode into Great Salt Lake City at the head of the Second Dragoons, a regiment in Albert Sidney Johnston's Utah Expedition.

The Mormon Battalion's chosen few would go on to write their names everlastingly in the history of California and the West in ways historians only now are beginning to recognize and understand. It is difficult to find many noteworthy events in Western history between the critical years 1846 to 1848 in which members of the Mormon volunteers did not somehow take part. They made possible Brigham Young's 1847 pioneer expedition to Utah, occupied California for the United States, took part in the 1848 discovery of gold at Sutter's Mill, opened the Mormon-Carson Emigrant Trail over the Sierra Nevada, and drove the first wagons over the Spanish Trail and Hensley's Salt Lake Cutoff of the California Trail.

These and other exploits have been more or less recognized over the years. Not so well known or understood, however, has been the larger role the Mormon Battalion performed in American and Western history. Too often historians seemed to adopt the limited outlook of Company C's Third Sergeant, Daniel Tyler, as reflected in his highly partisan and outdated account, *A Concise History of the Mormon Battalion in the Mexican War, 1846–1847,* first published in 1881. From that perspective, the march of the volunteers appears to go forward as a kind of heroic, self-contained epic possessing little relation to the world around it. For Latter-day Saints, the story is without question inspirational and faith promoting. But the failure to step back and see it in relation to the larger picture of American history has resulted in the undervaluing or forgetting altogether of some of the command's most notable contributions.

To focus, for example, on the battalion's Battle of the Bulls as a significant event in itself overlooks the important relationship that exists between this bovine encounter on southern Arizona's San Pedro River and President James Polk's plan to take over the region that now forms most of the American Southwest. The connection between the bullfight and Manifest Destiny lies in the answer to an obvious question: Where did the wild bulls come from in the first place?

All those belligerent bulls came from an abandoned ranch one Ignacio Perez established in 1822 under a grant from the Mexican government to create a buffer against Apache incursions from the east. By 1846 the invading warriors had overrun the region and turned Perez's 73,240-acre spread and its animals into their own game preserve, where they hunted the cattle left behind as they did any other game. Easiest to bring down safely were the cows and calves, which left the bulls to grow older, wilder, and more aggressive.

As this episode illustrates, except for a little island of Mexican soldiers and their suffering families at Tucson, the northern Sonoran region had reverted to Indian control by 1846 as the Hispanic frontier effectively retreated south of the present international border between Arizona and Mexico. The Mormon Battalion's march across the Southwest demonstrated that Mexico's claim on the region was hollow and that an expansionist president's bid for sovereignty was as good as that of anyone else except native Indians, including the Pima and Tohono O'odham but not including the Apaches, who were themselves not original inhabitants.

Nor was the brief but exciting fight with these dangerous animals on the San Pedro River the only evidence that the land would belong to whoever had the will to occupy, govern, and defend it. Mexico's failure to protect its northern provinces, following independence from Spain in 1821, exposed its colonies in New Mexico and southern Arizona to a prolonged bloodletting. As Colonel Cooke noted in his December 1846 letter to Sonora's governor, the Mexican government had done nothing to defend his province against this incessant attack. Despite the remarkable courage of a handful of local Hispanic soldiers, by 1846 the actual dividing line between Mexican authority and control by hostile Indians lay far to the south of any border drawn on maps of the period.

Even at the time, many Americans felt that the United States had unjustly acquired today's New Mexico, Arizona, and California from its weaker neighbor to the south. Yet the march of the battalion demonstrated that Mexico's claim to the Southwest was at least as problematic as that of the United States, which purchased this region under the Treaty of Guadalupe Hidalgo. Mexico's power was in decline. Independence movements in New Mexico and California challenged the authority of the remote central government. Bands of Navajo and Apache Indians, friendly at first to Americans, were implacably hostile toward Mexican intruders and other tribes. Increasingly, these native inhabitants ruled the land east of California and west of the Rio Grande.

Without firing a shot, the Mormon infantry marched across the width of Mexico's northern provinces and built a wagon road as they went. The invasion of Kearny's little Army of the West suggests that the claim of an expansionist president, James Polk, was at least as good as any other, with the possible exception of the oldest native peoples, who were themselves being displaced by Navajo and Apache invaders. The most effective means of conquest, employed by both Cooke and General Stephen W. Kearny, was not muskets or money but the promise to protect the inhabitants from hostile Indians. The American claim gave Mexican colonists not only a promise of political freedom, but hope of safety. Easily given, such pledges took forty years to fulfill.

Cooke's decision to leave the old Spanish road that ran between the abandoned Santa Rita copper mines and Janos, Mexico, was not taken in answer to the prayers raised by the unit's spiritual leader, Levi Hancock. Instead of taking the roundabout road to Janos, Cooke headed due west from the Rio Grande. His purpose was to find a shortcut to

San Bernardino Spring, a historic oasis on the present border between Mexico and the United States in southeastern Arizona—the destination Cooke had in mind all along. The alternative was to go the long way around by known roads to the south, via Janos and Fronteras, where the battalion might be exposed to military garrisons at both places.

Cooke's report and the subsequent California Gold Rush pointed up the importance of the Gila River's southern tributaries, the San Pedro and Santa Cruz rivers. By demonstrating the significance of the region south of the Gila as a corridor of commerce and travel, the battalion's march influenced the Senate's decision in 1854 to acquire for ten million dollars a block of Mexican territory of almost incomparable worth. Seldom has the nation gained so much for so little. Known as the Gadsden Purchase, this 29,640-square-mile section, taking in Tucson, encompassed a natural railroad corridor and a treasure house of silver, gold, copper, and other valuable metals.

More immediate dividends came from the battalion's work to open a wagon road from New Mexico to California, but it also paid off in another often overlooked respect. In opening a direct southern road to the Pacific, the Mormon footmen constructed a new thoroughfare known as Cooke's Wagon Road that cut almost straight across the historic north-south flow of commerce and travel on existing Spanish highways. Three years later, the route became part of the Southern Trail to California, followed by thousands rushing to the gold fields along the Sierra Nevada. Cooke's new road demonstrated that a route west, well to the south of the Gila River's upper reaches, was not only feasible but the way of the future. Portions of the new route would become thoroughfares for emigrants on the Southern Trail, as well as for the San Antonio–San Diego Mail Line, and for the Butterfield Overland Stage.

In California Cooke's command arrived too late to take part in the last battles of the American occupation but just in time to carry out President Polk's orders to treat the people of the region as fellow citizens, not as subjugated enemies. As time goes on, it becomes increasingly clear that the occupation of New Mexico and California during the Mexican-American War was among the most decisive chapters in all of American history. Polk had authorized Kearny to establish civil governments in

New Mexico and California but had cautioned him to "act in such a manner as best to conciliate the inhabitants." Unfortunately, glory-seeking countrymen had gotten to California first and grossly violated the letter and spirit of the president's instructions.

Commodore Robert F. Stockton, commander of the U.S. Navy's Pacific Squadron, combined forces with John C. Fremont and the California Battalion—a rough mix of freebooting mountaineers, Indians, and emigrant volunteers—to occupy strategic points and set up their own government by right of conquest. The people they presumed to govern had been largely independent for decades. At first they had seen little to gain from opposing the American takeover. But oppressive actions by Stockton and his ambitious underlings soon provoked the Californians to take up arms against the Yankee intruders. Before the revolt was defeated, it would claim the lives of several promising U.S. Army officers and leave a legacy of bitterness among the former citizens of Mexico.

The subsequent arrival of Colonel Cooke and his Mormon foot soldiers after their epic march put armed weight behind General Kearny's assertion of his authority to command American forces and establish a civil government in California. Prior to the Gold Rush, the non-Indian inhabitants of California numbered fewer than fifteen thousand. Some 336 Mormon muskets under a capable officer like Cooke were more than enough for Kearny to uphold his authority against rebellious Californians, hostile natives, insubordinate officers, or reckless Americans.

The good behavior and industry of battalion members would accomplish far more than the muskets they shouldered in restoring trust in the new government and its desire to defend the rights and interests of all its citizens. They protected local leaders, who had supported the American occupation and were seen as traitors by some of their former countrymen. They guarded ranches against attacks by hostile natives, who were once pacified under the Spanish mission system but had become increasingly warlike since the 1833 secularization of the missions. And they dug wells, made bricks, and built new buildings to improve community life at Los Angeles and San Diego.

Although few in number, the Mormon volunteers were an important reason the United States was able to pacify a region of proud and independent people as large as California. Colonel Richard B. Mason, who replaced Kearny as military governor, praised the unit's "patience, subordination, and general good conduct." From local citizens, he said, "not a syllable of complaint has reached my ears of a single insult offered, or outrage done, by a Mormon volunteer." For the nation's citizen soldiers during the War with Mexico, it was a singular record. Elsewhere, General Zachary Taylor said "extensive depredations and outrages" had been committed upon the peaceful inhabitants. "Were it possible to rouse the Mexican people to resistance," he went on, "no more effectual plan could be devised than the very one pursued by some of our volunteer regiments."

If their good conduct contributed to the peaceful acquisition of California, it was not the only noteworthy achievement by battalion members. Fifteen men selected from four companies escorted General Kearny and party, including John C. Fremont, to Fort Leavenworth and Fremont's court-martial for insubordination. Near Donner Lake in 1847, they buried the bodies of Donner Party members who had perished over the previous winter.

Months later, battalion members in California would witness an event of such historic importance it would transform the nation almost overnight and set off a massive population shift west, which continues, to the consternation of some, still today. Two of these men—and two only—would record the discovery of gold at Sutter's Mill on the day it happened. Nineteen-year-old Azariah Smith and Henry William Bigler were employees of James Marshall and John Sutter. Their journals establish beyond doubt the name of the discoverer, James Marshall, and the date of his find, January 24, 1848. And they stamp as false the claims of many self-professed discoverers who later tried to win a share of the limelight.

Two other battalion veterans, Sidney Willes and Wilford Hudson, soon afterward scored the first major gold strike when they discovered the rich Mormon Island placer diggings at present Folsom, which became the destination of the 1849 Gold Rush. Samuel Brannan, then California's head Mormon, imposed a 30 percent "rent" or "tax"—not a tithe—on the gold his fellow Latter-day Saints harvested from the American River in return for undefined services to secure the claim. William Tecumseh Sherman recalled that a miner asked military governor Richard Mason, "what business has Sam Brannan to collect the tithes here?" Colonel Mason answered, "Brannan has a perfect right to collect the tax, if you Mormons are fools enough to pay it."

As Brannan laid the foundation of his wealth, and fortune seekers around the world braced themselves to risk life itself to get to the gold fields, a company of battalion veterans and Mormons from the ship *Brooklyn* turned their backs on the riches of the earth. Instead they headed east on the line of present State Highway 88 to rejoin their families and faith in Salt Lake Valley. In going, they blazed a new wagon road, which crossed the Sierra Nevada at Carson Pass and became in 1849 the main thoroughfare of the rush to the new El Dorado. And this was only one of many western routes opened by battalion members and followed today by federal and state highways.

In the beginning, the Mormon Battalion was an unhappy command that seethed with resentment and outright rebellion. Not only did its members assign their allegiance to a higher authority, they instinctively rebelled against the notably harsh discipline of the antebellum U.S. Army. At the time, most gave little thought to the momentous events they took part in. They simply desired to return to their families, make new homes, and establish God's Kingdom in the American West. Only in later years did they come to realize what they had accomplished and take pride in their service.

Until 1996, when Norma Baldwin Ricketts published her landmark work, *The Mormon Battalion: U.S. Army of the West, 1846–1848*, the story was usually told as an inspirational, faith-building religious epic with little relation to surrounding events or the rest of the world. Now historians have at last begun to appreciate the larger role of the Mormon volunteers in the history of California and the American West and value the vast store of firsthand accounts about this region and its people they left behind. Ricketts related the experience and placed it in the context of the times, using a rich selection of original documents, most written by the volunteers themselves and never before published. Such primary sources open a priceless window on the Southwest and California and its inhabitants between 1846 and 1848. They offer eyewitness accounts of great events—the occupation of New Mexico and California, the opening of major transportation routes, the discovery of gold, and Mormon plans for an independent state in the West—that make this period one of the most important in U.S. history, a time that affects in ways unimagined the lives of Americans still today.

NORMA BALDWIN RICKETTS: AN APPRECIATION
by Will Bagley

Born in Holbrook, Arizona, on September 23, 1921, Norma Baldwin Ricketts grew up on the Navajo, Hopi, and Apache reservations. At age eight her grandfather, John Ramsay, baptized her in the river at Snowflake. She graduated from Winslow High School in 1938 and earned a bachelor's degree in business administration from Woodbury University in Los Angeles. During World War II, Ms. Ricketts worked at Lockheed Aircraft, and she served in the Church of Jesus Christ of Latter-day Saints' North Central States mission. She spent her career as a journalist with the McClatchy Company's *Sacramento Union* as a reporter, music and drama critic, and columnist. Ms. Ricketts joined nine other women to organize Sacramento's first company of the Daughters of Utah Pioneers and served as its first president. With her husband, Monte Fremont Ricketts, she raised two sons and a daughter.

Her pioneering work in early California history uncovered the forgotten role Latter-day Saints played in the California Gold Rush, especially when they blazed the Mormon-Carson Emigrant Trail over Carson Pass in 1848. Her definitive history of the Mormon Battalion won three national awards, including Westerners International Co-Founders Best Book Award. In his Foreword to *The Mormon Battalion*, Mr. Bigler noted that Norma Baldwin Ricketts's landmark work at last gave the story of the Mormon Battalion the comprehensive treatment it merited. Exceptional gifts as a researcher and writer and a heartfelt interest sustained over many years made her uniquely qualified to write a history that placed the battalion in the larger context of the history of the American West. She provided invaluable new information about the company and its members, including an accurate roster, an accounting of dependents, and insight into "who went where by name and number over the three-year period from 1846 to 1848 and beyond." Her treatment of a subject too long ignored, the women of the Mormon Battalion, was especially noteworthy. *The Mormon Battalion* cast "new light on the role of battalion members or veterans in the early history of California. In the process, she has demonstrated that she is a foremost authority on this important subject and has made a significant contribution to Mormon, western, and American history."

Upon her death at age eighty-eight on February 25, 2010, in Polson, Montana, six grandchildren, two great-grandchildren, and an enduring historical legacy survived Norma Baldwin Ricketts.

❧

Eyewitness to Discovery: Azariah Smith

Address at the James Marshall Gold Discovery State Historic Park, Coloma, California, June 12, 1999.

WHEN HE WAS ONLY NINETEEN YEARS OLD, A LIKEABLE YOUNG man from upstate New York was working at this place next to the American River's South Fork on January 24, 1848, 151 years ago today. As an employee of James Marshall and John Sutter, Azariah Smith was an eyewitness to what happened that day. It was an event of such importance that it continues to shape the lives of Americans down to the latest generation. Few seem to recognize it today, but the discovery of gold makes Coloma and this park one of the most historic places in our country, especially in view of what happened less than two weeks later. On February 2, 1848, the United States, under the treaty that ended the Mexican-American War, acquired all or most of present California and two other states, plus parts of four others. Can you name them?

Hardly anyone knew it at the time, but these momentous events would change the face of our nation almost overnight. Not only did they add to our continental domain the entire Southwest, encompassing all or most of present New Mexico, Arizona, California, Nevada, and Utah, plus much of Wyoming and Colorado, they also touched off a massive shift of population west that continues (to the consternation of some) to the present day.

Azariah Smith was not the only eyewitness to the discovery here that started the Gold Rush, whose sesquicentennial we celebrate this year throughout California. He was one of the two men—and two only—who recorded this event as it happened in a personal diary. The other was Henry W. Bigler, a slender Virginian in his early thirties. For more than a century, historians have recognized the importance of Bigler's account, but only in recent times have they come to know and appreciate young Smith's record.

Thanks to these two—Smith and Bigler—we can know for sure that January 24 was indeed the day of the gold discovery in 1848. And thanks to them, there can be little doubt that the one who discovered it was the very man after whom this historic park is named—James Marshall.

Now, to know for certain *when* and *who* is important because failing memories and the desire for attention can cause people to do and say funny things—and some not so funny. At the time, hardly anyone here gave much thought to such details. But as the years passed and the importance of the gold discovery increasingly sank in, those who were here that day—and some who weren't—began to tell all kinds of stories. Marshall himself thought he had found the precious metal on January 19, five days before the right one. And a small parade of self-professed discoverers literally came out of the woodwork to claim some of the limelight.

On these questions, however, Smith and Bigler allowed no room for doubt. Over more than a decade of interrogation by historians, they never wavered about the truth, as they knew it, or claimed for themselves any credit or glory. One especially appreciates such integrity when it comes from relatives, if somewhat distant. Bigler is a first cousin three times removed and Smith is a great-uncle (his sister, Esther Smith Anderson, is my great-grandmother). This is not to suggest that all of my ancestors were such notables.

The story of how Azariah Smith came to be at this place began with the dream of one of our most important, if least appreciated, presidents. I'll give you some clues. See if you can tell who he was.

The eleventh president of the United States was known as a "pure, whole-hogged Democrat." In Congress, where he served as speaker of the House of Representatives, his loyalty to Andrew Jackson earned him the name, "Young Hickory." The first dark horse ever nominated for president, he was chosen at his party's convention as a compromise candidate in 1844 only after he promised to serve for only four years—one term.

He won by less than a majority of the popular vote. Unlike presidents today was his approach to the job. "I prefer to supervise the whole operations of the government myself rather than entrust the public business to subordinates and this makes my duties very great," he said.

Who was he?

A stickler for details, he was at the same time a remarkable visionary. For James Knox Polk of Tennessee dreamed of an American nation much as it is today, with enough new territory to encompass all or part of a dozen future states and more than fifteen hundred miles of Pacific Ocean front. At the center of his dream was the place he wanted more than any other—California.

Mr. Polk was prepared to pay what was for him the princely sum of forty million dollars for this land, but Mexico stubbornly refused to sell. So, intentionally or not, he forced the issue by placing a small American force under a future president, General Zachary Taylor, on a disputed strip at the mouth of the Rio Grande claimed by both Mexico and Texas. At this provocation, Mexican cavalry crossed the river and ambushed U.S. dragoons, American blood was shed, and the War with Mexico was on. It was like an answer to the Methodist president's prayers.

In waging it, the president's strategy was two-fold. First, he sent a little American army under First Dragoons colonel Stephen Watts Kearny to occupy New Mexico and California for eventual annexation under a peace settlement. At the same time, he ordered American volunteers to strike hard at the heart of Mexico and end the war quickly—for he had to accomplish all this before his single term of office ran out in less than three years.

Such great designs by those in high office eventually affect the lives of individual citizens—and so it proved for Azariah Smith. On August 1, 1846, his eighteenth birthday, he marched into Fort Leavenworth, where he became a soldier in Kearny's little Army of the West and began to keep a journal of his adventures. Mr. Polk's call for volunteers had been oversubscribed, but on learning that the destination of the Mormon migration from Illinois would be California, he had approved the enlistment of five hundred soldiers as a Mormon battalion to keep the controversial religious movement loyal to the United States.

What he got for troops at first was a cross-section of the refugees who crowded Mormon emigration camps across Iowa that year. They ranged in age from gray-haired old men to youngsters in their teens. There were men with wives and dependent children in tow, some in wagons, too sick to walk. By the time the command marched west from Santa Fe, regular officers had trimmed it into a fairly efficient body of some 336 muskets. Not many, but more than enough to occupy the land we now know as California, whose entire population that year was less than 15,000, not counting Indians.

Smith's writings during the march of some two thousand miles to California and later occupation duty reveal a young man of many admirable qualities. He was better educated than most of his fellows, including his father, Albert Smith, a sergeant in the Mormon Battalion's Company B. He was a gentle spirit who liked to write poetry, was sensitive to the beauty of nature, and uniformly generous and kindhearted. He was also lonely and missed his mother terribly.

Of all his unsoldierly qualities, perhaps the most endearing was an optimistic spirit that no hardship or complaint by his companions could overcome. Where others saw godforsaken wilderness, arid and barren, his eyes would behold "a beautiful prairie." And when his companions saw themselves as the victims of adversity or unfair treatment, as they often did, he would chirp, "all in good health and spirits."

At the end of their enlistment in 1847 at Los Angeles, Azariah Smith and his father joined a party of other Mormon veterans who journeyed north through the Central Valley to Sutter's Fort at present Sacramento. They then followed the new wagon road over the mountains that crossed the Sierra Nevada at today's Donner Pass on the line of Interstate 80. At the site of present Truckee, they met messengers from the new settlement of their faith in Utah who instructed the younger, unmarried members of the party to go back and work for a year in California before coming on to Zion in the Great Basin.

So young Smith said goodbye to his father, who went on to meet the rest of his family in Salt Lake Valley, and retraced his steps back to Sutter's Fort, where John Sutter apparently never refused anyone who needed a job, whether he could afford to hire them or not. On October 3 that year,

Smith wrote, "Sutter sent after some hands to go up in the mountains, about thirty miles; to work at his sawmill and I with several others went."

True to character, he described this valley as "a beautiful place," but he came here in circumstances that put his positive spirit to a test from which Job might have shrunk. "I feel like a cat in a strange garrit," he said. But more than this, he was hurt—badly hurt—having suffered an injury that would have put him today in the intensive care ward.

Typically, he said nothing about it at the time, but his father, Albert, years later described the accident after his oldest son had begun to suffer from seizures. After their discharge, the two had purchased wild horses to save money, and one of the animals had thrown the younger Smith. He landed on his head, striking a large rock and suffering what was probably a circular fracture of the skull, literally a dent in the skull with bone pressure on the brain. Often sick with pain, Azariah Smith worked as best he could on the millrace and sought simple pleasures to keep his spirits up. One of these pastimes was to climb the hill on the other side of the river and roll down rocks, some weighing as much as a ton. It's amazing how many pioneers practiced this sport wherever they could find a mountain high enough to roll a rock down.

So it went through Christmas and into the New Year, 1848, until the day arrived that would change the course of American history. "Monday 24," Henry Bigler wrote in his diary, "this day some kind of mettle was found in the tail race that that [sic] looks like goald, first discovered by James Martial, the Boss of the Mill."

Six days later in an entry dated January 30, Azariah Smith wrote, "This week Mr. Marshall found some pieces of (as we all suppose) Gold, and he has gone to the Fort, for the Purpose of finding out." After writing this, he inserted, between the words "This week" and "Mr. Marshall," the date, January 24.

How long afterward did he put the exact date in? No one really knows for sure, but some historians have generally assumed that it was decades later—when the question of the date became a hotly disputed issued. But not necessarily. I have found later entries in his journal, never considered before, that make me think otherwise. More on that in a moment.

In the meantime, Smith and others here had no idea they were participants in one of America's most historic events. He worked at the mill and looked in his spare time for what he called "the root of all evil" as news of the discovery spread. Across the country and around the world, men braced themselves to risk life itself to get to the place where Azariah Smith was—and all he wanted to do was go home to his mother. "I was home-sick as well as physically sick," he later said. "I wanted to see my mother and I did not care whether there was gold in the locality or not."

So as soon as the snow melted in the mountain passes that year, Smith and a party of battalion veterans, including Henry Bigler and other Mormons, headed east over Carson Pass to rejoin their families. In going, they opened a new trail over the Sierra Nevada, the Mormon-Carson Emigrant Trail, which in 1849 became the main line of the California Gold Rush. The story of this trail is told by our friend Frank Tortorich in his book, *Gold Rush Trail*.[1]

In Utah Azariah Smith and his family colonized the little town of Manti, some 120 miles south of Salt Lake City, where he lived the rest of his life. Henry Bigler later settled at St. George, near the state's borders with Nevada and Arizona. And their eyewitness accounts of western America's most important event were largely forgotten—stuck under the mattress, up in the attic, or on a shelf in the granary for the mice to chew on.

In California, meanwhile, the gold discovery was celebrated on January 18 and 19, according to the recollection years after by Marshall and others, including some who had no business getting in the act at all. Probably the first time the correct date appeared in print, although largely unnoticed at the time, came 1881 with publication of the classic work, *A Concise History of the Mormon Battalion in the Mexican War* by Daniel Tyler. This account, based on journals and remembrances of battalion veterans, including Smith and Bigler, featured a few pages on the gold discovery, which it prudently dated "on or about January 24."

Four years later, California's great journalist-historian, John S. Hittell, was asked to give a talk on the gold discovery before the annual dinner

1   Frank Tortorich, Jr., *Gold Rush Trail: A Guide to the Carson River Route of the Emigrant Trail* (Pine Grove, Calif: Wagon Wheel Tours, U.S.A., 1998).

of the Society of California Pioneers. Having heard that Henry Bigler was still alive, he sent a copy of his talk to him with a request to correct any errors. Bigler replied it generally looked good to him, except for the date, which did not square with his diary. Bigler referred Hittell to Azariah Smith.

So it came about that Smith, who kept a journal all his life, recorded on January 15, 1886, at the end of more important events that day, such as buying his wife some "good Lindy Cloth for a dress," the following entry, which I found recently for the first time:

> And I also receaved a letter from J. S. Hittell, and a printed lecture, delivered by him, at the An[n]iversary of the California Pioneer Society San Francisco concerning the finding of the first peace [sic] of Gold, wishing some information concerning it, as I was there to work at Sutter and Marshalls Saw mill; when the first peace was found 24th of Jan,y 1848. I sent him a letter.

Now how could he be so sure about the date after thirty-eight years? It is possible that he had a remarkable memory. In 1879, he listed from memory in alphabetical order the names of 61 of the 102 original members of the Mormon Battalion's Company B. Or he simply looked it up in his own journal where the date was written. If the latter, as I believe was the case, he had probably entered the date when he transcribed the original entry from his pocket diary to his larger journal, or soon after.

Either way, throughout his life Azariah Smith never showed the slightest uncertainty about the date. In 1887, when applying for disability benefits for the injury he suffered as a result of his Mexican-American War service, he wrote that he had gone "with some others up in the mountains to help Mr. Marshall build a Saw Mill. But I was unable to work, for nearly two months being very Sick, but finally I got able to work some, until the 24th of Jan'y 1848 as I was working with Mr. Marshall, he found the first peace of Gold found in Cal."

And included with his papers today is a short, handwritten history of the first twenty years of his life from 1828 until he rejoined his family in 1848. This document is undated, but its appearance and the period it covers make it probable that it was written when he was twenty years old or soon after. In it, he says, "And with a few others I went up in the mountains, to a place now called Caloma [sic] and built a Saw mill. And while dig[g]ing the talerace the first nugget of Gold was found on Jan'y 24th 1848 by Mr. Marshall."

So much for the date. Equally certain seems the discoverer after whom our park is named, except for the hint of mystery unintentionally imparted by Smith himself on this score.

On December 19, a full month *before* the gold discovery, Smith dutifully recorded his day's work on the sawmill, then added, "this morning I missed a basin and knife off from my shelf, stolen by some one." Now the two main tools at that time for gathering gold were a pan, or basin, to pan for it and a pocketknife to dig the nuggets out from crevices in the rocks. Interestingly enough, these were the very implements stolen from young Smith.

Six weeks later, on February 2, ten days *after* the discovery, James Marshall brought Sutter back to Coloma to show his partner where the gold had been found. Accompanying the pair from Sutter's Fort was twenty-three-year-old William Johnstun, another of the six Mormons normally employed at the mill. The very next day, Smith said, "What should I find on the shelf but my knife and basin having been brought by Johnstun and put there by him, when we previously had asked him if he knew anything about it, and he af[f]irmed that he did not. Still he had it himself and kept it hid untill the present time."

Johnstun always claimed that he was an eyewitness to the gold discovery, but the evidence suggests he was not actually at Coloma at the time. It indicates instead that he was absent most of the time from the day Smith's knife and basin were stolen until the day he returned from Sutter's Fort with Marshall.

So I leave it to you. Was William Johnstun the one who took Smith's knife and basin? Why were they stolen? Was it to wash the culprit's face and whittle sticks? Or did Johnstun or someone else use them secretly to harvest the precious metal before Marshall discovered his nugget? Could it be that this mysterious thief thereby became the true gold discoverer, but too ashamed of his misdeed to admit it?

Someday we may know the answer.

In the meantime, having at last found a home in Manti, Azariah Smith never ventured far from that place for fifty years. Then in 1898, he and

AZARIAH SMITH AND "THE COMPANIONS OF MARSHALL"
Fifty years after the California gold discovery in 1848, San Francisco celebrated Henry Bigler, William J. Johnstun, Azariah Smith, and James S. Brown. AUTHOR'S COLLECTION.

three other surviving eyewitnesses received invitations to attend the Golden Jubilee of the Gold Discovery at San Francisco. It was the most spectacular event to hit the city prior to the great earthquake and fire, eight years later. As many as fourteen thousand men and women marched in the parade or rode in the great cavalcade on nearly a thousand horses. Some six hundred musicians played in thirty bands. It took two hours and twenty-five minutes for the procession to pass the Chronicle Building.

At the center of the festivities and excitement, quite overwhelmed by all of the unaccustomed attention, was the gentle spirit, now age seventy-one, who described it all with amazement in his journal, published as the final section of my book. Afterward, at the request of the Society of

California Pioneers, Smith signed an affidavit verifying that January 24 was in fact the date of the gold discovery. For in the midst of the fifty-year celebration, the San Francisco newspaper, *Mining and Scientific Press*, challenged the date and said it actually happened on January 19.

Azariah Smith lived another fourteen years, keeping his journal up to date all the time, until 1912, when he died quietly at age eighty-six at his home in Manti, Utah. Everyone in town knew that he had witnessed the gold discovery, and over the years the myth had grown up that he had a fortune in gold nuggets hidden away somewhere in his little house. So after waiting a respectable length of time after the funeral—say fifteen minutes or so—family members descended on his dwelling to look for the gold. But not all of them went for what Smith himself always called "the root of all evil."

His younger sister, Esther Smith Anderson, my great-grandmother, knew that he possessed something of far greater value than gold. While the others looked for nuggets, she found and recovered his journals, passing them on to her daughter-in-law, Annie Watt Anderson, my grandmother, who gave them to my mother, Hazel Anderson Bigler. Why is it that the truly precious things of life are always preserved by women?

Whatever the reason, let us be thankful it is so, as I thank each of you for the opportunity to come here today and tell you about this remarkable man and what he saw at this place over a century and a half ago.

❖

Seeing the Elephant in Utah: The Gold Rush and the Mormon Kingdom

Remarks to the University of Utah Libraries Annual Banquet, Salt Lake City, April 13, 1999.

ONE HUNDRED AND FIFTY YEARS AGO THIS MONTH, thousands of men, wagons, and animals gathered at five major jumping-off places along the Missouri River from present Kansas City to Council Bluffs. About to roll west was a great tidal wave of people. In California it would inundate almost overnight a sparsely settled land of old Spanish missions, vast cattle ranches, and superb horsemen. To new Mormon settlements in Utah, it would bring economic survival and an end to isolation. But it would also introduce nearly fifty years of cultural conflict with the rest of the nation. Eventually the massive population shift west, begun in 1849, would bring lasting change to an aspiring Mormon theocracy in the American West.

George Orwell once said, "To see what is in front of one's nose requires a constant struggle." This observation indicates that it is an appropriate time for an honest look at the earliest points of conflict between leaders of a defiant territory and the other Americans who passed this way during the nineteenth-century migration known as the Gold Rush, whose sesquicentennial the nation observes this year.

Only twenty months before it began, the professed people of Israel in the Last Days, better known as the Latter-day Saints or Mormons,

63

had moved to the Great Basin of North America, then in Mexico, to lay a theocratic base for the mission they would perform as a condition of Christ's coming again. What was this calling? Said Brigham Young, "We will roll on the Kingdom of our God, gather out the seed of Abraham, build the cities and temples of Zion, and establish the Kingdom of God to bear rule over all the earth."[1] The Kingdom he spoke of was not some vague spiritual ideal to be fulfilled on a far-distant day. It was a theocratic state also known as Deseret, ruled by God through inspired men, which would sweep to world dominion in its founders' days on earth. It was the stone cut without hands, foretold by the prophet Daniel, that would consume all other kingdoms and stand forever.[2]

Those who undertook this visionary endeavor were unlike any other emigrants in America's move west. Faith and destiny drove them, not land or gold. Like their leaders, most were young. The average age of the eight general authorities in their 1847 pioneer company, all apostles, was under age thirty-nine. The oldest were Brigham Young and Heber C. Kimball, both age forty-six. George A. Smith was the youngest, only thirty years old, having already served in this office for eight years. Revolutions are made by the young, and the crusade they led, "to reduce all nations and creeds to one political and religious standard," was a revolutionary aim.[3]

Yet even as they laid out their new city, events occurring elsewhere in 1847 would change for all time their design to establish the Kingdom of God in the West. That summer an American army under General Winfield Scott was closing in on Mexico City. And in California, Swiss entrepreneur John Sutter and his partner, James Marshall, began to build a sawmill on the American River's South Fork, east of Sacramento. On January 24, 1848, workmen turned the river into the millrace to test the flow of water on the wheel. That night, Henry Bigler, one of six Mormon Battalion veterans hired to build the mill, wrote the words that would

---

1   Brigham Young, July 8, 1855, *Journal of Discourses*, 2:317.

2   See Daniel 2:34–45.

3   *Proclamation of the Twelve Apostles of the Church of Jesus Christ of Latter-day Saints . . .* (New York: Pratt and Brannan, 1845), 1, 6.

electrify men's hopes around the world: "This day some kind of mettle was found in the tail race that looks like goald."[4]

Less than two weeks later under the terms of the Treaty of Guadalupe Hidalgo, Mexico surrendered to the United States ownership of California, as well as a large region comprising today's states of New Mexico, Arizona, Nevada, Utah, and parts of Wyoming and Colorado, all for $15 million, plus $3.5 million to settle claims of American citizens against that country.

The peace treaty with Mexico ended one war but opened another, a struggle for sovereignty between a Great Basin theocracy and an American republic that never quite realized that its supremacy was under challenge in the name of religious freedom. The quarrel would make one of the first places settled west of the Missouri River one of the last admitted to the Union. It was given the unwanted name of Utah.

So it came about that only six months after the first Mormon pioneer company arrived in Salt Lake Valley, latter-day Israel was right back in the United States again. What is more, a horde of curious gold-seekers were about to overrun the ramparts of its new Kingdom, all of them hellbent to "see the elephant," as they called it, an expression that meant to "see it all." But before many of them met a pachyderm in California, they would first see a Mormon elephant in the Rocky Mountains.

Historians differ somewhat over the number who traveled overland to the West Coast via South Pass from 1849 through 1856, but their estimates average well over two hundred thousand. Most emigrants used alternate trails to the north to bypass Mormon settlements, especially if they came from Missouri or Illinois, scenes of earlier conflicts between the millennial movement and its neighbors. But an estimated seventy thousand or so took the Mormon Trail from Fort Bridger to rest and re-supply in Salt Lake Valley. They then traveled north via the Bear River to reach the California Trail in the Silent City of Rocks, near Almo, Idaho, or south on the line of Interstate 15 to pick up the Spanish Trail

---

4   Rodman W. Paul, *The California Gold Discovery: Sources, Documents, Accounts and Memoirs Relating to the Discovery of Gold at Sutter's Mill* (Georgetown, Calif.: The Talisman Press, 1966), 33.

to Los Angeles, near Cedar City. A few (to their later regret) wound up in Death Valley or headed due west on the Hastings Cutoff, also known as the Salt Desert crossing.

One way or the other, more than twice as many people passed *through* Utah over these eight years as came *to* Utah. If one thinks traffic is bad today, one emigrant in 1850 said that after crossing Little Mountain his party was delayed for two hours in Emigration Canyon "by an accumulation of teams, entirely filling the road for two miles."[5]

For Mormon settlements, the economic impact of this stream of early tourists was a lifesaver. Understandably many of the emigrants would see it differently. John Hawkins Clark said coming to Salt Lake City in 1852 was "something like taking in the Irishman's show; it cost nothing to get in, but a great deal to get out."[6]

In fact, the cost to get in began to add up long before they arrived. A steady flow of cash poured from emigrant pockets into Kingdom coffers from Mormon ferries at river crossings on the overland trails. As Dale Morgan and Brigham D. Madsen have shown, the tolls varied, depending on time of year and traffic volume. But for a rough idea of how much money the ferries generated, let us join George Shepard from Mill Creek, Illinois, and his party in 1850 as they travel with two wagons to California, via Salt Lake Valley.

On June 5 they arrived at the Mormon ferry on the North Platte River, at present Casper, Wyoming. The toll was $4.00 per wagon and 25 cents for a horse, a total of $9.75. On they went to Green River, where the Mormon ferrymen charged $5.00 a wagon and $1.00 a horse to cross. On June 22 they came to the Weber River, near Henefer. "There are some Mormons here to ferry emigrants over," Shepard said. "They have a raft instead of a boat and take 3 dollars to carry over a wagon." Later, going north from Salt Lake, they struck the Weber again, near Ogden, where the ferryman imposed $3.00 a wagon. Next came Bear River, near Collinston: $5.00

---

5   Franklin Langworthy, *Scenery of the Plains, Mountains and Mines; or a diary kept upon the overland route to California, by way of the Great Salt Lake* (Ogdensburgh, N.Y.: published by J. S. Sprague, Book-seller; Hitchcock & Tillotson, Printers, 1855), 83.

6   John D. Unruh, Jr., *The Plains Across: The Overland Emigrants and the Trans-Mississippi West, 1840–60* (Urbana: University of Illinois Press, 1979), 312.

per wagon and $1.00 per horse. Ten miles took them to a stream that was only a rod wide, but its depth and soft banks made it hazardous to cross. But on the Malad there was a bridge "and a man standing by it," Shepard said, "to charge $1 for each wagon that passed over it."[7]

Now that year alone, about 10,000 wagons, 25,000 horses, and 32,000 oxen took the Oregon-California Trail. Not all went by Salt Lake after the North Platte and Green rivers, but these numbers illustrate the income produced by Mormon ferrying operations. One might agree with the emigrant who said, "This I think is better than gold digging."[8]

It would be misleading to suggest, as some have done, that Mormon entrepreneurs ran these ferries. Theocratic systems are communitarian in nature, not based on Milton Friedman's ideas of free enterprise. Well before the first Forty-Niner reached the North Platte, church authorities agreed that Brigham Young would "appoint the men and have the ferries under his entire control."[9] Later, when some outsiders tried to horn in on this moneymaking enterprise, a Utah militia force, including the feared Mormon gunman William Adams Hickman, discouraged competition at the lower Green River crossing by shooting "two or three mountaineers."[10]

Similar control was harder to impose on commerce between the overlanders and Mormon settlers. Gold Rush emigrants came to Salt Lake to buy flour and vegetables, find a blacksmith, get a home-cooked meal, exchange worn-out animals for fresh ones, trade oxen for horses, and replace heavy wagons with lighter ones that would go faster to the gold diggings. To lighten their loads, they were eager to dump manufactured products of every kind at any price. Said Mormon Joseph Holbrook, "It literally seemed that the Lord inspired them to load down their wagons

7   For Shepard Diary quotes, see David Bigler, Donald Buck, and Merrill J. Mattes, eds., "'O Wickedness, Where Is Thy Boundary?': The 1850 California Gold Rush Diary of George Shepard," *Overland Journal* 10:4 (Winter 1992), 2–33.

8   Dale L. Morgan, "The Ferries of the Forty-Niners," *Annals of Wyoming* 31:1 (April 1959), 12.

9   Journal History, March 3, 1849.

10   William A. Hickman, *Brigham's Destroying Angel; Being the Life, Confession, and Startling Disclosures of the Notorious Bill Hickman, the Danite Chief of Utah* (New York: George A. Crofutt & Co., 1872), 91–93.

WILLIAM A. HICKMAN
William Adams Hickman appears perfectly
capable of committing cold-blooded
murders, including killing Green River
ferrymen and Aiken Party member Horace
Bucklin, as described in *Brigham's Destroying
Angel; Being the Life, Confession, and Startling
Disclosures of the Notorious Bill Hickman, the
Danite Chief of Utah.* COURTESY OF THE
UTAH STATE HISTORICAL SOCIETY.

with everything that the saints need for tools, to wear as clothes, for
food."[11]

Given such temptation, it would have taken Saints indeed to obey the
counsel they received from their leaders. According to one emigrant,
when he tried to strike a bargain with a local farmer, a woman in the
house opposite came to the door and "squalled out" at the top of her
voice, "that man is a gentile, you know that Brigham says we must not sell
flour to the gentiles for less than $25 a hundred."[12] Maybe so, but most
ignored Young's repeated attempts to control prices and trade.

As California's Gold Rush gave a bloom of prosperity to Utah settlements, it also drew an army of curious sightseers. Depending on their
length of stay and whether their contacts were with average settlers or
Mormon authorities, most arrivals reacted favorably to what one called
"the Mormon halfway house." Especially inspiring after weeks on the
trail was the first view of Salt Lake City. "For a moment not a word came

11   Joseph Holbrook History, in Brigham D. Madsen, *Gold Rush Sojourners in Great Salt
      Lake City, 1849 and 1850* (Salt Lake City: University of Utah Press, 1983), 54.
12   *The Oregonian*, Portland, Oregon Territory, May 1, 1852, 1.

from a single member of the company," an Ohioan said, "all were speech-less at the grand scenery before us."[13] For Ansel McCall, the memory of his first meal with a Mormon family would live forever. It was, he said, a "sumptuous feast of new potatoes, green peas, bread and butter, with rich, sweet milk."[14] And as Forty-Niner James Hutchings got ready to pull out, he lamented, "Tomorrow we leave civilization, pretty girls, and pleasant memories."[15]

At the same time, emigrant opinions perceptibly worsened the longer they stayed beyond the average six or seven days. And many who spent the winter here for seasonal or financial reasons protested bitterly the treatment they received at the hands of Mormon authorities.

Over a hundred Oregon-bound emigrants, who lived in their tents and wagons near Ogden during the winter of 1850–1851, vowed that if they ever again breathed "the air of freedom" they would expose the injustices they had suffered. They elected one of their number, forty-one-year-old Jotham Weeks Goodell, an "old school" Presbyterian from Vermilion, Ohio, to tell their story. He did so in nine angrily detailed letters, published in 1852 by *The Oregonian* newspaper at Portland and later sent to Washington.[16]

After the same winter, 115 California emigrants petitioned Congress to replace Utah's territorial government with military rule. They named Nelson Slater, a forty-five-year-old New York schoolteacher, to describe at even greater length the injuries they had endured here.[17] Published

---

13 Charles Brown Voorhis, From Lake Erie to the Pacific: An Overland Trip in 1850–51, in Madsen, *Gold Rush Sojourners in Great Salt Lake City*, 34.

14 Ansel James McCall, *The Great California Trail in 1849* (Bath, N.Y., 1882), 57.

15 Shirley Sargent, ed., *Seeking the Elephant, 1849: James Mason Hutchings' Journal of His Overland Trek to California; Including his Voyage to America, 1848 and Letters from the Mother Lode* (Glendale, Calif: The Arthur H. Clark Co., 1980), 156.

16 The letters appeared in *The Oregonian* from April 3 to June 26, 1852, under the heading, "The Mormons." Mr. Bigler subsequently edited these letters as *A Winter with the Mormons: The 1852 Letters of Jotham Goodell* (Salt Lake City: Tanner Trust Fund and the Marriott Library, 2001).

17 Slater was a graduate of New York's Union College and Auburn Theological Seminary. He and his wife had three children, ages 14, 12, and 9, when they wintered in Utah. He became superintendent of schools for Sacramento County and died in Sacramento in 1886. See the *(Sacramento) Daily Bee* and *Sacramento Union*, May 10, 1886.

in 1851, his book, *Fruits of Mormonism*, was the first copyrighted in California.[18] Similar offerings include Franklin Langworthy's *Scenery of the Plains, Mountains and Mines*, published in 1855.[19] Such works cannot be dismissed as just anti-Mormon rhetoric. In understanding Utah's theocratic society, which existed in its purest form before 1858 and later caused conflict between Utah Territory and the United States, they are of primary importance. As Brigham Madsen has indicated in his groundbreaking work, *Gold Rush Sojourners in Great Salt Lake City*, they must be considered among the reasons President Buchanan ordered an American army to Utah in 1857. At the head of the grievances that they point up stands the question of law, which Slater and many other emigrants stamped as "informal, illegal, and unjust."[20]

It would be misleading to suggest, as some have done, that the exercise of law in Utah at the time was typical of the rough-and-ready forms of justice found on the frontier. One emigrant claimed he heard Apostle Willard Richards say, "what was law one day, was not law another day; that they, (the Mormons) were governed by the Holy Ghost."[21] That might not be as funny as it sounds.

The "free and independent" State of Deseret, established in 1849, provided that justices of its courts would be appointed by the legislature or chosen by popular election. The same generally applied in Utah Territory, created by Congress in 1850, except that the territorial organic act required the president to appoint the judges of the three highest district courts, who were usually not Mormons.

Since all this seems so democratic, how could it become so objectionable to many emigrants? First, the system rested on elections that either were never held or with with voters who were not permitted to cast their ballots in secret. In 1849 Hosea Stout became a legislator "by

---

18   Nelson Slater, *Fruits of Mormonism, A Fair and Candid Statement of Facts Illustrative of Mormon Principles, Mormon Policy, and Mormon Character, By More than Forty Eye-Witnesses* (Coloma, Calif.: Harmon & Springer, 1851)

19   Langworthy, *Scenery of the Plains, Mountains and Mines: or a Diary kept upon the Overland Route to California, by way of the Great Salt Lake*, ed. by Paul C. Philips (Princeton: Princeton University Press, 1932), esp. 80–95.

20   Slater, *Fruits of Mormonism*, 12.

21   Ibid., 20.

ASA CYRUS CALL
This image was taken about the time Call wintered in Utah in 1850–1851. Call was among the overland emigrants who petitioned Congress in June 1851 to "protect United States citizens, and secure to them their lawful and inalienable rights of life, liberty, and freedom of speech, guaranteed to them by the Constitution of the United States" in Utah Territory. COURTESY JOHN CALL.

what process," said he, "I know not."[22] Utah lawmakers later outlawed two cornerstones of American justice—legal precedence and common law. Finally, they ignored the intent of Congress and vested original criminal and civil jurisdiction in the probate courts, ruled by Mormon judges, which left appointed district justices with empty courtrooms.

In a theocratic society, where perfect justice is dispensed by inspiration, one does not put his trust in the rulings of men. Even so, it is no wonder some emigrants found the exercise of theocratic law "informal, illegal, and unjust."

William Fuller thought so in 1852 when he and twenty-three others protested "one of the grossest impositions ever practised upon travelers in a civilized community." They had forded the Weber and Ogden rivers rather than use the toll bridge that lawmakers had given James Brown the exclusive rights to build and operate. But Brown, who was the founder of the city of Ogden, had imposed the toll anyway. An officer and "twelve

---

22   Juanita Brooks, ed., *On the Mormon Frontier: The Diary of Hosea Stout, 1844–1861*, 2 vols. (Salt Lake City: University of Utah Press, 1964), 2:358.

or fifteen men armed to the teeth" overtook them on the Bear River. With the posse came the judge who imposed on the spot fines and costs totaling $120, no small fortune in those days. When they protested "the injustice and illegality" of this ruling, he informed them "there was no appeal from his court." No doubt equally in vain, they reported all this to Brigham Young and asked him to return their money at Sacramento.[23]

Not so willing to settle were the Oregon pioneers, including Jotham Goodell, his wife, Anna, and seven children, ranging in age from two to nineteen, who had wintered in 1850–1851 in Weber County. "Were Brigham to come in person and tender back the money he robbed us of, there is not a man among us but would exclaim: '*Your money perish with you! In our distress and anguish of soul, you robbed us of our all, and exposed our wives and little ones to the danger of perishing with famine, amid the wastes of the desert!*'" he wrote. "Never, NEVER, NEVER!"[24]

Twenty-nine-year-old Dr. Thomas Flint from Maine, who drove sheep and cattle to California in 1853, had better luck. On the way he gave some Mormon families, who had been robbed by Indians, enough supplies to take them to Utah. When Flint got to Salt Lake City, he received royal treatment, but his fortune did not extend to neighboring trains on the Southern Trail. At Nephi, authorities seized the horses of another company and fined the owner twenty dollars for damage to wheat stacks, but they refused to show Flint the alleged damage. Moreover, Flint said, "they threatened to double the amount if he found fault or swore."

At Fillmore, Flint found one Edward Potter from the train of William Hollister, after whom Hollister, California, is now named. Potter had come back to help two girls who wanted to return to Ohio rather than become wives of Bishop Noah Bartholomew. Their parents convinced them not to go at that time, so their rescuer returned to his train. But at Parowan an armed posse arrested Potter for seduction and threatened to take him back to Salt Lake for trial. They let him go only after he gave up his horse, and Hollister paid an additional fine of $150 in cash.

---

23   See Fuller to Young, July 23, 1852, Brigham Young Papers, LDS Archives; also available on Reel 6, Brigham Young Collection, Marriott Library, University of Utah.

24   *The Oregonian*, June 12, 1852, 1. Goodell and his family were incorrectly entered on the 1850 census for Weber County under the name Jackson Goodale, but later sources in Oregon and Washington confirm their identity.

While his own party was "kindly received," Flint said, other trains were harassed "in most every conceivable manner, particularly if they were from Illinois or Missouri." Fines were imposed for every infraction, "real or fictitious—enforced by men with rifles on their shoulders." Then he added: "The Mormons that joined us were so much in fear of the 'Destroying Angels' that they did not dare to venture away from the camp fire at night."[25]

Any Mormon who wanted to head for the gold fields would find few chances to join wagon trains from Missouri or Illinois because most of them kept well to the north for the reason pointed to by a homeopathic physician from Illinois. Dr. Israel Shipman Pelton Lord said that a Mormon ferryman told him "none of their persecutors would be safe in passing through the city; and while he told of their wrongs, he ground his teeth so [hard] as to be heard two or three yards." "Yet," Lord added, "he was not naturally a violent man; rather the reverse."[26]

Serious or not, such warnings seemed to frighten some emigrants. On being told of their danger, two alleged Illinois persecutors reportedly took off in such a hurry they forgot to take anything to drink. According to one of this pair: "They crossed the Great Desert 83 miles without water, and lost their horse; saving their own lives by eating or drinking, perhaps, the blood of a dead creature."[27] The customary Mormon response to stories like this was to quote Proverbs 28:1: "The wicked flee when no man pursueth."

Of all the protests over early Utah law, perhaps one case drew the widest notice: the killing of a non-Mormon emigrant, Dr. Thomas Vaughn, who wintered at Manti in 1851. There was no doubt about who did it. In February of that year, thirty-nine-year-old Madison Hambleton, one of Brigham Young's North Platte River ferrymen, shot the self-styled physician after church in front of everybody in town for seducing his wife. As Hambleton afterward said "the children was all that saved his wife,"

25   All quotes are from "Diary of Dr. Thomas Flint," *Annual Publications, Historical Society of Southern California*, 1923, 91–110.

26   Necia Dixon Liles, ed., *"At the Extremity of Civilization": A Meticulously Descriptive Diary of an Illinois Physician's Journey in 1849 Along the Oregon Trail to the Goldmines and Cholera of California* (Jefferson, N.C.: McFarland & Co., Inc., Publishers, 1995), 158.

27   Ibid.

according to settler Azariah Smith.[28] It appears that the victim of the alleged seduction was his first wife, Chelnicia, age thirty-three, not his new second wife, Maria Jane, age nineteen. At a March hearing before the Deseret Supreme Court (itself an illegal bench since Utah was by now a territory), Brigham Young showed up and pronounced Hambleton justified. His was always the last word. Except in this case, not quite.

Two full years later, Andrew Love at Nephi gave the affair a seasoning of Old Testament law. Said he: "Saw Brother Madison Hamilton of Sanpete which it appears has forfeited his life & Priesthood by taking back his Wife after Killing Vaughn for seducing her."[29] Since Hambleton was alive and well, he managed to escape such Biblical consequences for taking his wife back after shooting Vaughn to death.

If the unpredictability of theocratic justice at times troubled even the faithful, not far behind it as a cause of emigrant protest was the accusation that Mormon leaders were disloyal to the United States. On this score, it would be misleading to suggest, as some have done, that the outspoken devotion to the U.S. Constitution, often voiced by Brigham Young and other leaders, amounted to evidence of such allegiance. Not necessarily.

Mormons then believed that God had inspired the framers of the Constitution to create a land of religious freedom where His Kingdom would be restored and supersede, as it prevailed to universal dominion, the American republic and all other earthly realms. The Constitution thus was a steppingstone to a higher, millennial form of government, not an end in itself. It was cherished as the founding document of the Kingdom of God. The State of Deseret was its true heir and champion, not the government that frustrated the fulfillment of its divine purpose.

So reverence for the nation's founding document was not, by itself, evidence of loyalty to the republic. Without contradiction, Brigham Young could avow his devotion to the Constitution on one hand and excoriate the national government and its officials on the other. His allegiance was first, last, and always to the Kingdom of God. But his outspoken opinions offended many emigrants. "[The Mormons] deny

---

28   Azariah Smith Journal, February 11, 1851, LDS Archives, copy in author's possession.
29   Andrew Love Journal, May 8, 1853, LDS Archives, copy in author's possession. See Leviticus 20:10 and Deuteronomy 22:22.

the authority of the United States, and gasconade around as if they were able to maintain themselves against any force that might be sent against them," said one.[30]

Franklin Langworthy from Illinois shared this view. In 1850 he attended July 24th observances in the bowery where he heard speakers "read a paper entitled 'Declaration of Independence of Deseret,' and another, 'The Constitution of Deseret.' The Declaration of American Independence was also read." "They said many hard things against the Government and people of the United States," he went on. "They prophesied that the total overthrow of the United States was near at hand, and that the whole nation would soon be at the feet of the Mormons, suing for mercy and protection."[31]

Another emigrant said that Brigham Young said from the stand that his followers would "meet any force sent from the United States, and bid them God speed with musket and grape shot!"[32] And in 1851, William Singer, a former army officer, said that Young "denied the right of jurisdiction on the part of our government, and pledged himself that if a Governor came there and attempted its extension, he would resist it to the death!"[33] True or not, these allegations appear to reflect Young's attitude toward the U.S. Army expedition and new governor ordered to Utah by President Buchanan in 1857.

Such belligerence apparently led some to believe that the post office at Salt Lake routinely opened their letters and destroyed those that made unflattering comments about their Mormon hosts. One emigrant said he visited some outhouses near the post office and saw pieces of one of his letters in the waste paper. It is not clear whether his letter's ultimate destination resulted from its contents or a shortage of toilet paper in Utah.[34]

30   Dale L. Morgan, ed., "Letters by Forty-Niners Written from Great Salt Lake City in 1849," *Western Humanities Review* 3 (April 1849), 114.

31   Langworthy, *Scenery of the Plains, Mountains and Mines* (1932 edition), 80.

32   Slater, *Fruits of Mormonism*, 83.

33   See "About the Mormons," *St. Louis Intelligencer*, August 7, 1851, 2/3; and Bigler, ed., *A Winter with the Mormons*, 207–210. Although unsigned, the writer no doubt was former Major William Singer, who wintered with his wife and three children in Weber County in 1850–1851. Singer later became mayor of Marysville, California, and practiced law in San Francisco.

34   *Oregonian* (Portland, O.T.), May 13 [15], 1852, 1.

It would also be misleading to suggest, as some have done, that friction between Mormons and migrating Americans can be traced mainly to polygamy. True enough, the marriage doctrine did outrage some emigrants. Lucena Parsons, a twenty-eight-year-old Wisconsin schoolteacher, said that "spiritual" wives were "a poor heart broken & deluded lot" who have "not as much liberty as common slaves in the south."[35] And to show her independence in the male-dominated society, emigrant Hannah Keziah Clapp, an early feminist from Michigan, brazenly wore her "bloomer dress" to a meeting in the tabernacle. She also wore a pistol on her hip, presumably to stop some polygamist from trying to make her one of his wives.[36] But the marriage doctrine was less a source of conflict during this period than it would become in later years, when enemies of the Mormon Kingdom used it as a weapon to destroy theocratic rule.

Few of the nearly sixty documents President Buchanan sent to Congress in 1857 to justify sending an American army to Utah even mention polygamy. Forty-six, or three-fourths of them, came from the Office of Indian Affairs. Written mainly by U.S. Indian agents over a six-year period, they suggest that historians should not dismiss out of hand a rising chorus of accusations during the mid-1850s that Mormon agents, intentionally or not, encouraged Indian depredations against emigrant trains on the overland trails.[37]

Even before the tragedy at Mountain Meadows, other Americans had taken alarm at Mormon beliefs that the Indians, or Lamanites, were the seed of Joseph, a remnant of Jacob in the New World, and their own cousins by blood. Hardly comforting to settlers on the frontier or emigrants on the overland trails were the Book of Mormon prophecies that in the Last Days this remnant of Israel, meaning the Indians, would be in the midst of unrepentant Gentiles "as a young lion among the flocks

35   "Journal of Lucena Parsons," Kenneth L. Holmes, ed. and comp., *Covered Wagon Women: Diaries & Letters from the Western Trails, 1840–1890*, 11 vols. (Glendale, Calif.: The Arthur H. Clark Co., 1983), 2:274.

36   Hannah Keziah Clapp, "A Salt Lake City Stopover, July 1859," ibid., 7:245–254.

37   For examples, see *Oregonian*, June 26, 1852; *Alta California*, September 10, 1854; *Sacramento Daily Union*, September 10, 1857; *Daily Alta California*, October 18, 1857; *San Francisco Evening Bulletin*, October 28 and November 2, 1857; and *San Francisco Herald*, November 2, 9, and 12, 1857.

of sheep."[38] Such doctrines, plus Mormon resentment at past wrongs, almost made it predictable that charges of tampering with the Indians would be raised.

These and other conflicts with Gold Rush emigrants were only the opening shots in a verbal war between incompatible political systems that could never coexist in peace. Such protests over theocratic law, disloyalty, denial of free speech, undemocratic forms of government, lack of economic freedom, and other issues would only intensify over the years. As the world rushed through Utah, it would transform a revolutionary creation that was compelled to gain universal dominion within the lifetime of those who established it, or not at all, short of the millennium. It could not permanently endure as an independent state or distinctive culture limited by the confines of the Great Basin.

The history of this struggle, and the honorable men and women on both sides who waged it, has been largely lost, as the title of my book *Forgotten Kingdom: The Mormon Theocracy in the American West, 1847–1896*, points up, which is indeed unfortunate. For it is not only America's longest conflict between church and state and a unique chapter in its history. It is also essential to understanding society today in one of our nation's fastest growing states, yet one still divided by cultural lines drawn during the nineteenth century.

This largely forgotten quarrel between the American republic and a theocratic territory began with the Gold Rush, 150 years ago, when a mighty flood of fortune-seekers, hell bent to "see the elephant" in California, opened the ramparts of the Kingdom of God and beheld a Mormon elephant in the Great Basin. The sudden, massive population shift west would make inevitable the sweeping changes, initiated in 1890 by church president Wilford Woodruff, that would place Utah on the road to statehood and growth.

---

38   The Book of Mormon, 3rd Nephi 20:16.

⚜

Garland Hurt,
the American Friend
of the Utahs

This is an edited version of an article that first appeared in
Utah Historical Quarterly *62:2 (Spring 1994), 149–170.*
The Utah State Historical Society honored Mr. Bigler
with the Dale L. Morgan Award for this article.

To the Utah tribe, he was known as "the American," a name that set him apart in native minds from the early Mormon settlers of Utah Territory. And he was probably the only person, at that time or since, to challenge Brigham Young's often repeated dictum that it was cheaper to feed the Indians than to fight them. He was Garland Hurt of Virginia, a committed Jacksonian Democrat, self-taught physician, and devout member of the Methodist Episcopal Church (South) who came to Utah in 1855 at age thirty-five to serve as U.S. Indian agent. Over the next five years, he would become not only a trusted friend of the Utah tribe but also one of the most controversial figures in the territory's early days. His story points up the importance of Indian relations during the first decade of Utah's history and throws needed light on the causes of conflict between Mormon leaders and federal authorities during this period.

The year after he arrived, Hurt charged that Young's feeding-or-fighting policy had made the Indians "clamorous and insolent" and "imposed upon the people of the Territory a most oppressive burden."[1] And in forwarding to Washington the claims of Utah settlers for losses suffered during the Walker Indian War of 1853, he was even more outspoken:

> If half the amount that is here presented had been appropriated and used in a proper manner for the civilization of the Indians during the last three years, the whole of this same Utah tribe, and all others in the vicinity of these settlements might, by this time, [have] been happily located and in the enjoyment of many, if not all, the comforts of civilized life, and that, too, without the complaint of a single individual in the Territory for losses.[2]

Born on December 27, 1819, Garland Hurt was reared on a frontier farm in the Old Dominion's Russell County, the fourth of ten children born to William D. Hurt, a War of 1812 veteran, and his wife, Elizabeth Crabtree.[3] At age nineteen he began his formal education at Emory and Henry College in Emory, Virginia, a four-year liberal-arts institution founded in 1836 by the Holston Conference of the Methodist Church, where he studied from 1838 to 1841.[4] There he met John Milton Elliott, whose influence would later win his appointment as Indian agent in Utah.

Meanwhile, Hurt taught school at nearby Tazewell in southwest Virginia and studied medicine as an apprentice of one Dr. Henry F. Peery.[5] In 1845 Hurt joined Elliott in eastern Kentucky, where his school friend practiced law, and offered his services as a physician. As the only doctor in the place, he successfully amputated a man's gangrenous foot without ever having seen the procedure, using a honed butcher's knife and small

1   Hurt to J. M. Elliott, October 4, 1856, Letters Received by the Office of Indian Affairs, 1824–81, Utah Superintendency, National Archives, reels 897–898. Microfilm copies of this correspondence are located in the USHS Library, Salt Lake City.

2   Hurt to Manypenny, November 20, 1856, "The Utah Expedition," House Exec. Doc. 71 (35-1), 1858, 183.

3   Mary Louisa Rice, "Biographical Sketches and Records of the Families: Leslie, Hurt and Rice or Mother's Scrap Book," 1926. This manuscript, owned by Mary Grace Rice Garland of Paintsville, Kentucky, was located and copied in 1992 for the USHS Library by Robert Castle of Auxier, Kentucky.

4   *Catalogue of the Officers and Students of Emery & Henry College* (Washington County, Virginia, 1840), copy in Kelly Library, Emory and Henry College, Emory, Virginia.

5   See Logan Uriah Reavis, *Saint Louis: The Future Great City of the World* (St. Louis: Gray, Baker & Co., 1875), 781–789, copy in Missouri Historical Society. Referred to hereinafter as Reavis, "Hurt biography."

GARLAND HURT
Dr. Garland Hurt won the affection of
the Utes, then known as the Utahs, who
called him "The American" during his
four years as a territorial Indian agent.
Hurt was the last non-Mormon federal
officer to leave Utah in 1857. He carried
word of the slaughter of an Arkansas wagon
train at Mountain Meadows to the army in
October. AUTHOR'S COLLECTION.

carpenter's saw. He later considered the operation one of his life's most
important achievements.

Besides medicine, Hurt was also interested in politics. In 1851 he won
the seat in the Kentucky legislature formerly held by Elliott, who was
elected to the U.S. House of Representatives. An astute politician, Elliott
soon became chairman of the powerful Committee on Public Expenditures. In September 1854 he delivered personally to Hurt a commission
from President Franklin Pierce, also a Democrat, to serve as U.S. Indian
agent in Utah Territory. Characteristically, the Virginian vowed "to reach
the field of my official duties before winter sets in."[6]

Hurt underestimated the distance and the weather. Before this he
had probably never ventured more than three hundred miles from his
birthplace on the west slope of the Appalachian Mountains. He now
began an overland journey of more than fifteen hundred miles at the
end of the emigration season, when travelers would be few. Reaching the
head of the Oregon Trail at Independence on November 15, he wrote to

---

6   Hurt to Mix, September 7, 1854, Office of Indian Affairs, Utah Superintendency.

the territorial governor and ex-officio superintendent of Indian Affairs, Brigham Young, that he had been held up by weather, but would come as early as possible in the spring.[7] He did better than that.

At 10 p.m. on Monday, February 5, the agent reached Great Salt Lake City with four "hardy mountaineers" who carried the first mail of 1855 from the East.[8] It included news that caused a "good deal of excitement through the city."[9] President Pierce had named Lieutenant Colonel Edward J. Steptoe, commander of a force then wintering in Utah, to replace Young as governor. Steptoe had been ordered to investigate the 1853 massacre of his 1837 West Point classmate, Captain John W. Gunnison, and seven others by Pahvant Indians on the Sevier River, near present Deseret, and bring the guilty natives to justice.[10] Nor was this the only news that could affect Hurt's new assignment.

Less than a week before the agent's arrival, Wacca or Wakara, widely known as "Walker," chief of a roving band of Utahs called the Cheveriches, had died suddenly of "consumption" at his camp near Fillmore. The charismatic chief's death followed six years of intermittent conflict between Mormon settlers and the native people who inhabited the Utah and Sanpete valleys and the Uinta Basin. Both sides had perpetrated atrocities: cruel ambushes by one and outright executions, sometimes billed as "skirmishes," by the other.

For centuries the Utahs had lived in scattered bands close to Utah Lake, then one of the most productive fisheries in western America, whose waters yielded an abundance of cutthroat trout, suckers, chub, and whitefish.[11]

---

7   Hurt to Young, December 1, 1854, Brigham Young Papers, LDS Archives.

8   Reavis, "Hurt biography," 783.

9   Scott G. Kenney, ed., *Wilford Woodruff's Journal*, 10 vols. (Midvale, Utah: Signature Press, 1983), February 6, 1855, 4:304.

10   Steptoe would decline the appointment as governor of Utah Territory, but not before he became convinced that the Mormons had been tampering with the Indians against the interests of the United States. See David H. Miller, "The Impact of the Gunnison Massacre on Mormon-Federal Relations: Colonel Edward Jenner Steptoe's Command in Utah Territory, 1854–55" (Master's thesis, University of Utah, 1968).

11   For more on this important but neglected subject, see Joel C. Janetski, "Utah Lake: Its Role in the Prehistory of Utah Valley," *Utah Historical Quarterly* 58:1 (Winter 1990), 4–31; and D. Robert Carter, "Fish and the Famine of 1855–56," *Journal of Mormon History* 27:2 (Fall 2001), 92–124.

The earliest European explorers in 1776 had marveled as they watched natives catch fish in thousands by hand. The stable food supply had enabled the tribe to employ horses, acquired from the Spanish, for purposes other than simply eating them. The Utahs used their new technology to become the haughty overlords of the Great Basin and to oppress lesser tribes.

Before Brigham Young's followers reached Salt Lake Valley, mountain man James Bridger had warned them that the "Utah tribe of Indians are a bad people; if they catch a man alone they are sure to rob and abuse him, if they don't kill him."[12] Hurt himself, no romantic when it came to his native charges, would say there was "not a braver tribe to be found among the aborigines of America than the Utahs, none warmer in their attachments, less relenting in their hatred, or more capable of treachery."[13]

Especially abhorrent to the white newcomers had been Walker's custom of raiding lesser Great Basin tribes to steal their children and trade them to Spanish slavers from Taos and Santa Fe for horses. The destructive practice had driven desert bands along the Virgin River and its tributaries into decline and potential extinction. Though baptized by the Mormons in 1850, Walker had been infuriated when Young put a stop to the slave trade in Indian children. But the Mormon leader's action had won the friendship of oppressed tribes, mainly the Paiutes, in southern Utah.

Meanwhile, no sooner had Hurt arrived in Utah than he was called to placate the Pahvants at Corn Creek near Fillmore after their chief, Kanosh, had been forced to turn over six of his followers for killing Gunnison and his party.[14] Nor was this the only problem Hurt faced that spring. Bloodied by the Mormon militia, threatened by more advanced fishing methods, and increasingly displaced from the lands around their

---

12   Journal History, June 28, 1847.

13   J. H. Simpson, *Report of Explorations across the Great Basin of the Territory of Utah* (Reno: University of Nevada Press, 1983), Appendix O, 459–464.

14   Pahvant chief Kanosh said he "threw them away." Initially he agreed to surrender seven from his tribe, one for each of the slain Gunnison Party, minus one for the native killed in 1853 by an immigrant party en route to California. Six Indians were finally turned over, including a woman and two old men, one blind. See Miller, "The Impact of the Gunnison Massacre on Mormon-Federal Relations."

Utah Lake food source, the once-dominant Utahs were growing desperate and ready to go to war against Mormon newcomers.[15]

Hurt's first move was to call on Brigham Young for an "outfit and funds" to visit the tribes. He found the governor anxious for him to go but with no money on hand "to defray the expenses of the Agency."[16] Forced to negotiate a loan, the dedicated agent issued a draft for fifteen hundred dollars against the credit of the Office of Indian Affairs and, as he needed money, continued this practice. In the absence of administrative oversight by the governor to control agency expenditures, however, it would bring Hurt to the edge of financial ruin.

With these funds, the Virginian provided presents for Pahvant chief Kanosh in exchange for the surrender of tribe members accused of the Gunnison massacre, and he attended the trial in March at Nephi.[17] There he also acted as a physician in treating a "violent epidemic" among the tribe, which had moved to the outskirts of the settlement to follow the court proceedings.[18] The agent reported that several natives had died of the disease, including Chief Walker himself some weeks before.

Hurt had found the Indians of the territory "exceedingly destitute . . . and turned upon the white settlers to beg for their subsistence," despite earlier Mormon efforts to establish Indian farms.[19] Convinced these conditions would lead to future conflict, he named William Maxwell in Utah County, Jeremiah Hatch at Nephi, and John Ray at Fillmore to furnish tools and teach the Indians how to farm. For their services, Hurt pledged a "reasonable compensation" and only afterward asked the head of Indian Affairs if he would fund this promise.[20]

---

15   Mormon Indian agent George W. Armstrong in 1855 reported, "the chiefs complained to me that they could not catch their usual supply of fish, in consequence of some of the citizens using sein[e]s and nets to their disadvantage." To pacify the natives, he requested one of the Mormon "fishing companies" to catch a supply of fish for them, which it did. See Armstrong to Young, June 30, 1855, in Sen. Doc. 1, (34-1), 1855, 521–528.

16   Hurt to Mix, February 25, 1855, Utah Superintendency, National Archives.

17   The trial was a farce. An all-Mormon jury under Nephi bishop Jacob G. Bigler, foreman, ignored Judge John F. Kinney's orders and found three guilty of the lesser offense of manslaughter. Sent to the territorial penitentiary at Salt Lake, they walked away and went back to Corn Creek as soon as the soldiers had gone.

18   Hurt to Manypenny, April 2, 1855, Office of Indian Affairs, Utah Superintendency.

19   Hurt to Young, March 1855, Office of Indian Affairs, Utah Superintendency.

20   Hurt to Manypenny, April 2, 1855, Office of Indian Affairs, Utah Superintendency.

Fortunately, Commissioner George W. Manypenny did approve, providing the Indians would not be encouraged to think "they will be fed & clothed and cared for" without working for these benefits. Payment to farmers would be sanctioned, he said, so long as they performed valuable work and were not permanently employed. Too often, he said, "employees have rendered little service to the Indians or government, in comparison with the salaries allowed them."[21]

As he began these projects Hurt found his work directly affected by a development among the millennial-minded settlers of Utah that was unlike anything known to the Indian service of his day. On April 7, two months after the agent's arrival, the man he reported to as superintendent of Indian Affairs observed the twenty-fifth anniversary of the founding of the territory's dominant faith by making a significant announcement: "Prest. Young said the day has come to turn the key of the Gospel against the Gentiles, and open it to the remnants of Israel," reported one; "the people shouted, Amen, and the feeling was such that most present could realize, but few describe."[22] It meant the time had come for the "remnant of Jacob," believed by Mormons to be the American Indians, to hear the gospel of their fathers and return as foretold by the Old Testament prophets to build up Zion before Christ came again.[23]

To gather the natives, known as Lamanites, some 160 missionaries were named at the April 1855 General Conference of the church in Salt Lake City—the first of many who would be sent to the Absarokas (better known as the Crows), the Cherokees, Hopis, Shoshones, Southern

---

21 Manypenny to Hurt, June 20, 1855, Indian Office Letterbook, Records of the Office of Indian Affairs, Letters Sent, 52:189, National Archives, microfilm copies in University of Utah Library, Salt Lake City. Referred to hereinafter as Indian Office Letterbook.

22 Juanita Brooks, ed., *Journal of the Southern Indian Mission* (Logan: Utah State University Press, 1972), April 21, 1855.

23 This doctrine had a dark side: When the Lord gathered His people for the last time, the "remnant of Jacob shall be among the Gentiles . . . as a lion among the beasts of the forest . . . [who] both treadeth down, and teareth in pieces" (Micah 5:7–15). Also see Parley P. Pratt, *The Essential Parley P. Pratt* (Salt Lake City: Signature Books, 1990), 23. An early patriarchal blessing said: "And when the remnants of Jacob go through the Gentiles like a lion among the beasts of the forest, as the Prophets have spoken, thou shall be in their midst and shall be a captain of hundreds." See Journal of John Borrowman, digital copy of typescript at Cache Valley Diaries, Utah State University Digital Collections, 5.

Paiutes, Gosiutes, Navajos, Bannocks, Utahs, Northern Paiutes, Nez Perces, and other North American tribes. This important millennial prelude followed the work of some two-dozen Mormon missionaries who had gone the year before to the destitute tribes in southwestern Utah. There they had protected the desert natives from their predatory kinsmen to the north, taught them to farm, and baptized them by the hundreds.

For those called to take up the hard life of an Indian missionary, Mormon apostle Orson Pratt held out the hope of a shining reward: When the time came to gather the remnant of Israel, it had been promised, "then the Lord should appear unto them." So they should "not be faint-hearted when they go hungry and thirsty," he said, for the time was not far distant when "the face of the Lord will be unveiled."[24] Lorenzo Brown, soon to be called on a mission to the Indians at Las Vegas Springs, summed it all up: "The Gentiles have rejected the truth & lo we turn to Israel."[25]

At this, the Methodist agent was not favorably impressed. Before leaving to visit tribes in the south, he fired off a confidential report to the commissioner of Indian Affairs. Portraying the missionaries as "a class of rude and lawless young men," he warned, "there is perhaps not a tribe on the continent that will not be visited by one or more of them." His description suggested that some Mormon bishops may have taken advantage of an opportunity to rid their flocks of unwanted elements. More serious was Hurt's opinion that the Mormons had created among the natives a distinction between themselves and "the people of the United States, that cannot act otherwise than prejudicial to the interests of the latter." He urged the commissioner to alert agencies across the country to keep the missionaries under close scrutiny and ensure that federal laws "to preserve peace on the frontiers" would "be properly enforced."[26] His alert touched off a spate of reports over the next few years, alleging Mormon tampering with the Indians.[27]

---

24 *Deseret News*, May 16, 1855.

25 Journal of Lorenzo Brown, April 8, 1855, BYU Library.

26 Hurt to Manypenny, May 2, 1855, "The Utah Expedition," House Exec. Doc. 71 (35-1), 176–177.

27 For some examples see ibid., 124–205; Senate Exec. Doc. 1 (35-2), 1859, 335–339; Senate Exec. Doc. 42 (36-1), 1860, 1–139; House Exec. Doc. 38 (35-1), Vol. 9, 1857–58, 2–13; House Exec. Doc. 102 (35-1), Vol. 12, 1857–58, 1–3; and House Exec. Doc. 1, Vol. 2, pt. 2 (35-2), 1859, 282.

Meanwhile, the dirty palls of smoke that draped the western slopes of the Wasatch Mountains in 1855 demonstrated that at least one tribe had little love for the religionists who had taken over its land and fishing grounds. "Almost all of our kanyons, north and south, have been burned," Mormon leader Heber C. Kimball reported, "some by the Indians, and some by the carelessness of the whites."[28] And a settler at Nephi that summer said, "a destructive fire in our pinerry has been burning for several days." According to the Indian arsonists, he reported, "the Mormons cut their timber & use it & pay them nothing for it, & they prefer burning it up."[29]

As Hurt set out to help the angry Utahs, he moved at the same time to improve understanding between the Mormons and the national government. Invited to speak during July Fourth observances at Salt Lake City, he began by extolling the American Constitution, sure to please his Mormon audience.[30] He allowed that he was not surprised at "the delicate relations that exist between the United States and the little colony of Utah," given the persecution his listeners had suffered. And he was "ready and willing," he pledged, to "consecrate his life and his feeble energies for the conciliation of your rights."[31]

Hurt tried at first to establish good relations with Brigham Young. Soon after his Independence Day speech, he acknowledged Young's "general supervisory role over conduct of his agents" and pledged to cooperate "in all your efforts to advance the interests of the Territory."[32] Two months later, on returning from a trip to Gravelly Ford on the California Trail, he seemed genuinely touched by a gift from Young of some "very delicious grapes" which "filled my heart with gratitude to the donor."[33]

---

28 *Latter-day Saints' Millennial Star*, November 17, 1855, 730.

29 Diary of Andrew Love, July 26, 1855, LDS Archives, photocopy in author's possession.

30 Mormons believed the Constitution was divinely inspired but regarded it as a stepping-stone to a higher form of theocratic rule, not as an end in itself.

31 Remarks by Garland Hurt on July 4, 1855, as reported by J. V. Long and revised by Hurt in his own handwriting, Brigham Young Papers.

32 Hurt to Young, July 6, 1855, Brigham Young Papers.

33 Hurt to Young, September 15, 1855, Brigham Young Papers. Emigrants often came under attack near Gravelly Ford, where the California Trail crossed the Humboldt River about five miles east of present Beowawe, Nevada. There Hurt negotiated a simple treaty with the Indians that was never ratified. A. P. Haws, a Mormon, operated a farm on the south bank of the river.

The agent further demonstrated an ability, which other federal officials often lacked, to win the friendship and respect of his peers of whatever faith. Reporting on Hurt's visit to the Humboldt River natives, his interpreter C. L. Craig said, "my comrades will join me in saying that they never have traveled with a more perfect gentleman than Doctor Hurt whose energy and aim was always for the best."[34]

The Virginian now set his course between the two extremes of feeding or fighting. He undertook to teach the suffering Utahs how to feed themselves and, in so doing, to win their loyalty for the United States. His first move was to inform Brigham Young of his plan to establish farms for the natives "whose lands the whites have occupied" and "who have placed themselves almost entirely in a state of dependency on the white settlements." Hurt requested Young's views "in regard to this enterprise" and advice as to suitable locations.[35] The governor's response was prompt and unqualified. Not only did Young "highly approve" the idea, but he said he was gratified that the agent's views "so strongly coincide with my own upon this subject." He recommended suitable sites for Indian farms in Utah, Sanpete, Juab, Millard, and Iron counties.[36] Given Young's hearty approval, the agent moved with a zeal that bordered on recklessness. On November 27, 1855, he and a party of six left Salt Lake City "to select suitable places to establish and locate Indian reservations, with a view to persuade the poor unfortunate Indians to forsake their nomadic [ways] for a civilized life."[37]

Over the next three weeks, Hurt laid out an entire township, 36 square miles, for an Indian farm at Corn Creek, some ten miles south of Fillmore, where he found good soil and enough water "to irrigate 700 or 1,000 acres." In Sanpete County, he quadrupled this spread, marking off four full townships, or 144 square miles, from a point about five miles south of Manti to the mouth of the San Pitch River. The site bordering the Sevier River was large enough to encompass Chief Arapeen's favorite

---

34 *Deseret News*, August 30, 1855; Journal History, August 27, 1855.

35 Hurt to Young, November 20, 1855, Brigham Young Papers.

36 Young to Hurt, draft in handwriting of Daniel H. Wells, November 23, 1855, Brigham Young Papers.

37 See report by Lyman S. Wood, Indian interpreter, in Journal History, December 14, 1855.

hunting grounds in the rugged canyon of Twelvemile Creek and today's towns of Gunnison, Mayfield, Redmond, and Centerfield. More modest at first was the 640-acre farm set aside on the west bank of the Spanish Fork River in Utah County, but this was enlarged the following April into a "reservation" covering 12,380 acres.[38]

In his fourth-quarter report, Hurt told Governor Young he intended "to stock these reservations during the ensuing season with such stock and implements . . . as may be necessary to carry on a vigorous system of agriculture." Moreover, he said, "I wish through you to have an act passed by Congress confirming these reservations as the future home of these bands." He asked that farming instruction be extended to the territory's other tribes before they were forced to "starve, or subsist by rapine and murder." To pay for these grandiose plans, he called for an appropriation of $75,000 to $100,000, plus an additional $30,000 to cover his commitments to neighboring bands.[39]

All of this was probably more than Brigham Young had in mind when he first approved the farming scheme, which may explain why it took nearly four months for Hurt's request to reach Washington without the governor's endorsement. It may also have been the reason why Young asked the agent in February 1856 to go off on a side trip of more than a thousand miles to visit tribes along the California Trail between Salt Lake City and Carson Valley.[40]

Meanwhile, as he waited for the weather to break, Hurt took up the study of law, unaware that his ambitious plans were heading into trouble on the fiscal front. On November 14, a month before the agent laid out his farming sites, Commissioner Manypenny had cautioned that "the

---

38   Spanish Fork eventually became Utah's main farm, reaching from a point about two miles west of Spanish Fork to West Mountain and Utah Lake and taking in today's town of Lake Shore. See David A. Burr, "Map of a Survey of the Indian Reservation on Spanish Fork Cr., Utah Territory, Showing Its Connection with the U.S. Survey of the Territory," National Archives, photographic copy of original in BYU Library. Also see Kate B. Carter, ed., Heart Throbs of the West, 12 vols. (Salt Lake City: Daughters of Utah Pioneers, 1939–1951), 1:126–128; and Elisha Warner, The History of Spanish Fork (Spanish Fork: Press Publishing Company, 1930), 60.

39   Hurt to Young, December 31, 1855, Office of Indian Affairs, Utah Superintendency, 1856–58.

40   Young to Hurt, February 11, 1856, Brigham Young Papers, LDS Archives.

rate of expenditure indicated by your accounts cannot be sanctioned."[41] Even more forcefully, Manypenny on March 19, 1856, called on Hurt to reach an understanding with Governor Young and Mormon subagent George Armstrong on their expenditures. Otherwise, he warned, Hurt's drafts might be rejected in future.[42]

Hurt saw these letters for the first time after his return from Carson Valley when copies arrived on August 28 with the commissioner's notification, dated July 9, that funds for the Utah agency had run out and his most recent drafts had been rejected.[43] The agent's own zeal to help the Utahs, the lack of administrative control, and the unreliable nature of the mail service, mainly during winter, combined to put him in real financial jeopardy. For any unpaid drafts, which represented loans against the Office of Indian Affairs, he alone was responsible.

Faced with disaster, the Virginian mounted a spirited defense. In his work, he told the commissioner, he had tried to correct the distinction Indians made "between Mormons and Americans, which was calculated to operate to the prejudice of the interests and policy of government toward them." He had applied through the governor, "for I supposed that the proper channel," for an appropriation to meet the costs of the Indian farms and had been encouraged to go ahead with this venture. Then Young had asked him to visit the natives along the Humboldt, Carson, and Truckee rivers that would require nearly four months and an expenditure of up to six thousand dollars. Contrary to Manypenny's earlier charge that he had failed to consult with the governor and Agent Armstrong, Hurt said he had told Young he feared there "would not be funds enough to meet our engagements for farming purposes" if he went to Carson Valley. Young's only reply, the agent said, "was that he had no doubt but my drafts would all be paid."[44]

It measured Hurt's desperation that he now sent two appeals to his friend in Congress, one by the eastern mail and the other four days later by the southern route to California. In both missives, the agent sharply criticized Mormon doctrines and policies toward the Indians. He told John Elliott that Indian lands had been occupied and the game killed off,

41 Manypenny to Hurt, November 14, 1855, Indian Office Letterbook, 53:42.
42 Manypenny to Hurt, March 19, 1856, Indian Office Letterbook, 53:517.
43 Manypenny to Hurt, July 9, 1856, Indian Office Letterbook, 54:454.
44 "The Utah Expedition," House Exec. Doc. 71 (35-1), 179–181.

leaving the natives "to starve or fight." Although a few chiefs had been baptized into the church, he said, they had "about as much knowledge of Christianity as brutes." Admitting he had overrun his receipts by as much as twenty thousand dollars, he urged the lawmaker to "use your influence to secure an appropriation at the next session of Congress."[45]

The Kentucky congressman jumped to Hurt's defense. "From long personal acquaintance," he told Commissioner Manypenny, he knew his friend to be "a man of not only fine ability but great prudence." Said the powerful committee chairman: "I will be at your office on Monday in regard to the matter."[46] As it turned out, his influence was not needed. In September, Manypenny had notified Hurt that a new appropriation had made it possible to cover his drafts. It took six months for his letter to reach the worried agent.

After this incident, Hurt dropped any pretense of trying to get along with Brigham Young. The agent was outspoken in protesting an incident at Fillmore, where the house of Edwin Pugh was stoned because he had invited two members of Hurt's visiting party, Richard James and James White, both Mormons, to stay overnight with him. The rowdies demanded to know, the agent said, what Pugh "was doing with those damned Americans about his house." Furthermore, he told Young, Mormon express riders had falsely warned the local Pahvant natives that "the Americans were coming to tie them." On learning that the Indians in Utah "made a distinction between the Mormons and Americans," Hurt went on, he had always tried "to teach them that there is no distinction ... but that we were all the Great Father's people." He then made a prediction that would come to pass sooner than he realized: "If they believe me they will accuse the opposite party with lying and attempting to deceive them, and then how easy it will be for men to imagine that I am stirring up prejudices among the Indians against the people."[47]

---

45   Hurt to Elliott, October 1, 1856, Office of Indian Affairs, Utah Superintendency, 1856–58, National Archives.

46   Elliott to Manypenny, December 20, 1856, Office of Indian Affairs, Utah Superintendency. An ardent southerner, Elliott gave up his seat in Congress in 1859 to organize Confederate support in eastern Kentucky and to serve in the 1st and 2nd Confederate Congresses. After the war, he became a prominent judge before an angry litigant assassinated him in 1879. Kentucky's Elliott County preserves his memory.

47   Hurt to Young, October 31, 1856, in "The Utah Expedition," House Exec. Doc. 71 (35-1), 182.

His blunt protest was returned in spirit by Mormon leaders as relations rapidly worsened during the time of Israel's cleansing, known as the Mormon Reformation, prior to an armed confrontation with the United States in 1857. Before the Reformation of 1856, "all was peace, sobriety and good order," Hurt later wrote. In October, he said, "a proclamation issued from the Lord's anointed, announcing the solemn fact that the people had violated their covenants with God and commanding them indiscriminately to bow at the Confessional, and repair to the streams of the mountains and be rebaptized forth with." He went on, "I have seen men and women, weeping in the utterest agonies of soul, and when I attempted to console them would say, they abhorred the idea of being forced into a confessional but dare not refuse."[48]

Earlier in 1856 Wilford Woodruff had told what happened when Hurt, along with U.S. surveyor general David H. Burr and some "smaller fry," tried to exercise his newly acquired legal skills in defending the primacy of federal law in the district court at Salt Lake City. Some of them, the apostle said, "went out of the house in the form of a sled, using the seat of their honor for runners."[49] To such undignified treatment the agent was not long in responding.

On February 16, 1857, four spent Indian missionaries, whose "trail could be followed by the blood from our horses legs," reached the Utah settlements after a heroic, 380-mile midwinter ride from Fort Limhi, northernmost Mormon outpost on the Salmon River's east fork, near present Salmon, Idaho.[50] They delivered to Brigham Young a report

---

48   See Hurt to Cumming, December 17, 1857, U.S. Territorial Papers, Utah Series, roll 1, vol. 1, April 30, 1853–December 24, 1857, National Archives, copy on microfilm A-59, USHS Library.

49   Woodruff to Smith, Journal History, April 1, 1857. This incident, which apparently occurred on February 14, 1857, was among the immediate causes of the armed confrontation between Utah Territory and the United States known as the Utah War. See Juanita Brooks, ed., *On the Mormon Frontier: The Diary of Hosea Stout*, 2 vols. (Salt Lake City: University of Utah Press, 1964), 2:622.

50   L. W. Shurtliff, Life and Travels of Lewis Warren Shurtliff, microfilm of handwritten copy made in 1926 from original manuscript owned by Elsie Van Leuven of Emmett, Idaho, in Idaho Historical Society, Boise, photocopy in author's possession. The four express riders were Shurtliff, mission president Thomas Smith, Pleasant Green Taylor, and Lachoneus Barnard.

and map of an exploration of the Bitterroot Valley by a party under Benjamin Franklin Cummings, who envisioned the rich region to the north as the future "abode of the saints."[51] Less than a week later, Young announced he would go "to Salmon River in Oregon" as soon as the weather allowed.[52] This gave Hurt the opening he had been looking for.

His riposte was delivered on March 30, in a letter marked "private," to the commissioner of Indian Affairs. Hurt said he had learned unofficially that Governor Young planned to take up most of the current appropriation and throw the burden of settling agency expenditures "without the means of liquidating them" on him. Coming to the main reason for his confidential note, Hurt reported that "His Excellency is now arranging an outfit of goods to be expended by him on an exploring expedition through the Territories of Oregon, Washington, and perhaps British Columbia." It was impossible, he concluded, for him to serve any longer "under the supervision of one who would decoy me into ruin."[53]

Later that year Young himself was treated to a cutoff of funds and an unaccustomed dressing-down by then commissioner of Indian Affairs J. W. Denver. It was the governor's obligation, Denver said, "to keep a supervisory control" over the agents and keep their expenditures "within the appropriations made for your superintendency." Young had failed to do this; moreover, Denver said, "you fitted out an expedition yourself, and conducted it northward, out of your superintendency, to give presents to Indians not under your control."[54] Nor was that the end of it.

President James Buchanan included Denver's rebuke among nearly five-dozen letters and reports covering a six-year period that he submitted to Congress to justify his ordering in May 1857 a U.S. Army expedition to escort a new governor to Utah and to enforce federal law in the territory. Of this number, forty-six came from files of the Office of Indian Affairs. And of those, Garland Hurt had written six, with two more unpublished because they were marked "private."

---

51 Cummings, Biography and Journals, November 19, 1857, typescript, BYU Library.
52 Brooks, *On the Mormon Frontier*, 2:623.
53 Hurt to Manypenny, March 30, 1857, Office of Indian Affairs, Utah Superintendency.
54 Denver to Young, November 11, 1857, in "The Utah Expedition," House Exec. Doc. 71 (35-1), 186–188.

As other federal officials fled Utah Territory in 1857 and Brigham Young declared martial law and called up the Nauvoo Legion, Hurt stuck to his post. Apparently putting his trust in the tribe he had served and the friendship of local Mormon leaders, probably including Spanish Fork bishop John Butler, he moved to the Spanish Fork Indian farm where a two-story adobe building had recently been completed.[55] From this sanctuary he urged the Utahs to reject Mormon overtures to form an alliance against U.S. forces, offering himself "as a hostage for the peaceful intentions of the troops."[56]

Hurt's control over the militant tribe, however, made him a potential threat to the heart of the Mormon settlements as up to five thousand Nauvoo Legion troops mobilized to blockade the Echo Canyon approach to Salt Lake Valley from the east. As it became less likely that the invading U.S. Army expedition would make it through the mountains that fall, the agent became more and more isolated and fearful for his own safety.

His decision to escape came soon after he heard that a party of California immigrants had been attacked on the Santa Clara River in southern Utah by Piede Indians, especially when the natives "insisted that Mormons, and not Indians, had killed the Americans." Hurt sent a native youth named Pete off by a secret route to discover the truth of what had happened. On September 23 the young warrior came back with an awful tale of blood. His report, as repeated by Hurt three months later, was the first essentially accurate account to the point of naming John D. Lee as instigator of the massacre by Mormons and Indians of some 120 emigrants from Arkansas at a quiet place on the Spanish Trail known as Mountain Meadows.[57]

---

55   Bishop John Butler was later accused of being a friend of Hurt, a charge he hotly denied. But he credited the agent with doing "a great deal of good at that time in giving employment to about fifty hands and in putting a little money in circulation." See John Butler, Autobiography, 1808–1861, typescript copy, USHS Library. A Daughters of Utah Pioneers monument about two miles south of Spanish Fork on State Highway 115 marks the site of the two-story adobe building where Hurt made his headquarters.

56   Reavis, "Hurt Biography," 785. Verifying Hurt's claim, Indian interpreter Dimick B. Huntington recorded on September 1, 1857, that he told Chief Ammon and other Utahs that "they [the soldiers] have come to fight us & you for when they kill us they will kill you they sayd the[y] was afraid to fight the Americans." See D. B. Huntington, Journal, September 1, 1857, MS1419-2, LDS Archives.

57   Hurt to Forney, December 4, 1857, in "The Utah Expedition," House Exec. Doc. 71 (35-1), 199–205.

The agent now decided to get out, but the question was which way to go. At the Spanish Fork farm he was hedged in to the north and south by Mormon settlements. He had been told that no one could leave the territory or cross the mountains unless he applied to Brigham Young for a passport, which Hurt refused to do. The answer arrived with a party of Utah chiefs who had come from the Uinta Basin to urge the agent to go back with them and investigate the possibility of establishing a farm there. But one or more of the natives also told local Mormon lookouts what Hurt had in mind.

So it was that early on September 27 a half-dozen Indians rushed into Hurt's office crying, "Friend! friend! the Mormons will kill you!" The Virginian looked out his window. He saw about one hundred armed men on horseback guarding the road to Spanish Fork Canyon on the east. As Hurt grabbed his papers, more natives rushed in to report that another body of armed men was on the road from Springville and still more were gathering in Payson. Then his interpreter came into the room and said, "Doctor, you're gone in!" The agent vowed to escape or "die in the attempt."

The troops that Hurt saw had been ordered to arrest him by anxious Nauvoo Legion officers who feared he might get away before General Aaron Johnson, head of the military district, returned from Salt Lake City with orders from Brigham Young on how to handle the troublesome agent. Colonel John S. Fullmer, who commanded the force from Spanish Fork, was joined by mounted companies from Payson and Springville under Colonel Charles B. Hancock and Major A. B. Wild, about three hundred men in all. Expecting the natives to fight for their agent "at the drop of a hat," the Mormon officers had tried to raise enough men "to awe them into submission" and make Hurt "a prisoner this day."

But within eighty rods of the Indian farm, the Nauvoo Legion troopers ran into a growing swarm of Utah warriors, "armed and much excited." Two other companies of ten men each, ordered to block the Spanish Fork Canyon escape route, rode into more militant natives "who would not let them pass" at the mouth of the canyon. Meanwhile, an Indian boy saddled Hurt's horse, and off he rode with three young warriors, Pete, Sam, and Showers-hockets, heading first to West Mountain on Utah Lake to confuse his pursuers, then back that night for supplies before riding up Spanish Fork Canyon.

Having been ordered to avoid an Indian war as a U.S. Army expedition near ed Mormon settlements, Bishop Butler dismissed the troops. Too late, General Aaron Johnson arrived with orders from Brigham Young on September 28 to "convey the Indian Agent Dr. Garland Hurt to this place." Finding the Indian farm a "perfect scene of waste and confusion," he regretfully reported, "the bush had been shook and the bird flown."[58]

The "bird" and his native lifeguards soon flew into a heavy snowstorm that "pelted without mercy the naked skins of my shivering escorts," and in crossing the mountains they waded "through snow knee deep."[59] Before they reached their destination, Brigham Young on October 7 reported to Commissioner Denver that Hurt "saw fit to leave the field of his official duty on the 26th of September last." He enclosed a copy of an alleged letter in which he had noted the agent's intention to take off "by some unfrequented route, and in company with certain Indians." Calling this course "very unsafe and highly improper," Young said he had pledged "a comfortable carriage" for Hurt's "speedy and safe transportation" to the American troops then approaching the territory.[60]

Hurt never said why it took twenty-seven days for him to go from Spanish Fork to South Pass on the Oregon Trail where he met Colonel Albert Sidney Johnston, commander of the U.S. Army expedition, on

58   Quotations and other information on the escape of Garland Hurt are taken from Hurt's report in "The Utah Expedition," House Exec. Doc. 71 (35-1), 205–208; "Autobiography of John Lowe Butler," 28–30; and Report of Genl. A. Johnson to Lt. Genl. D. H. Wells in regard to the flight of Dr. Garland Hurt, U.S. Indian Agent, Oct. 1857, Territorial Militia Records, 1849–1875, Utah State Archives, copy in author's possession. The latter document complements Hurt's own account and raises questions about Brigham Young's forthrightness in reporting the episode.

59   Hurt to Johnston, October 24, 1857, in "The Utah Expedition," House Exec. Doc. 71 (35-1), 208.

60   Ibid., 209, 210. In Dale Morgan's 1948 article, "The Administration of Indian Affairs in Utah, 1851–1858," *Pacific Historical Review*, 17:4, he suggested the possibility that Young's letter to Hurt "was written after rather than before his departure, as a good joke on Hurt." Aaron Johnston's report, cited in note 59, which came to light after Morgan's article, makes this post-dating even more likely, but as a joke it was surely not intended. A longer draft of this letter on September 26 in the handwriting of Daniel Wells is located in the Brigham Young Papers. Another draft of a letter to Hurt, with the same date, handwriting, and place, suspends him for alleged misconduct, but it apparently was not delivered or made public.

October 23. Nor did he describe his route. But it is more than likely that his Indian guides took him from Spanish Fork Canyon up Diamond Fork on the Escalante Trail of 1776 to cross the rim of the Great Basin into the Uinta Basin where he probably waited in the Indian camps, near present Vernal, Utah, until the way ahead was clear. They then rode over Diamond Mountain into Brown's Hole, following an Indian trail later known as the Outlaw Trail, up Green River to reach the Oregon Trail at the mouth of Big Sandy River. From there it was an easy ride over South Pass to the army camp on the Sweetwater River.

Hurt stayed with the army as Johnston ordered his scattered command to concentrate at Fort Bridger as November blizzards swept the high plains in today's southwestern Wyoming. The march from Hams Fork near present Granger, Wyoming, to the trading post on Blacks Fork, a distance of thirty-five miles, took fifteen days and cost the lives of some three thousand cattle, horses, and mules. To replace his losses to winter and Mormon raiders, Johnston sent Captain Randolph Marcy of the Fifth Infantry and a handpicked party on a hazardous winter journey to Fort Union near Las Vegas, New Mexico, to obtain mules, horses, and beef cattle.[61]

Marcy's task gave Hurt a final opportunity for service when the agent heard of Johnston's concern over reports that the Mormons were organizing a mounted force of three hundred to intercept Marcy at the Green River on his return. Volunteering to serve as the eyes of the army in a region he now knew, in January 1858 Hurt and five young Utah warriors rode back to the Uinta Basin, where Hurt lived with the Indians for nearly three months on such food "as they were able to procure by hunting." At times he survived for days "upon roots alone" before returning to Fort Bridger in mid-April to find that his sacrifice had been in vain and the "Utah rebellion" was over.[62]

Hurt returned to Utah in 1858 with the army, assisting Johnston in selecting a suitable location for Camp Floyd, near present Fairfield, and

---

61 For the story of this expedition, see Randolph B. Marcy, *Thirty Years of Army Life on the Border* (Philadelphia and New York: J. B. Lippincott Co., 1963), 198–243.

62 Reavis, "Hurt Biography," 786, 787. Hurt's duty as a scout became unnecessary when Marcy was ordered to return from Fort Union by a different route. From the Arkansas River, near present Pueblo, Colorado, Marcy took the line of the Cherokee Trail north to the Oregon Trail on the North Platte River.

eventually returning to the Spanish Fork farm. Much of the rest of his career as an Indian agent was spent defending himself against various charges, including running away without cause, misapplication of public funds, inciting the Indians, and even sleeping with mountain man Miles Goodyear's widowed native wife and fathering a child by her.[63] Typically, Hurt allowed none of these accusations to pass unnoticed and took the offensive whenever possible.

The most serious allegation was a charge by territorial secretary William H. Hooper, a Mormon, that Hurt had caused the Utah Indians "who had always been friendly" to become abusive and threatening. Furthermore, Hooper told Utah's new governor, Alfred Cumming, that Hurt had spent the winter in the Uinta Basin where he had urged the Utahs to "come out and join in the onslaught upon the Mormons."[64]

Johnston, by now a general, rejected the accusation. But Governor Cumming and Jacob Forney, the new superintendent of the Utah agency, not wishing to stir up trouble, simply ignored Hurt's repeated demands over the next eighteen months for an investigation to clear his name. Forney even tried to demean Hurt's projects, finding his operations in a run-down state "with scarcely any stock or farming implements on any of them."[65] He also reported that inhabitants in the neighborhood of the Spanish Fork farm denied that the agent had had any reason to take off the way he did.

With little or no support, Hurt fought back as best he could, even to the point of gathering testimonials to his character from Mormon

63   Miles Goodyear in 1846 had built a trading post, Fort Buenaventura, near the confluence of the Ogden and Weber rivers within the present city limits of Ogden, Utah, where he lived with his Utah common-law wife, Pamona, until he sold the location in 1847 to Mormon settlers and left the area. Considering Hurt's religious faith and his earlier report on the high incidence of venereal disease among the Utahs, the story that Hurt had taken up with Goodyear's former mate is highly unlikely. It was recorded in Huntington, Journal, May 1858, LDS Archives.

64   Hooper to Cumming, April 15, 1858, Office of Indian Affairs, Utah Superintendency.

65   Bishop John Butler's detailed inventory of the Spanish Fork farm immediately after the agent's escape listed many items, including livestock, farming implements, and agricultural produce, as did an inventory Hurt himself prepared from memory after joining the army. Except for the building and irrigation ditch at Spanish Fork, these items had largely disappeared by the time Forney visited the farms. For Butler's inventory, no doubt the best because it was done on the scene rather than by recollection, see Aaron Johnson's Report. Also see James C. Snow to George A. Smith, February 8, 1858, Journal History.

leaders in Manti, Fillmore, and Utah Valley. Testifying to the agent's "prudence, justice and moderation" were such local luminaries as Warren Snow, Isaac Morley, John Lowry, Parmenio A. Jackman, Joseph Pugmire, Samuel Bennett, and more than a dozen others. Hurt also struck back at the man he saw as his chief tormentor. In a "private" letter direct to Commissioner Denver, Hurt reported on January 6, 1859, that he had learned unofficially that Brigham Young had prepared a large number of claims for improvements on the Indian farms. The agent did not wish "to delay or defeat the prompt payment of any just claims," but he feared some of the charges "do not come under that category."[66]

Hurt spent most of 1860 in Washington, D.C., settling his own records.[67] But a year later his letter to Denver and his prior report of Young's 1857 Oregon venture had their intended effect when Congress directed the Office of Indian Affairs to examine Brigham Young's accounts. Hurt also may have encouraged such an investigation while he was in the nation's capital. If so, the result only showed how much he had underestimated his old adversary.

Benjamin Davies, then Utah superintendent of Indian Affairs, admittedly "a comparative stranger" in the territory, examined dozens of witnesses under oath about Young's activities and reported back that he had never seen "in a practice of many years at the bar" a time when so many "concurred with such precision and exactitude." Their "perfect recollection" and testimony, he said, "could not have failed to convince the most skeptical of the truthfulness of their statements."[68] Young was fully cleared of any wrongdoing.

By then Garland Hurt had closed the Utah chapter of his life and moved to Missouri, where he completed his medical education at St. Louis Medical College and won election to the Missouri General

66   Hurt to Denver, January 6, 1859, Office of Indian Affairs, Utah Superintendency.
67   Reavis, "Hurt Biography," 788.
68   See "Accounts of Brigham Young, Superintendent of Indian Affairs in Utah Territory," in U.S. Congress, House Exec. Doc. 29 (37-2), 1862, which offers a rich source of material for further study. John D. Lee and Dimick B. Huntington both swore under oath that they saw more than three thousand dollars in listed goods distributed to Indians at Mountain Meadows less than three weeks after the massacre. Contradicting his own testimony, Lee later said, "Brigham Young never spent a dollar on the Indians in Utah, while he was Indian Agent." See William Bishop, ed., *The Life and Confessions of John D. Lee* (St. Louis: Bryan, Brand & Company, 1877), 257.

Assembly, in which he served two sessions. In 1874 he became president of the St. Louis Medical Society.

"Exceptionally pure in life and thought, his temperament is joyous, and his manners dignified, though gracious," wrote a biographer of Hurt in 1875. Moreover, "The marks of confidence and esteem that have been bestowed upon him, by his profession and by the people of St. Louis, could have had no more worthy recipient."[69]

Late in life Garland Hurt married for the first time. He was nearly seventy when his only child was born, a son also named Garland, who apparently left no descendants of his own. Soon after, he moved to his wife's home in Newport, Arkansas. There, "the American" friend of the Utahs died of pneumonia on December 9, 1903, less than three weeks short of his eighty-fourth birthday. By the members of his church he was remembered as "one of the saintliest and sweetest spirits we have ever known." They had lost, they said, "a man of sterling worth and upright-ness, and faithful to every trust put upon him."[70]

---

69   Reavis, "Hurt Biography," 789.

70   Rice, "Biographical Sketches," 56. The late Susan B. Park of Carson City, Nevada, provided information on Hurt's later life.

✿

The Great Reformation: Prelude to the 1857–1858 Utah War

Presentation to the 2006 Annual Meeting of the
Utah State Historical Society, September 15, 2006.

THE NOTED HISTORIAN JAMES C. COBB HAS SAID, "THE PAST is not static or finite, but dynamic and fluid. It is subject neither to closure nor containment, but flows unchecked through the present and into the future."[1] This is usually true, but sometimes what flows through seems more to resemble the past described by novelist George Orwell. "When it has been recreated in whatever shape is needed at the moment," he said, "then this new version is the past, and no different past can ever have existed."[2]

Consider the Great Reformation that broke in territorial Utah in September 1856. One historian has called it just "a much needed moral and spiritual awakening."[3] Another compared it to a "a religious revival."[4]

---

1   James C. Cobb, "For the South, There Is No Closure," *Wall Street Journal*, May 8, 2001, A26.

2   Irving Howe, *Orwell's Nineteen Eighty-Four: Text, Sources, Criticism* (New York: Harcourt Brace Jovanovich, Inc., 1963), 142.

3   B. H. Roberts, *A Comprehensive History of the Church of Jesus Christ of Latter-day Saints*, 6 vols. (Salt Lake City: Deseret News Press, 1930), 4:119.

4   Orson F. Whitney, *History of Utah: Comprising Preliminary Chapters on the Previous History of Her Founders Accounts*, 4 vols. (Salt Lake City, 1892–1904), 1:565.

BRIGHAM YOUNG, CIRCA 1869
For more than three decades as
territorial governor, ex officio
superintendent of Indian affairs, and
prophet, seer, and revelator of the LDS
Church, President Brigham Young ruled
a Rocky Mountain empire. CHARLES R.
SAVAGE STEREOGRAPH, COURTESY
YALE COLLECTION OF WESTERN
AMERICANA, BEINECKE RARE BOOK
AND MANUSCRIPT LIBRARY.

To a third, it was a period when "moral principles were urged with great
intensity."[5] Still others thought it was only a "call to repentance."[6] And
none tied it directly to the 1857–1858 Utah War.

Most attributed the Reformation to Jedediah Morgan Grant, possibly
because it featured the harrowing doctrine that certain sins could only be
atoned by human blood. Perhaps to distance Brigham Young from such
an upsetting idea, most fail to mention Grant was his second counselor.
But one did go so far as to admit he was a member of the First Council
of Seventy.

Now it takes a lot of self-confidence for an independent historian who
stands on the often-quoted wisdom of Yogi Berra ("It's amazing what
you can see by just looking") to take issue with such an impressive array
of scholars as those quoted. But even without looking, he discovered a
more reasonable explanation of what the Reformation was about than

5   Leonard J. Arrington, *Great Basin Kingdom: An Economic History of the Latter-day
      Saints, 1830–1900* (Cambridge, Mass.: Harvard University Press, 1958), 161.

6   Andrew Love Neff, *History of Utah, 1847 to 1869* (Salt Lake City: Deseret News Press,
      1940), 550–551; Gustive O. Larson, "The Mormon Reformation, *Utah Historical Quar-
      terly* 26:1 (January 1858), 45–63.

all these authorities combined. (Coincidentally, it came from his great-great-grandfather, Jacob G. Bigler, the bishop of Nephi in the 1850s.)

In December 1856, Bishop Bigler attended legislative meetings at Great Salt Lake and was shaken and fearful of what he witnessed. "The fire of God is burning here and I command you and your quorums to scour up your armor both temporally & spiritual[l]y," he wrote to the priesthood leaders of his settlement. "Prepare yourselves to stand by me when Israil is to be cleansed," he said, "for this has got to be done that the Gentile bands may be Broken."[7]

What "Gentile bands" was he talking about, anyway?

Thomas Kane had spoken of them seven years earlier, when he had acted on his own initiative and withdrawn the initial Mormon memorial for a territorial government. "You must have officers of yourselves," he told Apostle Wilford Woodruff, "not military Politicians who are strutting around in your midst usurping Authority over you." He said, "You are better without any Government from the hands of Congress than a Territorial Government."[8]

In the end, it made no difference. Obsessed with slavery, Congress established a territory. One senator reportedly thought the requested name, Deseret, sounded too much like "desert." So Congress bestowed a name of its own choosing that no one else wanted—Utah. President Millard Fillmore signed the measure on September 9, 1850, and a forty-year struggle, of which the Utah War was only the hot phase, was born that day.

Just as Kane had predicted, Congress's imposition of government by presidential office seekers became intolerable by 1855. In his message to the legislative assembly that December, Governor Brigham Young used such words as "odious" and "tyrannical" to describe the colonial system.[9] Without asking Congress for permission to go ahead, he ordered Utah lawmakers to convene a constitutional convention and create the sovereign State of Deseret, a synonym for the Kingdom of God.

7   Bigler to Pyper and Webb, December 22, 1856, Record of the Nephi Mass Quorum of Seventies, 1857–1859, MSS SC 3240, Special Collections, BYU Library.
8   Kenney, ed., *Wilford Woodruff's Journal*, 3:515–516.
9   "Annual Governor's Message," December 11, 1855, *Deseret News*, December 19, 1855, 2/1.

Delegates were elected in February under a marked balloting procedure that usually produced the desired results unanimously. Just before they met in March 1856, Brigham Young explained their task. While the world did not understand, he said, "the Lord is building up his kingdom on the earth, is gathering his Israel for the last time, to make a great and mighty nation of this people." The constitutional convention was to "give them a free and independent State, and justly make them a sovereign people."[10]

Completed in only eleven days, the constitution of Deseret created a sovereign state equal in size to the sweep of Young's vision. The area its borders enclosed would have placed it third among today's states. An alleged census put its population at nearly eighty thousand, about double the actual number, not counting Indians. With high hopes, Young instructed Utah's delegate to Congress, John M. Bernhisel, to work with apostles John Taylor and George A. Smith in gaining the support of Congress for the new state charter.

If well planned, the 1856 bid for statehood—the most comprehensive prior to the Civil War—was surprisingly ill timed. Washington refused even to consider the idea. The new Republican Party had won control of the House on a platform to abolish slavery and polygamy. If this was not bad enough, Bernhisel told Brigham Young "that an effort was being made to procure your removal from office."[11] That suddenly freed his mind of any illusions that Washington favored him or his sovereignty aspirations.

Young got the bad news on August 28, 1856, and from that day his position was one of defiance toward the national government. "Let them rip and let them roll while the devil pops them through, for truly their time is short," he exploded to Taylor, Smith, and Bernhisel.[12] "As the Lord lives, we are bound to become a sovereign State in the Union, or an independent nation by ourselves," he told his followers. From the beginning, God's Kingdom had been "a terror to all nations," he said, but it would "revolutionize the world and bring all under subjection to the law of God, who is our law giver."[13]

10   Brigham Young, "Discourse," March 16, 1856, *Deseret News,* March 26, 1856, 18/3.
11   Bernhisel to Young, July 17, 1856, Brigham Young Papers, LDS Archives.
12   Young to Smith, Bernhisel, and Taylor, August 30, 1856, ibid. The author is indebted to Ardis E. Parshall for this item.
13   Brigham Young, "Remarks," August 31, 1856, *Deseret News,* September 17, 1856, 219/4, 220/1–3.

Less than three weeks after learning Deseret's sovereignty aspirations were dead on arrival, Young in a dramatic fashion made it apparent the time had come to break the Gentile bands, as Bishop Bigler said, and stand before humankind as a free and sovereign people. But there was an important prelude to this pivotal event in history. What could it be? The answer takes one to the plains of Moab, opposite Jericho.

Before ancient Israel crossed the Jordan, God through Moses promised that if His people obeyed His commands, He would "set you high above all the nations on earth." But "if you do not obey," the Lord also promised, "all these curses will come upon you." He then named them. For latter-day Israel, some had a familiar ring. There was famine, as suffered in 1855–1856; swarms of locusts, much like the grasshopper hordes that stripped their fields in 1855; and a nation coming against them, "like an eagle swooping down," a reminder of past treatment by a republic, whose symbol was the very bird the Almighty mentioned.[14] These calamities did not speak of an acceptance with God, but of standing on the wrong promises.

To offer before the Lord a godly people, worthy of favor in a confrontation with the United States, which Brigham Young foresaw, the Moses of latter-day Israel touched off a great revival, as described by the Nephi bishop, to cleanse the body of Israel in the Last Days. It called on members to confess their sins and be rebaptized, purify their lives and homes, and flush federal officials, apostates, Gentile merchants, and other corruption out of the body of God's people. It was indeed a spiritual renewal or call to repentance, as historians have said. But it was much more than that. For sinners and the righteous alike, it was also a fearful time.

As the Reformation's voice of Leviticus, Young chose Jedediah Morgan Grant, known to the faithful as "the sledgehammer of Brigham." By any name, Young's forty-two-year-old second counselor was an impressive and at times a frightening figure. He stood over six feet, bore not an unneeded ounce on his lanky bones, and appeared a little like a young Abraham Lincoln. He had six wives, treated them well, and was modest and kindly by nature. But what set the long-faced New Englander apart from other Mormon leaders was the indignation that burned in his innards at seeing filth and imperfection in God's chosen people. With a tongue sharpened by verbal combat with Gentile ministers, he was a

---

14   Deuteronomy 28:1, 15, 49.

fire-breathing preacher who frightened the congregation into a right standing before God. And when Grant and Young spoke of shedding human blood for the remission of certain sins, it "made the Harts of many tremble," understated Apostle Wilford Woodruff.[15]

U.S. Indian agent Garland Hurt said he had "seen men and women weeping in the utterest agonies of soul, and when I attempted to console them would say, they abhorred the idea of being forced into a confessional but dare not refuse."[16] According to Hannah Tapfield King, one of the many remarkable women in Utah history, "The people shrunk, shivered, wept, [and] groaned like whipped children. They were told to get up in meeting and confess their sins. They did so 'till it was sickening, and brought disease."[17]

By October Brigham Young's handcart experiment had collapsed into catastrophe as hundreds of members of the last of two of the five companies died of starvation and exposure near South Pass. The Reformation offered a welcome distraction from the disaster, overwhelming what a popular Mormon song called "the handcart scheme," and Jedediah Grant wore himself out, preaching in unheated halls and baptizing in cold mountain waters. Suddenly the "troubler of Israel" fell silent, struck down by typhoid and pneumonia, probably brought on by exhaustion. But his passing on December 1, 1856, only gave the Reformation new life as other leaders took up the torch he had laid down.[18] And it roared out of control.

During the legislative sessions Bishop Bigler attended that month, "the House was filled with the spirit of God almost to the consuming of our flesh," Apostle Woodruff said on December 23. The lawmakers resolved to forsake their sins and be rebaptized. The previous evening the apostles and Seventies had "Cut off from the Church" federal judge George P. Stiles for adultery, shortly before a mob broke into his office and pretended to destroy district court records.[19] Later dismissed as a prank, it was one joke that had far-reaching consequences. The apparent destruction of federal court records was a primary reason that President Buchanan acted to restore federal law in the territory.

---

15   Kenney, ed., *Wilford Woodruff's Journal*, 4:451.
16   Hurt to Cumming, December 17, 1857, Territorial Papers, Utah Series, USHS.
17   Journal of Hannah Tapfield King, October 8, 1856, LDS Archives.
18   1 Kings 18:17.
19   Kenney, ed., *Wilford Woodruff's Journal*, 4:519–20.

As the Reformation's cleansing flames roared into 1857, Utah's surveyor general looked up from his maps and saw three unannounced figures in his office. They thrust a letter in his face and demanded to know if he had written it. David H. Burr allowed he had. President Franklin Pierce had appointed the former geographer to Congress to survey the public land, of which Utah was comprised, prior to opening it for private purchase. Burr had told Washington that settlers were consecrating their holdings to the church through Brigham Young, as if to transfer ownership. America's land laws, created to transfer federal lands into private ownership, had been nullified in Utah, where the Lord owned the land, but Burr could not understand why settlers destroyed section and township markers when they had the most to gain from his work.[20]

The fifty-two-year-old cartographer, whose maps are collectors' items today, began to fear for his safety. Friends warned that his life was in danger, but he dismissed threats against him as idle menace until he heard about the killing of three men at Springville. Assassins had ambushed and apparently blood-atoned William Parrish and his son, Beason, as they sought to escape. "They were shot, *their throats cut, and their bowels ripped open,*" Burr told Washington.[21] Killed in the dark by mistake was their guide, Gardner G. "Duff" Potter, the Judas who led them into the ambush. Everybody in town knew who did it, but no effort was made to arrest or punish them.[22]

Now thoroughly frightened, David Burr told the General Land Office "the United States Courts have been broken up and driven from the Territory." The fact was, he said, "*these people repudiate the authority of the United States in this country and are in open rebellion against the general government.*"[23] The fear and desperation in these italicized words led Burr to escape and motivated an American president to take immediate action.

---

20 See "Report of the Secretary of the Interior," House Exec. Doc. 1 (34-3), 1856, v. 1, pt. 1, Serial 893, 543.

21 Burr to Hendricks, February 5, 1857, "The Utah Expedition," House Exec. Doc. 71 (35-1), 120.

22 For the story of the Parrish-Potter murders, see Polly Aird, "'You Nasty Apostates, Clear Out': Reasons for Disaffection in the Late 1850s," *Journal of Mormon History* 30:2 (Fall 2004), 129–207.

23 Burr to Hendricks, March 28, 1857, "The Utah Expedition," House Exec. Doc. 71 (35-1), 118.

By mid-April 1857 spring opened the trails and allowed David Burr, U.S. Marshal Peter K. Dotson and Judge George P. Stiles, to escape. Judge Stiles left believing that his court records had been destroyed, another reason Buchanan took action. He was the last of eight federal judges appointed by American presidents to Utah district courts. Five had fled out of fright or frustration; two died and one was not reappointed.[24] His departure left justice wholly in the hands of the probate courts, which meant Brigham Young.

The last of President Pierce's appointees to come and the first to flee was William W. Drummond, who gave all the rest of the federal judges a bad name. He left his wife in Illinois and arrived in 1855 with a Chicago prostitute on his arm. He took off ten months later, before the Reformation. But a year after he left, he added his voice to the uproar it caused with an inflammatory letter to the president filled with undocumented allegations.

"Nearly all the gentile and apostate Scurf in this community left for the United States," Hosea Stout rejoiced on April 15. "The fire of the reformation is burning many out who flee from the Territory afraid of their lives," he said, piously adding the Proverb, "The wicked flee when no man pursue[s]."[25] And Brigham Young said on returning from his excursion to Oregon Territory that spring, "Our city looks as though it had taken an emetic and vomited forth apostates, officials, and in fact all the filth which was weighing us down."[26]

But if all was now well in Zion, not so was it in the rest of the nation. Three days after Young returned from his journey north, four wagonloads of newspapers and letters rolled in. With the delivery from the East on May 29 came Apostle George A. Smith and Utah's congressional delegate, John M. Bernhisel. Two days later, they joined Young's Sunday prayer circle while one of them read aloud accounts on conditions in

---

24   The others were Perry Brocchus, Lemuel G. Brandebury, John F. Kinney, and William W. Drummond. Leonidas Shaver and Lazarus Reid died, and Zerubbabel Snow was not reappointed.

25   Juanita Brooks, ed., *On the Mormon Frontier: The Diary of Hosea Stout, 1844–1861*, 2 vols. (Salt Lake City: University of Utah Press, 1982), April 16, 1857, 2:625.

26   Young to Pratt and Benson, June 30, 1857, *Latter-day Saints' Millennial Star*, 19 (August 28, 1857), 556.

Utah in the eastern press. "We find that all hell is boiling over against us," said Apostle Woodruff.[27]

Three days earlier, Lieutenant General Winfield Scott, as directed by President Buchanan, had ordered a U.S. Army force of "not less than 2,500 men" to enforce federal law in the territory believed to be in full rebellion. Some say the Utah War started the day Scott issued the order, May 28. Others say it began with Brigham Young's declaration of martial law on September 15, 1857.

But the flow of events shows that it started a full year before: when Brigham Young on the last day of August 1856 threw down the gauntlet to the United States and vowed, "As the Lord lives, we are bound to become a sovereign state in the Union, or an independent nation by ourselves." It outruns credulity to think that the Reformation, which he himself ignited less than three weeks later, was simply a religious revival, unrelated to Young's declaration of self-government, if not independence.

Instead, it was the all-important spiritual component of a comprehensive move to break the bands imposed by Washington and arise either as a free and sovereign state of the Union—as state sovereignty was then understood—or an independent nation among the kingdoms of this world. Full sovereignty, not colonial rule, as represented by a territorial government, was the larger purpose it served. Only then could God's Kingdom fulfill its destiny to prepare the way for Christ to come again within the lifetime of its founders.

The great spiritual conflagration did not hasten this happy day, but it did bring about sooner than expected a dangerous armed showdown with the United States. It also led to crimes, before and after the president ordered troops to Utah, that are hard to admit and justify today, including the horrific atrocity in September 1857 at Mountain Meadows.

The early winter of 1857 announced an end to the worst year in Utah's history. In December, with a U.S. Army camped at Fort Bridger, preparing to advance on Salt Lake Valley as soon as spring opened the trail, Congress asked Buchanan why he had ordered troops to Utah, and the president began to look for a peaceful way out of the crisis he had precipitated. Silent, too, were the inflammatory voices that had stoked the fires of reform and brought the dangerous confrontation to a head.

27 Kenney, ed., *Wilford Woodruff's Journal*, 5:53–54.

One Sunday about that time, Hannah Tapfield King said, Brigham Young arose "peaceful and benign" and told the people to go to anyone they had wronged and confess to them alone, "but stop this confessing in public." He would have no more of it. She said his words fell "like balm on the spirits of the people."[28]

Which is how the speaker hopes the words "the end" will fall on the ears of his listeners as well. The Great Reformation, prelude to the Utah War of 1857–1858, was over.

---

28   Journals of Hannah Tapfield King, LDS Archives, 142.

⚜

"A Lion in the Path": Genesis of the Utah War 1857–1858

This is an edited version of an article that first appeared in
Utah Historical Quarterly 76:1 *(Winter 2008), 4–21.*

In December 1857, two American armies confronted each other in the snow on the high plains of today's southwestern Wyoming. At Fort Bridger, some eighteen hundred officers and men, including volunteers, of the U.S. Army's Utah Expedition—roughly one-fifth of the republic's regular soldiers available for frontier duty—waited for spring to clear the way to advance on Salt Lake Valley. Between them and the Mormon stronghold stood the hosts of latter-day Israel, also known as the Utah Territorial Militia, or Nauvoo Legion, as many as four thousand strong, ready to stop them in the winding Echo Canyon corridor through the Wasatch Mountains.

In Washington that month, Secretary of War John B. Floyd said the government could no longer avoid a collision with the Mormon community. "Their settlements lie in the grand pathway which leads from our Atlantic States to the new and flourishing communities growing up upon our Pacific seaboard," Floyd said. They stand as "a lion in the path," he added, defying civil and military authority and encouraging the Indians to attack emigrant families.[1]

---

1   "Report of the Secretary of War," December 5, 1857, Sen. Exec. Doc. 11 (35-1), 1858, Serial 920, 7, 8.

The lion in the nation's path was Brigham Young, Utah's first governor. And the grand pathway he stood in the way of was the overland line of travel and communications between the nation's eastern and western sections. Although replaced as territorial governor, he had declared martial law three months earlier in order to stop all travel without a permit across an expanse of western America that reached from the Rocky Mountains of today's central Colorado to the Sierra Nevada, west of Reno. It was an act of defiance, if not war, that would affect Utah's history for years to come.

The immediate impact of Young's actions fell on California. There a newly elected fifth governor voiced alarm that winter over the effect of the trails closure and "Mormons and Indians" on immigration. Governor John Weller said his people were "entitled to protection whilst traveling through American territory." To secure it, "The whole power of the federal government should be invoked," he said.[2] As he spoke, volunteer militia companies were forming in gold-mining towns along the Sierra Nevada, ready to march on Utah from the west.[3]

Noted historian David McCullough has said that nothing ever had to happen the way it happened. History could have gone off in any number of different directions at any point along the way.[4] But how could it come to this? To make the picture even more bizarre, both sides used the U.S. Constitution to justify their actions.

President James Buchanan in May 1857 acted under his executive authority and power as commander in chief of America's armed forces. He ordered the U.S. Army to escort a new governor to Utah and serve as a *posse comitatus* to enable appointed officials to enforce federal law in a territory that he believed to be in a state of open rebellion.[5] But his action touched off an armed revolt. "God almighty being my helper, they cannot come here," Brigham Young roared, declaring martial law.[6] The United

---

2   Governor John B. Weller, Inaugural Address, January 8, 1858, California State Library.

3   "More Volunteers for the Mormon War," *San Francisco Evening Bulletin*, January 5, 1858, 5:74, 2/1.

4   McCullough, "Knowing History and Knowing Who We Are," *Imprimis* 34 (April 2005), 4.

5   A *posse comitatus* is a force representative of all citizens to enforce the law under the legitimate authority of a political jurisdiction.

6   Young, "Remarks," September 13, 1857, *Deseret News*, September 23, 1857, 228/1.

States was breaking the Constitution, he said, and "we would now have to go forth & defend it & also the kingdom of God."[7] He believed God had inspired framers of the Constitution to create a land of religious freedom where His kingdom would be set up in the Last Days as foretold by the Old Testament prophet Daniel. Young and his people had established God's Kingdom. The U.S. Constitution was its founding document. They were its true defenders, not corrupt Washington politicians.

Meanwhile, a Nauvoo Legion lookout on Bridger Butte, eyeing the federal camp on Blacks Fork, may have thought that he had seen all this before. He was now engaged in the nation's first civil war, but it was also the third Mormon war within twenty years. And the causes of all three—the 1838 Mormon War in Missouri, the 1845–1846 Mormon War in Illinois, and now the one in Utah—had a familiar look.

What could they have in common? These similar observations point to the answer:

"The Mormons instituted among themselves a government of their own, independent of and in opposition to the government of this state."[8]

"They openly denounced the government of the United States as utterly corrupt, and as about to pass away and to be replaced by the government of God."[9]

"Their hostility to the lawful government of the country has at length become so violent that no officer bearing a commission from the Chief Magistrate of the Union can enter the Territory or remain there with safety."[10]

Who spoke those words? All were elected heads of state; each sent troops to put down a perceived Mormon rebellion; and they used the word "government" five times in three sentences to identify the problem.

---

7   Scott G. Kenney, ed., *Wilford Woodruff's Journal*, 10 vols. (Midvale, Utah: Signature Books, 1983), 5:78.

8   "Extracts from Gov. Boggs' Message of 1840," in *Document Containing The Correspondence, Orders, &c. In Relation To The Disturbances With the Mormons; And The Evidence Given Before The Hon. Austin A. King* (Fayette, Mo.: Office of the Boon's Lick Democrat, 1841; published by order of the Missouri General Assembly), 9–10.

9   Thomas Ford, *A History of Illinois from its Commencement as a State in 1818 to 1847*, ed. Milo Milton Quaife, 2 vols. (Chicago: S. C. Griggs and Co., 1854; reprinted R. R. Donnelley & Sons, Lakeside Classics Edition, Lakeside Press, 1945–1946), 2:158–159.

10   James Buchanan, "A Proclamation," House Exec. Doc. 2 (35-2), Vol. 1, Serial 997, 69–72.

In order of mention, they were Lilburn W. Boggs, governor of Missouri; Thomas Ford, governor of Illinois; and James Buchanan, our fifteenth American president. What government did they refer to?

When the heavens opened in the early nineteenth century and God spoke again to humankind as He did in the days of Moses, He reinstituted a system of rule, known as a theocracy, defined as divine rule through inspired spokesmen. Theocratic rule bestows many blessings. No longer need one bear the anguish of uncertainty and an endless quest to discover who he is, why she came to be at this point in time, and how one can be sure of self-awareness hereafter.

With such blessed assurance, however, comes an unwelcome corollary. For prior to the millennium, a theocracy, ruled from heaven above, cannot co-exist with a republic, governed by its people from earth below, without civil warfare. History has shown that the two governing systems are incompatible and cannot live together in peace. Instead there will be a struggle for supremacy until one compels the other either to bend or be gone.

Brigham Young knew of this incompatibility from experience by 1846, when he led his people west from Nauvoo toward the place that his predecessor had chosen before Joseph Smith was murdered in 1844. The Great Basin was a vast region of interior drainage, outside the United States and hundreds of miles from the nearest outpost of rule by its professed owner, the Republic of Mexico. In this empty and isolated area, Young would do again what had been done before in Missouri and Illinois.

In Missouri, land possession was volatile even before 1831, when the Almighty named Jackson County as Zion, and Independence—its frontier seat, a booming jumping off place on the Santa Fe Trail—the site of New Jerusalem. The plan of Zion's city was a picture of millennial order (theocratic government) and communal economic purpose. It resembled a beehive with a central square mile, or hive, of identical lots, where the working bees of Zion lived, and plots on the outskirts for them to go out to and harvest. Everywhere else, people lived on the land they farmed and were widely scattered outside smaller towns.

On paper, the planned urban center seems harmless, but a closer look reveals its confrontational nature. The City of Zion was exclusive, even hostile toward outsiders for whom it held no room. The collective agri-cultural concept was intimidating to next-door farm families, whose land spelled their survival. The command to "fill up the world" with cities of the same design bears the compulsion of divine rule to prevail over, rather than coexist with, its neighbors.

All of which mattered little in the summer of 1847, when Brigham Young laid out at the lowest eastern point of the Great Basin almost a true copy of Zion's City, today's Salt Lake City, which became a model for future Mormon towns. Land belonging to the Lord would not be bought or sold, he said, but assigned as inheritances. Having begun the task to establish God's Kingdom as an earthly dominion, Young headed back over the trail to wave on a parade of wagons and prepare to return the next year.

While he was gone, the earth moved. Taking place were events so momentous that they would change forever Young's vision of God's western Kingdom, as well as the destiny of the nation itself, in ways still beyond our powers to discern. Six months after Young's 1847 company arrived in the Salt Lake Valley, two Mormon Battalion veterans recorded the discovery of gold in California. A human tsunami was about to trans-form an isolated land into the Crossroads of the West. And ten days later, an even more pivotal event occurred. On February 2, 1848, the United States acquired all or most of five present southwestern states, including Utah, plus parts of two others, under the Treaty of Guadalupe Hidalgo, which ended the War with Mexico.

One cannot overstate the impact of these happenings on Utah history. No longer were Zion's working bees, with a lot in the city and a plot on the outskirts, trespassers on land claimed by Mexico. Instead, at a stroke, they became squatters on the public domain of the United States. To the features that made Zion's City unwelcome in Missouri was added an even more controversial one: the exclusive communitarian design on divinely held property conflicted with both the land laws and policies of a republic that transferred two-thirds of its public domain into private ownership during the nineteenth century. All it took for an outsider to acquire the right to buy 160 acres of the Lord's domain was clearance of the Indian claim and an authorized survey. For federal surveyors, life in early Utah would be an adventure.

Not yet ready to adopt a sovereign position, Mormon leaders now faced the need to reach an interim accommodation with the nation they had just left. Why at first they decided to seek a territorial form of government, the least favorable for establishing a sovereign realm, is unclear. On May 3, 1849, John M. Bernhisel headed to Washington with a memorial scroll of signatures twenty-two feet long asking Congress to create a territory named Deseret. If the region staked out by fewer than ten thousand settlers appeared extravagant—it was roughly twice the size of Texas—it reflected the expectation of future growth.

At the same time, Mormon leaders created a "free and independent" state of the same name to stand until territorial status was granted. This soon evolved into a memorial for statehood. Two months after Bernhisel left to request a territory, territorial secretary Almon W. Babbitt took off to seek full entry into the Union. Deseret now had conflicting petitions. It would take months to get orders from the Great Salt Lake Valley, so in November 1849 Apostle Wilford Woodruff and John Bernhisel went to Philadelphia to seek counsel from the faith's faithful advocate, Thomas L. Kane.

Kane told them he had applied to President James Polk for a territorial government at Brigham Young's request, but that Polk had refused to accept the condition that he would "appoint men from among yourselves," probably referring to Young as governor. At this, "I had to use my own discretion and I withdrew the Petition," he said. "You must have officers of yourselves, & not military Politicians who are strutting around in your midst usurping Authority over you," Kane told Apostle Woodruff. "You are better without any Government from the hands of Congress than a Territorial Government." Kane next revealed his own prophetic powers. Under a territory, "corrupt political men from Washington would control the land and Indian agencies," he said, "and conflict with your own calculations."[11]

True to his prediction, President James Buchanan in 1858 handed Congress over sixty letters and reports over a six-year period to justify sending a military expedition to Utah. All but four were written by officials from the two agencies Kane had put his finger on—the U.S. Land Office

---

11   Kenney, ed., *Wilford Woodruff's Journal*, 3:515–516.

and the Office of Indian Affairs. In the end, it mattered little. Obsessed with slavery, Congress created a territory, took away its seaport, and gave it an unwanted name, Utah. President Millard Fillmore signed the bill on September 9, 1850, and it could be said the Utah War started on that date. One emigrant said he heard Brigham Young say, "If they send a governor here, he will be glad to black my boots for me."[12] Thanks to Kane's influence, President Fillmore inadvertently handed the job of blacking Young's boots to one of the prophet's wives: He named Young himself Utah's first governor.

Other presidential appointments over the next six years were a mixed lot, but not noticeably different from those of other territories. Perhaps the best was Franklin Pierce's choice as Utah's surveyor general. Fifty-two-year-old David H. Burr was nothing like the controversial figure he would become. One of the nation's leading mapmakers, he had served as cartographer for the U.S. Post Office and official geologist of Congress. Over a long career, he had surveyed and mapped most of the states and many cities and counties and published the first map of North America incorporating the discoveries of Jedediah Smith.

But as Kane predicted, Burr got no respect in Utah. And he had not seen anything like it when he came in 1855. Patterned after Zion's City, Mormon settlements were twice the size that federal law allowed for preemption entry on occupied town sites, a half-section, 320 acres. Great Salt Lake City topped that limit by six times.[13] The year before Burr arrived, settlers began to consecrate their holdings to the church through trustee-in-trust Brigham Young.[14] And Utah legislators ignored Indian rights and granted by law canyons, water and timber resources, and herd grounds to Mormon leaders as if to convey ownership. But these oddities hardly compared to the hostility Burr's crews met in the field. According to his deputy, local settlers told native chiefs that "we were measuring out the land" to claim it and "drive the Mormons away and kill

---

12 David L. Bigler, ed., *A Winter with the Mormons: The 1852 Letters of Jotham Goodell*, 50.
13 See "An Act for the relief of the citizens of towns upon the lands of the United States, under certain circumstances," *The Public Statutes at Large of the United States*, Vol. 5, 453–458.
14 "Report of the Commissioner, General Land Office," House Exec. Doc. 1 (34-3), 1856, Serial 893, 210–211.

the Indians."[15] Burr was seen as "an enemy, and an intruder upon their rights."[16] In the past, his work had opened the way for settlers elsewhere to own their land. He could not understand why rural Mormons removed the mounds and posts that marked section and township corners and hoped they would realize "how important it is to them to perpetuate these corners."[17] When the day came, Mormon officials would blame him for not setting them properly.

Thomas Kane's prophetic powers in relation to land ownership also proved true when it came to the U.S. Office of Indian Affairs. In the house divided that was Utah, the federal agency's aim was to keep peace on the frontier. The mission of God's Kingdom, on the other hand, was to teach the Indians, or Lamanites, the gospel of their forefathers and become partners with them in building New Jerusalem on the American continent. Appointment of Brigham Young as ex-officio superintendent of Indian Affairs placed the Mormon leader in charge of conflicting objectives.

It is not surprising that Young, to the alarm of U.S. Indian agents, favored one at the cost of the other. Nor would it have mattered, except when Zion was redeemed, said the prophet Micah in words repeated in the Book of Mormon, the "remnant of Jacob," or Lamanites, would be among unrepentant gentiles "as a young lion among the flocks of sheep, who, if he go through, both treadeth down and teareth in pieces."[18] People on the frontier could figure out that the "remnant of Jacob" referred to the Indians, while the flocks of sheep this young lion would go through, tearing people to bits, if they did not repent, probably meant them. So it was that Mormon overtures to the tribes on the Missouri frontier had been a source of rumor, misunderstanding, and conflict.

The same fear can be seen in Secretary of War Floyd's 1857 report, as well as in California governor Weller's inaugural address soon after. The call of hundreds of Indian missionaries to tribes west of the Mississippi

15   C. L. Craig to David H. Burr, August 1, 1856, "The Utah Expedition," House Exec. Doc. 71 (35-1), 1858, Serial 956, 115–116.
16   Ibid., David H. Burr to Thomas A. Hendricks, June 11, 1857, 120.
17   "Annual Report of Surveyor General of Utah," September 30, 1856, House Exec. Doc. 1 (34-3), 1856, Serial 893, 543.
18   Micah 5:8; The Book of Mormon, 3 Nephi 21:12.

River, starting in 1855, set off alarm bells in Washington, D.C., and across the West. And true to Kane's prediction, most of the documents Buchanan handed Congress to justify his ordering a U.S. Army expedition to Utah came from the Office of Indian Affairs.

Aware of such fears, Brigham Young at times seemed to encourage them. "O what a pity they could not foresee the evil they were bringing on themselves, by driving this people into the midst of the savages of the plains," he said in August 1857.[19] Even then, the territory's senior general ordered his militia commanders to "Instruct the Indians that our enemies are also their enemies & how they are continually fighting against them somewhere and that it will be come upon them as well as the Sioux & Cheyennes in due time, that they must be our friends and stick to us, for if our enemies kill us off, they will surely be cut off by the same parties [the U.S. Army]."[20]

Whether a creature of federal imagination or real, the lion that the War Department saw in the nation's path in 1857 was an alliance of Mormons and Indians, Ephraim and Manasseh in the Mormon theological parlance. Lending credence to such fears had been attacks on small emigrant parties the summer before on the California Trail along the Humboldt River, on the line of today's Interstate 80, and a horrific atrocity at Mountain Meadows in southern Utah.

Thomas Kane did not spell out a third source of friction between the Great Basin theocracy and the American republic, but clearly referred to it when he said, "You do not want two governments with you."[21] In a theocratic system, God's will renders obsolete the imperfect human covenants on which social order depends, such as the rule of law.

In Illinois, Nauvoo's municipal council took advantage of a liberal city charter to create an exclusive court system for people who lived under higher law. Illinois governor Thomas Ford said they created courts to execute laws of their own making "with but little dependence upon the constitutional judiciary."[22] Utah legislators did the same. To short circuit

---

19   Young, "Remarks," August 2, 1857, *Deseret News*, August 9, 1857, 188/1–4.
20   Daniel H. Wells to William H. Dame, August, 13, 1857, William R. Palmer Collection, File 8, Box 87, Sherratt Library.
21   Kenney, ed., *Wilford Woodruff's Journal*, 3:515.
22   Ford, *A History of Illinois*, 2:66

the territory's district courts under judges appointed by the president, they created county-level probate courts and vested them with original civil and criminal jurisdiction, powers not meant by Congress, to establish an exclusive judiciary. They further banned common law and legal precedent.[23]

Such practices had caused violent opposition in Illinois, but stirred little complaint in Utah because its people accepted it as part of their faith. Passing emigrants were not so acquiescent. The first book copyrighted in California was an 1851 collection of emigrant grievances at random arrests, fines, punishment, and lawsuits. They called on Congress to institute military rule in Utah.[24] And district judges bombarded Washington with protests at being stripped of their function. Of eight appointed from 1850 to 1856, five fled, two died, and one was not reappointed.

By 1855 it had become clear to Mormon leaders that God's Kingdom could not live under territorial rule and fulfill its destiny as foretold by the Prophet Daniel.[25] They now opened the most determined bid for entry into the Union prior to the Civil War, when they would declare Deseret a state unilaterally. Repeatedly they had asked Congress for permission to hold a constitutional convention as the first step in the statehood process, but federal lawmakers had ignored their request. This time they would give Congress a choice: Take us as a self-governing state or leave us alone.

Describing territorial rule as an "odious, tyrannical, and absurd system of colonial government," Young in December 1855 called on Utah lawmakers to hold a convention to adopt a state constitution.[26] The delegates who assembled from across the territory in March 1856 had been elected unanimously under a marked ballot system that disallowed the opportunity to vote in secret. Another carryover from Nauvoo, such

---

23 For similarities between Utah's early probate courts and the county courts that evolved in New Mexico, see Howard R. Lamar, "Political Patterns in New Mexico and Utah Territories, 1850–1890," *Utah Historical Quarterly* 28 (October 1960), 363–387.

24 See Nelson Slater, *Fruits of Mormonism or A Fair and Candid Statement of Facts Illustrative of Mormon Principles, Mormon Policy and Mormon Character, by More than Forty Eye-Witnesses* (Coloma, Calif.: Harmon & Springs, 1851).

25 See Daniel 2:44.

26 Brigham Young, "Governor's Message," December 11, 1855, *Deseret News*, December 19, 1855.

voting practices had caused "bitter hatred and unrelenting hostility" in Illinois, as the *Quincy Whig* editor had predicted.[27]

Completed in eleven days was the constitution of a new state named Deseret that equaled in size, if not yet population, the sweep of Brigham Young's vision. Its borders enclosed an area exceeded only by today's states of Alaska and Texas. An alleged census counted nearly eighty thousand inhabitants, or about twice the true number, not counting Indians, an exaggeration Young would later elevate to nearly one hundred thousand. In high spirits, Young informed John Bernhisel of these preliminaries and dispatched Apostle George A. Smith to work with him and Apostle John Taylor, editor of *The Mormon* in New York, in winning the approval of Congress for the new constitution, which would be tantamount to statehood.

But the 1856 drive for sovereignty through statehood proved ill timed. Deseret's delegates found no interest in Washington even to consider the bid. The new Republican Party, now in control of Congress, won on a platform calling for the abolition of slavery and polygamy. If this news was not bad enough, Bernhisel's report cleared Young's mind of any illusions that Washington looked with favor on him or his desire for statehood. The Utah delegate told Governor Young "an effort was being made to procure your removal from office."[28]

From late August 1856, Brigham Young's position was one of defiance toward the national government. Less than three weeks after learning Deseret's sovereignty aspirations were dead on arrival, he made clear that the time had come to throw off Washington's yoke. On September 14, Young ignited a flaming revival to cleanse Israel and present before the Lord a godly people worthy of divine favor in an imminent showdown with the United States, which he foresaw. Known as the Reformation, it called members to confess their sins and be rebaptized, clean up their lives and homes, and flush federal officials, apostates, gentile merchants, and other manifestations of corruption out of the body of Israel. For sinners and the righteous alike, it was a fearful time.

---

27   Sylvester M. Bartlett, *Quincy Whig*, January 22, 1842, in John E. Hallwas and Roger D. Launius, eds., *Cultures in Conflict: A Documentary History of the Mormon War in Illinois* (Logan: Utah State University Press, 1995), 83–84.

28   John Bernhisel to Young, July 17, 1856, Brigham Young Papers, LDS Archives.

In December, the Nephi bishop attended legislative sessions at Great Salt Lake City and signaled the purpose of the spiritual conflagration. "The fire of God is burning here," Bishop Jacob Bigler told the leaders of his settlement. "Prepare yourselves to stand by me when Israil is to be cleansed," he said, "for this has got to be done that the Gentile bands may be Broken." The move to sovereignty also anticipated a possible military confrontation. "The Saints in Carson & Sanbernidino are called to Come Home Come Home Come Home," he wrote. As early as December 1856, these outlying colonies were called back to defend Zion.[29]

As the archer to shoot the Reformation's "arrows of the Almighty among the people," Young chose his lanky second counselor, Jedediah Morgan Grant. At age forty-two, he stood over six feet, loved his wives—all six of them—and was kindly by nature. What made Grant exceptional was the fire that burned in his belly at the sight of uncleanliness, personal or spiritual, in God's people. He was "pruning with a sharp two edged sword & calling loudly upon the people to wake up & repent of their sins," wrote Apostle Wilford Woodruff. As other leaders turned to the handcart crisis on the Wyoming plains, Grant wore himself out "preaching for several months calling upon the people to repent" in unheated halls and rebaptizing in cold mountain waters. Typhoid and pneumonia, probably brought on by exhaustion, struck silent the voice that had "been like the Trump of the Angel of God & he has labured night & day untill He was laid prostrate with sickness."[30] Grant's passing on December 1, 1856, only gave the Reformation new life as other leaders took up the torch he had laid down.

During territorial legislative sessions on December 23 at Great Salt Lake City, "the room was filled as with Consumeing fire" of the spirit of God "& many things were revealed which were marvelous," Apostle Wilford Woodruff recorded.[31] The lawmakers resolved a week later to forsake their sins and be rebaptized. They did not say whether such sins included breaking into the offices of Judge George P. Stiles the night before and pretending to destroy district court records. Some dismissed

---

29   Jacob G. Bigler to John Pyper, David Webb, and counselors, December 23, 1856, Record of the Nephi Mass Quorum of Seventies, 1857–1858, MSS SC 3244, BYU Library.
30   Kenney, ed., *Wilford Woodruff's Journal*, October 7 and 9, December 1, 1856, 4:469–470, 488.
31   Ibid, 4:520.

it as a prank. If so, it was one joke that had far-reaching consequences. The apparent destruction of federal court records was a primary reason President James Buchanan acted to restore federal law in the territory.

Overcome by religious zeal, the lawmakers also drew up memorials to President-elect Buchanan to justify the nullification of federal law. Accusing former presidents of sending officials who "threaten us with death and destruction," they swore to "resist any attempt of Government Officials to set at naught our Territorial laws, or to impose upon us those which are inapplicable and of right not in force in this Territory."[32] The doctrine of nullification had led South Carolina a quarter-century earlier to the brink of civil war.[33]

Like the 1856 statehood bid, the memorial and resolutions were ill timed as well as confrontational. John Bernhisel delivered them to President Buchanan two weeks after his inauguration in March 1857. He referred them to Interior Secretary Jacob Thompson, who called them "a declaration of war." The cabinet member rebuked Bernhisel and said he did not know how the memorials would strike the president, but that they made a very "unfavorable impression on his mind."[34]

Meanwhile, frightened and upset by the apparent destruction of his court records, Judge George P. Stiles satisfied the mob's intention in ransacking his office. He became the last of five district justices, appointed by Presidents Millard Fillmore and Franklin Pierce, who abandoned their posts in Utah from 1851 to 1857. He was also the last of Pierce's three judicial appointees, who took to their heels and left justice entirely in the hands of the probate courts, which meant Brigham Young.

---

32   "Memorial & Resolutions to the President of the United States, concerning certain Officers of the Territory of Utah and Memorial to the President of the United States," 1856–58, Memorials and Resolutions, General Assembly, Utah Territory, 1852–59, MIC 3150, Reel 3, Utah State Archives. Utah lawmakers apparently based the power to nullify federal laws on Sec. 17, "An Act to establish a Territorial Government for Utah," in *Statutes at Large of the United States*, Vol. 9, 458.

33   Civil war was narrowly averted in 1832 when South Carolina threatened to secede from the Union if the U.S. government tried to collect federal tariff duties in the state. President Andrew Jackson's threat to send troops to enforce the U.S. law eventually nullified John C. Calhoun's nullification doctrine, which held that states had the power to declare federal laws null and void.

34   John Bernhisel to Young, April 2, 1857, Brigham Young Papers, LDS Archives.

The first to flee had been John F. Kinney, who presided over the 1855 Gunnison murder trial and saw the Mormon jury nullify his instructions. He drew the wrath of Utah lawmakers by opposing legislation to outlaw common-law jurisdiction. They retaliated by assigning him to preside over a new district in Carson Valley, five hundred miles west of Great Salt Lake City, inhabited "by Indians, & destitute of the necessary comforts," the judge protested. For this "insult to me and my family," he took off on April 21, 1856, and went home to West Point, Iowa, where he came down with bilious fever.[35]

The last to come and next to go was William W. Drummond, who fully measured up to Utah's opinion of outside judges. He left his wife in Illinois and came to Utah with a Chicago prostitute on his arm (and at times at his side in court). After the lecherous judge told a Fillmore grand jury that Utah lawmakers had no power to bestow original civil and criminal jurisdiction on probate courts, he found himself indicted by the Millard County grand jury and arrested under a warrant issued by the probate judge at Fillmore. It was a charade, like the burning of Judge Stiles's court records, but it scared the judge, who took off with his lady friend in May 1856. He would be heard from again.

The cleansing fires of the Reformation roared into 1857. In late January, David H. Burr looked up from his maps and saw territorial officers Hosea Stout, James Cummings, and Alexander McRae standing before him. They showed him a copy of his letter to the General Land Office months before and asked if he had written it. He said yes. They then told the surveyor that "*the country was theirs,* that they would not permit this interference with their rights, and this writing letters about them would be put a stop to." Burr saw no reason for their visit except to intimidate him, he told the General Land Office commissioner Thomas A. Hendricks. The surveyor began to fear for his safety. "For the last three months my friends have considered my life in danger," he said, but he

---

35   John F. Kinney to Jeremiah Black, undated, U.S. Attorney General, Records relating to the appointment of Federal judges, attorneys, and marshals for the Territory and State of Utah, 1853–1901, PAM 14082 and MIC A 527–540, USHS. Kinney complained but learned his lesson. Again appointed chief justice in 1860, he did Young's bidding and found himself elected, almost unanimously, as Utah delegate to Congress from 1863 to 1865.

thought threats made against him and disaffected Mormons were idle menaces until he heard in March 1857 that three men had been killed at Springville. Assailants from the town ambushed, murdered, and disemboweled William Parrish and his son, Beason, as they tried to get away.[36]

Burr's cry of alarm reached Washington soon after the inflammatory resignation of Judge William W. Drummond, who wrote it almost a year after he and his mistress had taken off. Among other things, he charged that supreme court records had been destroyed "by order of the Church," that Indians had murdered Captain John W. Gunnison in 1853 under Mormon orders and direction, and his predecessor, Judge Leonidas Shaver, "came to his death by drinking poisoned liquors."[37] The absconded judge offered no evidence or witnesses to support these accusations and, contributing to the dubious nature of his reports, his estimate of Utah's population as a hundred thousand, about twice the actual number, was overblown.

Even so, the territory's top general made the most of the manpower he had as he pushed preparations for the anticipated military confrontation with the United States. On April 1, Lieutenant General Daniel H. Wells announced the militia's reorganization into companies of ten, fifty, and one hundred to pattern it after the hosts of ancient Israel. All able-bodied men from age eighteen to forty-five were ordered to sign up for military duty.[38] Wells also divided Utah into thirteen military districts and appointed an officer to enroll recruits in each of them.

As they began to march, spring opened the trails and allowed Burr, Judge George P. Stiles, Marshal Peter K. Dotson, and others to flee. "Nearly all the gentile and apostate Scurf in this community left for the United States," Hosea Stout said. "The fire of the Reformation is burning many out who flee from the Territory afraid of their lives," he went on, adding the proverb, "The wicked flee when no man pursue[s]."[39]

But, as he said, not all the "scurf" had flown. Perhaps less wicked than the rest or braver, U.S. Indian agent Garland Hurt, known to the Ute

---

36   David H. Burr to Thomas A. Hendricks, February 5, 1857, "The Utah Expedition," House Exec. Doc. 71 (35-1), 118–120.

37   Ibid., William H. Drummond to Jeremiah Black, March 30, 1857, 212–214.

38   For the new organization, see *Deseret News*, April 1, 1857.

39   Juanita Brooks, ed., *On the Mormon Frontier: The Diary of Hosea Stout, 1844–1861*, 2 vols. (Salt Lake City: University of Utah Press, 1982), April 15, 1857.

tribe as "the American," holed up on the Ute Indian training farm he had established on the Spanish Fork River, below the town of the same name. Before going to his sanctuary, he set a trap for Utah's superintendent of Indian Affairs. In a confidential letter posted by private hands, he told George Manypenny in Washington, D.C., that Brigham Young was gathering Indian goods for an "exploring expedition through the Territories of Oregon, Washington, and perhaps British Columbia."[40]

Brigham Young's northern expedition in the spring of 1857 was the longest of his career in the West. Hurt suspected that it was no pleasure junket, but he could not have known its purpose had to do with a possible confrontation with the United States. Young announced the journey less than a week after four half-starved riders, whose trail could be followed by the blood from their horses' legs, reached Salt Lake City in late February after a hazardous mid-winter journey of nearly four hundred miles from Fort Limhi, the Northern Indian Mission on the Salmon River.

The news and map they delivered were riveting. In October 1856, Young had ordered Indian missionary Pleasant Green Taylor to contact the Hudson's Bay agent in the Bitterroot Valley and investigate the purchase of Fort Hall on the Snake River, overlooking the Oregon Trail. The following month, Taylor and Fort Limhi companions Benjamin F. Cummings and Ebenezer Robinson crossed the Continental Divide by present-day Lemhi Pass on the 1805 Lewis and Clark Trail, and rode north to the great valley of the bitterroot, now in southwestern Montana.[41]

Young's agents from the Great Basin were stunned by the magnificence of the Flathead Indian homeland, guarded on three sides by high mountain ranges. They were especially impressed by its agricultural potential. The valley was not only richly fertile, but a thousand feet below Salt Lake Valley in elevation. Streams of water rushed from every side and timber resources appeared endless. One of the agents, Nauvoo Legion major Benjamin F. Cummings, learned that emigrants arriving by steamboats on the Missouri River could be transported from Fort Benton over a new wagon road to the Bitterroot Valley.

---

40   Garland Hurt to George Manypenny, March 30, 1857, Letters Received, Office of Indian Affairs, Utah Superintendency, microfilm, USHS Library.

41   Lemhi is a misspelling of Limhi, a Book of Mormon name.

"When considered with Mormonism," Cummings and his companions "could not help thinking that some day Bitter-Root valley, as well as other portions of the country over east of the mountains would become the abode of the saints."[42]

Brigham Young apparently thought so, too. He announced he would go north to Fort Limhi, then in Oregon Territory, now in Idaho, and made public the names of a large number of the territory's leading military, civic, and religious leaders to go with him. Later, with his prayer circle, he heard Cummings' journal read aloud and studied his map. "The price of freight will come down when settlements are made in the Land," Young said.[43]

On April 24 Young led a line of wagons, carriages, and animals over a mile long north from Great Salt Lake City. The parade included 115 men, 22 women, and 5 boys and numbered all three members of the faith's ruling triumvirate—the First Presidency of Brigham Young, Heber C. Kimball, and Daniel H. Wells—and other top religious, military and settlement leaders. Especially noteworthy was the presence of Ute chief Arapeen and his wife, Wispit. He could be counted on to recommend his hosts to northern native leaders.

Over the next thirty-three days, Utah's superintendent of Indian Affairs met with Indians of Oregon Territory, outside his legal jurisdiction, and gave them "many presents of blankets." He inspected the Lewis and Clark Trail that led from Fort Limhi to the waters of the Missouri River and an emerging wagon trace to the Bitterroot Valley. He also selected a location on the Salmon River's east fork, now Lemhi River, for a second fort to expand the colony near Salmon, Idaho. "The president felt well toward the brethren in this place and said the settlements must go north instead of south," wrote William Dame.[44]

Young did what he set out to do—"rest the mind and weary the body"—he told his followers on the eve of his fifty-sixth birthday, five days after he returned on May 26. "I have renewed my strength, renewed

---

42   Benjamin Franklin Cummings, Autobiography and Journals, November 16–19, 1856, BYU Library.

43   Kenney, ed., *Wilford Woodruff's Journal*, 5:26.

44   William H. Dame Journal, May 18, 1857, BYU Library.

the vigor of my body and mind."[45] He would need the entire strength of his mind and muscle to meet the dangers gathering on the course he had charted. Two days before, Apostle George A. Smith and John Bernhisel had arrived from the east to report that "all hell is boiling over against us," said Apostle Woodruff.[46]

It was hardly an overstatement. While Young was in Oregon Territory, President Buchanan confirmed rumors in the east as early as mid-April and ordered troops to Utah. On May 28, Lieutenant General Winfield Scott issued orders for not less than twenty-five hundred men to make up the expedition. He ordered its commander, Brevet Brigadier General William S. Harney, that the expedition was to act as a *posse comitatus* in aiding a new governor and federal officers to enforce the law in a territory considered to be in a state of rebellion. He was not to attack "any body of citizens whatever, except on such requisition or summons, or in sheer self-defence."[47]

On July 24, 1857, the tenth anniversary of his arrival in Salt Lake Valley with the first pioneer company, Brigham Young announced publicly that an American army was on its way. The news shocked a people emotionally stressed by the Reformation and murder of Apostle Parley P. Pratt. Excited and fearful, they filled the bowery on Sunday, two days later, and anxiously waited to hear Young tell what it meant for them and their families. Brigham Young began in a way he rarely, if ever, did. He opened his Bible and read aloud: "In the days of these kings shall the God of heaven set up a kingdom, which shall never be destroyed; and the kingdom shall not be left to other people, but it shall break in pieces and consume all these kingdoms, and it shall stand for ever."[48] They had established the kingdom Daniel envisioned in the Last Days, he told his people. It would never be destroyed, and "that is my testimony."[49] There was nothing to fear.

As American troops neared Utah, Young on September 6 swore that if the nation sent an overwhelming force in 1858, he would lay the territory

45   Brigham Young, "Remarks," May 31, 1857, in *Deseret News*, June 10, 1857, 107/1–3.
46   Kenney, ed., *Wilford Woodruff's Journal*, 5:53–54.
47   George W. Lay to William S. Harney, June 29, 1857, "The Utah Expedition," House Exec. Doc. 71 (35-1), 7–9.
48   Daniel 2:27–49.
49   Brigham Young, "Remarks," July 26, 1857, in *Deseret News*, August 5, 1857.

in waste and flee into the mountains. "Brother [Thomas] Smith is presid-
ing at [Fort] Limhi [on] Salmon River," he reminded his trusted associates, "Now do we not want a station about half way from here say near
Fort Hall?" he asked. "He said that the north is the place for us & not the
South," wrote Apostle Woodruff.[50] Two days later, a U.S. Army envoy
interrupted such contingency planning.

As a lieutenant, Stewart Van Vliet had led the charge that won the day
at Monterrey during the War with Mexico, but he was better known as a
peacemaker, who had established cordial relations with many Mormons
he had hired while serving as quartermaster at Fort Kearny on the Oregon
Trail. This was the reason General Harney chose the quartermaster, now
a captain, to go ahead of his command and arrange forage and supplies
for his expedition and find a suitable place for an army post.[51] To avoid a
collision, he bivouacked his dragoon escort on Hams Fork, near present
Granger, Wyoming, and traveled into the Great Salt Lake Valley with
Nathaniel V. Jones and Briant Stringham, who were returning from the
abandoned Mormon mail station at Deer Creek. He met that night with
Brigham Young, who gave his fellow Vermont native a cordial reception.

Over the next six days, the officer exercised all of his known diplomatic
skills. He had seen General Harney's orders, he told his Mormon hosts,
and they held no intimation that U.S. troops "would or could molest or
interfere with the people of Utah." He assured them the government's
intentions "were of the most pacific nature." Further, he had seen Utah's
new governor, Alfred Cumming, and was convinced he had no orders
"to interfere with the Mormons as a religious people."[52] At the same
time, Van Vliet warned "plainly and frankly" of the consequences of
their present course.[53]

It was all to no avail. He was told "with the greatest hospitality and
kindness" that the "troops now on the march for Utah should not enter
the Great Salt Lake valley." The officer left six days later convinced the
Utah Expedition would meet armed resistance. On his way east, he met

50   Kenney, ed., *Wilford Woodruff's Journal*, 5:90.
51   Pleasanton to Van Vliet, July 28, 1857, House Exec. Doc. 2 (35-1), II, Serial 943, 27–28.
52   Stewart Van Vliet to John B. Floyd, November 20, 1857, "Report on the Utah Expedi-
     tion," Sen. Ex. Doc. (35-1), v. 3, n. 11, Serial 920, 37–38.
53   Ibid., Stewart Van Vliet to Alfred Pleasanton, September 29, 1857, 25–27.

its new commander at the South Platte River crossing and gave him this word. Colonel Albert Sidney Johnston, Second U.S. Cavalry, had left his regiment in Texas in the hands of its capable second in command, Lieutenant Colonel Robert E. Lee. Van Vliet later told Secretary of War Floyd that Brigham Young had said if Cumming entered Utah, "he would place him in his carriage and send him back."[54]

The day after the officer left the Great Salt Lake Valley, Young did what he meant to do all along. Knowing that President Buchanan had appointed a new governor in keeping with the law—that his own appointment had expired three years before and he could claim the office only until replaced—and that U.S. soldiers were ordered to respect the rights of all citizens, act only in self-defense, and serve only to assist federal officers in upholding the law—he declared martial law on September 15, 1857. "We are invaded by a hostile force, who are evidently assailing us to accomplish our overthrow and destruction," he proclaimed. He prohibited armed forces of every kind from entering the territory and ordered the Nauvoo Legion to repel an imagined invasion. But his proclamation's most dangerous provision was that "no person shall be allowed to pass or repass into or through or from the Territory without a permit."[55]

It has been said that Young told Mormon troops just to burn grass, but shed no blood. But the Utah War was no game. Nauvoo Legion officers had orders to attack American soldiers if they pushed beyond Fort Bridger or attempted to enter the Salt Lake Valley from the north.[56] And when Brigham Young stopped all travel and communications "into or through or from" an area of the American West large enough to enclose New England, New York, Pennsylvania, and Ohio, he all but cut the nation in half and made bloodshed certain, if the lion in its path did not move off or back down.

In a blessing for both sides, Brigham Young chose the path of peace and allowed time to resolve the differences between the American republic and its theocratic territory, which it did over the next thirty years.

54   Ibid., Stewart Van Vliet to John B. Floyd, November 20, 1857, 38.
55   "Proclamation of Governor Young," in "The Utah Expedition," House Exec. Doc. 71 (35-1), 34–35.
56   See Daniel H. Wells to Lot Smith, October 17, 1857, Lot Smith Collection, University of Arizona Library, Tucson, and the Daniel Wells reports, LDS Archives.

Today, the 1857–1858 Utah War is largely forgotten, even in Utah. It should not be. For not only was it what Daniel Boorstin called America's first civil war, but it was also a dramatic chapter in the history of Utah and the nation, filled with episodes of sacrifice for faith, heroic rides, desperate winter marches, courage and commitment on both sides, and an Indian raid on the Mormon Indian Mission in Oregon that would affect the course of history in Utah.[57]

This unique conflict also holds many important lessons for our nation today. To benefit from them, the story of the Utah War must be a faithful account of its causes and outcome. As we observe its sesquicentennial, the telling of America's first civil war should respect the motives and judgment of the men and women on both sides, who waged it, and be as fair, and as balanced and, above all, as honest, as flawed historians can make it.

---

57   For the full story of this conflict, see William P. MacKinnon, *At Sword's Point: A Documentary History of the Utah War to 1858, Part 1* (Norman, Okla.: Arthur H. Clark Company, 2008); and David L. Bigler and Will Bagley, *The Mormon Rebellion: America's First Civil War, 1857–1858* (Norman: The University of Oklahoma Press, 2011).

Terror on the Trail: The Massacre at Mountain Meadows

Presentation to the 23rd Annual Convention,
Oregon-California Trails Association, Salt Lake City, Utah,
August 19, 2005.

SEPTEMBER 11, 2007, WILL MARK THE 150TH ANNIVERSARY OF the most horrific terrorist attack in U.S. history. I'm not talking about 9/11, 2001. I refer to September 11, 1857. On that day, white settlers and Indians in southwestern Utah deceived, betrayed, and murdered more than a hundred men, women, and children at a rest stop on the Spanish Trail to Los Angeles known as Mountain Meadows. No one knows for sure how many they killed that day because there were no survivors old enough to tell. But a good estimate would come to about forty unarmed men; some thirty women, most of them young mothers; and as many as fifty children, including about twenty girls between the ages of seven and seventeen.

It was the most horrific terrorist attack in our nation's history, not as figured by body count, but in the way its victims were slain. White men and Indians struck them down one at a time, up close and personal, with knives, hatchets, pistols, and muskets. Mercy was shown only to children too young to testify and young enough to come under a doctrinal exemption known as "innocent blood." Only seventeen children qualified.

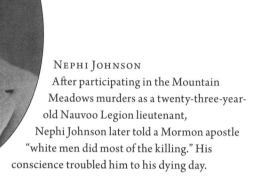

NEPHI JOHNSON
After participating in the Mountain
Meadows murders as a twenty-three-year-
old Nauvoo Legion lieutenant,
Nephi Johnson later told a Mormon apostle
"white men did most of the killing." His
conscience troubled him to his dying day.

For their mothers and fathers, brothers and sisters, it was all over in minutes. For the seventy or so white men involved in the killing, it would never be over. All belonged to the Church of Jesus Christ of Latter-day Saints, the Mormons. Most were God-fearing men, devoted husbands, caring fathers. The wounds they suffered that day were soul-deep and never healed. Sixty-one years later, Nephi Johnson lay dying. In delirium, the eighty-four-year-old Indian missionary preached in native languages, sang hymns, and prayed. Suddenly his eyes opened wide, staring straight up, and he cried, "Blood! *Blood*! BLOOD!" Sixty-one-years before, he had led the Indians in killing the women and children. He was reliving the horror, and he was afraid to die.

Noted historian David McCullough has said that nothing ever had to happen the way it happened. "History could have gone off in any number of different directions in any number of different ways at any point along the way," he said.[1] So why did it go the way it did in this case? How could God-fearing men do such a thing? A hundred and fifty

---

1   David McCullough, "Knowing History and Knowing Who We Are," *Imprimis* 34:4 (April 2005).

years of obstruction, cover up, denial, and falsification have obscured the answers to such disturbing questions.

Our limited time today also precludes a detailed examination of the events and since-forgotten beliefs behind the worst atrocity on our overland trails. But as I briefly recount these events and the conditions in which they took place, you may gain some insight into why it happened.

As you do, keep in mind something else McCullough said. He said there was never anything like the past. Nobody ever lived in the past. Our ancestors didn't go around saying, "Isn't this fascinating living in the past?" They lived in the present, just as we do, only it was their present, not ours. Just as we don't know how things are going to turn out, they didn't either. The two-time Pulitzer Prize winner and author of 1776 said it's easy to find fault with people for why they did this, or didn't do that, because we're not involved in it, we're not inside it, we're not confronting what we don't know—as everyone who preceded us always was.

The Arkansas emigrants who headed west in 1857 surely had no idea of what lay ahead. Not only would they be murdered, but forever after they would also be maligned, mischaracterized, and blamed for what happened to them. And they would be unable to defend themselves.

This defamation continues today, although we know better. We know that, unlike many of the parties that passed through Utah during this period, they were an orderly train, led by mature, experienced captains, fifty-two-year-old John T. Baker and Alexander Fancher, age forty-five, who surely knew their responsibility for the safety of some eighty women and children. Most of their wealth was tied up in a large cattle herd, but they also possessed thirty or forty wagons, horses, mules, tools, firearms, and cash for expenses. Their picture is not one of hell-raisers, but of prosperous farm families moving west to California to make new homes there.

After more than four months on the trail, they arrived in Salt Lake Valley near the peak of a flaming revival, called the Reformation, to purify God's people and merit divine favor in an imminent confrontation with the United States. Mormon leaders had seen it coming. The brief history of this fervent millennial movement had already shown that a people ruled by God through inspired men could never live in peace within a republic governed by the elected representatives of its citizens—the two governing systems are incompatible. The Reformation featured a fearful doctrine known as blood atonement.

In addition, some weeks after the train left Arkansas, Mormon Apostle Parley P. Pratt had been brutally murdered in that state. He was killed by the vengeful husband of a woman whom he had taken as his twelfth polygamous wife. But to believers, Pratt was a martyr of the faith, whose blood cried for vengeance—not on the man who had taken his life, but on the people of the nation and state, who allowed him do it with impunity. The popular apostle was killed in the same part of Arkansas that the emigrants came from.

Finally, less than two weeks before the doomed company arrived, news had struck Salt Lake City that an American military expedition had marched from Fort Leavenworth to escort a new governor to Utah to replace Brigham Young and assert federal authority in the theocratic territory.

In short, the emigrants came *to* the wrong place *from* the wrong place *at* the wrong time. Utah Territory was a place emotionally enflamed by excessive religious zeal, the thirst for vengeance, and the threat of war.

Malinda Cameron Thurston, who survived only because her husband decided to take the northern trail, while the rest of her family took Mormon advice and went south, fixed the day of the train's arrival as August 3, 1857. From that day, out of all the companies that had followed the southern trail since 1849, some with cattle or sheep, the company from Arkansas became a marked train, one singled out for special treatment.

Early that same day, Apostle George A. Smith left in a horse-drawn carriage on a flying visit to the string of Mormon settlements along the route that led to the Spanish Trail, near Cedar City, 250 miles to the south. At each settlement he delivered orders from Brigham Young to sell no food to the emigrants and to tell the Indians they have "got to help us or the United States will kill us both."[2] The latter order bore sobering implications.

Mormons then and today believe that American Indians, known as Lamanites, are a New World remnant of ancient Israel from the tribe of

---

2   Young to Hamblin, 4 August 1857, Juanita Brooks, *The Mountain Meadows Massacre,* 34–35.

Manasseh, the son of Joseph, son of Jacob. They also accept as true that most members of the faith also descend from Jacob through Joseph's other son, Ephraim. The conviction of common Hebrew ancestry made Mormons and Indians cousins by blood and natural allies.

These beliefs appear innocent enough today, but they were hardly non-threatening then. For the prophet Micah warned that when Zion was redeemed the "remnant of Israel" would be among the gentiles "as a young lion among the flocks of sheep; who . . . both treadeth down and teareth in pieces," a prophecy repeated by the Book of Mormon prophet 3rd Nephi.[3] Mormons then believed the "remnant of Israel" referred to the Indians and the prophecies to their own time and circumstances.

Today such teaching is not taken seriously. Then it was. In southern Utah, they took it very seriously. In a blessing on William H. Dame, then commander of Utah's Southern Military District, the Cedar Stake patriarch prophesied the officer's mission. "Thou shalt be called to act at the head of a portion of thy brethren and of the Lamanites in the redemption of Zion and the avenging of the blood of the prophets upon them that dwell on the earth," he promised. "The angel of vengeance shall be with thee."[4]

Unaware of the danger in their path, the emigrants followed Apostle Smith south along today's Interstate 15, but at a much slower pace. In a horse-drawn vehicle the apostle averaged forty miles a day, even after giving sermons and issuing orders along the way. Slowed by their herd, the emigrants journeyed at a little more than seven miles a day. After months on the trail, they needed flour and fresh vegetables, especially for the children, but they could not buy food at any price. At Provo and Nephi, sharp words were exchanged because the settlements refused to permit their cattle to graze on common fields. An inflammatory rumor spread that some train members had helped murder the Mormon prophets, Joseph and Hyrum Smith.

Ahead of them, the apostle issued instructions, written and verbal, to those who would soon murder them. He met with Colonel Dame; John D. Lee, ostensibly a lowly Indian farmer, but an adopted son of Brigham Young under a sealing ordinance long ago discontinued and

---

3   See Micah 5:8 and The Book of Mormon, 3 Nephi 20:15–16.
4   William H. Dame Papers, February 20, 1854, MS 2041, LDS Archives.

a main figure in the massacre; Isaac C. Haight, president of the Cedar Stake of Zion; and Major John Higbee, who would give the order to kill the emigrants. Lee later said that he always understood that Smith came to prepare the people for that bloody work.

If so, an important part of Smith's mission was to carry out Brigham Young's order to dismiss the moderate head of the Southern Indian Mission and replace him with frontier zealot Jacob Hamblin, who could be counted on to do as he was told. Smith ordered him to gather up the Southern Paiute chiefs and bring them back with him to Great Salt Lake to meet with Young.

Smith had done all this and was halfway home when he and his party, now enlarged by a dozen or so Indians, met the Arkansas train at Corn Creek in central Utah. The apostle camped within forty yards of the emigrants, who voiced fear at seeing Mormons and Indians together and doubled their guard. Smith later claimed the Arkansans poisoned the Pahvant Indian band at Corn Creek, but there is no evidence to support this charge. Like all the other tales of emigrant misbehavior, it is patently false, but still repeated, for no apparent reason than to convey the impression that "they got what they deserved."

The Corn Creek meeting actually had nothing to do with poison and everything to do with the emigrants' reaction at the sight of Mormons and Indians traveling north together. Up to this point, halfway between Salt Lake and Mountain Meadows, they had traveled at less than eight miles a day. But from Corn Creek to their final resting place, they hurried up to over twelve miles a day, or about as fast as they could go with a big herd after so long on the trail. They were not looking for trouble. They were trying to get away.

As they neared the Spanish Trail, Apostle Smith delivered the Paiute chiefs to Salt Lake, where they met with Brigham Young and his personal interpreter, Dimick B. Huntington. Afterward Huntington said he gave them "all the cattle that had gone to Cal[ifornia] by the south rout."[5] The gift was an invitation to attack the Baker-Fancher train with the implied promise of help if needed. The Paiute chiefs knew what cattle he referred to because they had seen them at Corn Creek. They left Salt Lake early

---

5   Dimick B. Huntington Journal, 1857–May 1859, LDS Archives.

on September 2 to be at Mountain Meadows when the first volley was fired five days later.

Meanwhile, the emigrants passed Cedar City and crossed the gradual swell that divides Great Basin waters from the head of the Colorado River. On September 6, a Sunday, they camped at the scenic Spanish Trail location named Mountain Meadows because it was more than a mile above sea level and provided ample water and grass. Here, some thirty-five miles from the nearest settlement, they felt secure enough to rest and recruit their cattle for the desert stretch ahead after driving them hard for almost two weeks. But the spot they selected—not close enough to a spring, and too close to the low hills around it—was indefensible.

Early Monday morning, a deadly burst of gunfire out of the pre-dawn darkness killed or wounded as many as ten men as they stood silhouetted by the campfire. The first volley's destructive impact suggests the involvement of white Indian missionaries under John D. Lee because the Paiutes had few firearms and little skill in using them. But the emigrants chained their wagon wheels together, dug rifle pits, and fought back. Their resolute defense led to one of the bizarre episodes in this story.

Worried by the standoff, the head of Zion's Cedar Stake sent a rider to notify Brigham Young that the Indians, real and disguised, had corralled the train and ask, "What should we do now?" Where else on the frontier would they send an Englishman with only one horse on a five-hundred-mile ride to inquire what to do about Indians attacking a party made up of mostly women and children? Anywhere else, they'd know what to do, and, without a "by your leave," do it. And where in western annals of heroic rides for help does the hero come back to find that the settlers have helped the Indians kill the emigrants? Only here.

On Wednesday night two young volunteers tried to slip out and seek help from the agon trains behind them. One had joined the train at Provo to get away from Utah. Mormon guards shot and killed him at a nearby spring. They wounded his companion, too, but he escaped to alert emigrants to white involvement. On Thursday, three other men slipped out after dark in a desperate attempt to reach California on foot. One got as far as Las Vegas Springs before he was tracked down and killed. Meanwhile, a plan was hatched that same night to disarm the Arkansans and decoy them into the open.

On Friday, 9/11/1857, John D. Lee and William Bateman drove two wagons into the little stronghold under a white flag. Lee said they found the emigrants almost out of ammunition, short of water, and becoming desperate. He told them their only hope was to turn over their arms, "so as not to arouse the animosity of the Indians," and place their lives under the protection of the Mormon military arm, known as the Nauvoo Legion, which did double duty as the territorial militia.[6]

Soon after, the most heartbreaking parade ever staged on American soil emerged from the camp. Leading it was a wagonload of children under six years old. Then came Lee on foot, followed by a second wagon bearing two or three wounded men and one woman. Some distance behind walked the women and older children. After them, a quarter mile or so to the rear walked in single file the disarmed men, each escorted by an armed guard. It was all carefully planned. As the women and children entered a narrow place in the hills, heavy with brush, Major Higbee called out: "Halt. Do your duty."

It was horrific. Each of the guards shot the man next to him. At the firing, Indians and painted whites swarmed out of the brush to kill women and children with knives, hatchets, and guns. The little valley was filled with gunfire and screams of women and children under murderous attack. Girls begged for their lives and cried out loud as they were dragged away to have their throats cut. As he killed two wounded men in the wagon with one shot, Samuel McMurdy reportedly prayed, "O lord, my God, receive their spirits, for it is for thy Kingdom that I do this."[7] Nephi Johnson later testified white men did most of the killing. Southern Paiute oral remembrance agrees.

Next morning they covered the bodies with a little dirt, which gave no protection from the coyotes. They then formed a prayer circle, Lee said, and thanked God "for delivering our enemies into our hands." And they swore to keep their role secret from everyone but Brigham Young, to always say the Indians alone did it, and to kill anyone who broke this oath. To excuse their Indian allies, the initial story blamed the victims for what happened to them. They had poisoned the Pahvants on Corn

---

6   William Bishop, ed., *The Life and Confessions of John D. Lee* (St. Louis: Bryan, Brand & Company, 1877), 240.

7   Ibid., 241.

Creek, 140 miles to the north, and brought it on themselves, the story goes. But no Pahvants from Corn Creek took part in the atrocity.

Four days after the killing, Brigham Young declared martial law. He stamped the U.S. Army expedition "an armed mercenary mob," ordered the territorial militia, or Nauvoo Legion, to repel an imagined invasion, and shut down all travel "into or through or from" an area of the American West large enough enclose New England, New York, Pennsylvania, and Ohio, without a permit. The massacre and closure of overland trails led California's newly elected fifth governor to voice alarm over the impact on immigration, "so essential in developing the state's resources." To protect citizens traveling through U.S. territory, Governor John B. Weller said, the "whole power of the federal government should be invoked."[8]

Nearly three weeks after the crime, John D. Lee reported to Brigham Young, who undoubtedly knew all about it by then. At this point, a historian meets a familiar phenomenon. In each of many nineteenth-century conflicts between the Mormons and their neighbors, one almost always discovers two squarely opposing, mutually exclusive, and highly credible versions.

In his later confessions, Lee said he told Young all there was to tell, including the names of those who took part. According to Apostle Wilford Woodruff, Lee only told Young that the emigrants had poisoned the Indians, who became enraged and alone killed them, sparing only a few children for sale to the Mormons. Years later, Young swore that Lee came two or three *months* after the massacre and began to tell him about it, but he had stopped him. He'd heard rumors about it and didn't want his feelings "harrowed up" by a recital of the horrid details.

The end of the Utah conflict in 1858 introduced a period of cover-up, obfuscation, appeasement, and bureaucratic bungling. To avoid bloodshed, Young's replacement as governor, Alfred Cumming, scotched an attempted investigation by the fearless federal judge John Cradlebaugh. It seemed that everyone west of the Missouri River—except federal officials in Utah and Washington—knew the truth. The California newspapers had it right almost as soon as the first reports reached the West Coast.

---

8   Inaugural Address, Governor John B. Weller, January 8, 1858, California State Library.

Yet for twenty years, only the U.S. Army investigated the massacre. In 1859, Major James H. Carleton, who later commanded Union forces in the Southwest during the Civil War, led a mounted company from Los Angeles to Mountain Meadows. He saw at once that "a great and fearful crime" had been committed. The officer called the men who did it "relentless, incarnate fiends," but his report was largely ignored in the events leading to the Civil War.[9]

Carleton and his men of Company K collected and buried some of the bones, erecting over them a monument of stones twelve feet high topped by a cedar cross that bore the words: "Vengeance is mine: I will repay saith the Lord."[10] The soldiers had gone off to the Civil War two years later when Brigham Young visited the site. He read these words and said, "It should be vengeance is mine and I have taken a little."[11] His escort tore down the cross and scattered the stones. Three years later Captain George Price and Company M, Second California Volunteer Cavalry, camped there and built it up again.

After the Civil War, pressure grew from the outside, and from church members as well, for an investigation and punishment of the crime. So it was that one would pay the price for all. The excommunication of John D. Lee came in 1870. To get him out of the way, he was sent off to run the ferry at a remote location on the Colorado River, now called Lee's Ferry. A year later, guilt-ridden former Cedar City bishop Philip Klingensmith appeared before the district court in Pioche, Nevada, and broke the oath of silence.

Still nothing happened—and for good reason. The only man with the power to conduct an investigation and punish the guilty simply chose not to unless he controlled the outcome. Brigham Young took such authority from a unique legal system created by Utah lawmakers after Congress established the territory in 1850. In brief, a pre-millennial theocracy applied democratic processes to create an exclusive legal system for a people who lived under a higher law. But it gave little or no consistent equal protection to outsiders.

---

9   "Special Report of the Mountain Meadow Massacre, by J. H. Carleton, Brevet Major, United States Army, Captain, First Dragoons," House Doc. 605 (57-1), 1902, Serial 4377, 8–12, 13.

10   Romans 12:19.

11   Scott G. Kenney, ed., *Wilford Woodruff's Journal*, 5:577.

Not for twenty years did Congress dismantle the territory's controlled judiciary and restore the court system it had meant to create in the first place. Six months after it passed the Poland Act in 1874, a federal marshal arrested John D. Lee and others for the massacre.

Lee's two trials in 1875 and 1876 stand as remarkable examples of judicial string pulling, first to exonerate, then to convict the same defendant. The first twelve-member jury counted eight active and one inactive Mormons and three so-called gentiles. No faithful Mormon stepped forward to testify against Lee, but enough evidence did come out to convict him. As expected, however, the panel deadlocked, nine to three. Only the non-Mormons voted to convict.

The wave of indignation that now swept across the country alarmed church leaders. Something had to be done to close the book on Mountain Meadows without incriminating anyone else. At the same time, a new U.S. attorney was under pressure to gain a conviction. So the two sides struck a deal. The prosecutor agreed not to implicate Brigham Young and others. In return, Young sacrificed John D. Lee. He provided the witnesses to convict his adopted son and guaranteed a unanimous verdict. To make it look good, as well as work, the prosecutor empaneled Mormon jurors only.

As scripted, witnesses appeared out of the sagebrush at Lee's second trial in any number it took to seal his fate. The all-Mormon jury in less than four hours found their former friend and brother guilty, twelve to zip. It was all neatly done.

John D. Lee, scapegoat for the sins of many, sat on the edge of his coffin at Mountain Meadows in 1877 and was shot to death by firing squad. "The old man never flinched," one observer said. His reward was a passport to celestial glory awarded in 1961 when LDS officials restored his church membership and former blessings. He now lies under a marker enigmatically engraved "Know the truth and the truth shall make you free." With that, the book on Mountain Meadows was finally closed.

Except for the bones. The bones cried from the ground in 1859 when Major Carleton buried many from victims of all ages and erected over them a monument of stones and a cross. The monument was later torn down, but the bones would not keep silent. The men of Company M, Second California Cavalry, heard them and restored it. The bones again cried from the ground in 1999, when the LDS Church, in cooperation with the descendants of John D. Lee and family members of the emigrants, began work on a new memorial. A backhoe operator broke the earth and exposed the bones buried by Carleton's men—a young woman's skull with a bullet hole in the crown, broken children's bones, arm and leg bones scarred by coyote teeth. A self-disciplined county sheriff saw the children's bones and was deeply moved. "That was what really hit me hard," he said.[12]

The bones tell of beliefs, long ago outdated and forgotten: God's kingdom as a sovereign theocratic state, the immediate coming of the Son of Man, oaths to avenge the prophets' blood, unquestioning obedience to religious authorities, American Indians as instruments of divine justice, uncontrolled religious zeal, the shedding of human blood for the remission of certain sins, justice by inspiration, the law of adoption, and others.

The bones tell of Arkansas farm families who did not come to torment Utah settlers, but to pass through their country on their way to make homes in California. The bones rebuke the slanders and false testimony to justify and conceal the involvement of those who killed them. The bones speak of vengeance that fell on the wrong heads. They tell of innocent men, women, and children, deceived, betrayed and slain for no rational reason or purpose.

On the 142nd anniversary of the massacre, September 11, 1999, over a thousand attended the dedication of the new monument. In dedicating it, LDS Church president Gordon B. Hinckley said he came as a peacemaker. We cannot comprehend what happened here so long ago, he said. It was not a time for recrimination, but a time to leave "the matter in the hands of God," he said.

The day before the dedication, several hundred family members of the victims—Bakers, Mitchells, Fanchers, Dunlaps, Tackitts, and others—came from Arkansas and across the country to attend special services in the valley on the headwaters of the Santa Clara River. They came to honor their slain early relatives and return to the earth their troubling bones. Reverently they bore them in little handmade arks to the new monument, where they placed them in soil from Arkansas.

12   *New York Times*, August 15, 1999, 22.

Afterward a Baptist preacher from the town of Springdale, Arkansas, concluded his sermon with a lesson from Mountain Meadows for the living, including you and me, one that seems especially appropriate as we come three weeks from today to 9/11/2005, the 148th anniversary of the massacre and the fourth of the worst terrorist attack in our history in terms of the number killed.

No one knows the hour or the way he will be called home, Reverend Stanton Cram said. If for you, it would be today, at this place, as it was for them, he asked, "Are you ready?"

That's a good question to think about, as well as end my talk on, and I do both now with thanks to each of you for your kind attention.

✤

The Aiken Party Executions and the Utah War 1857–1858

Six men rode into Salt Lake Valley
and disappeared during the 1857–1858 Utah War.
Their fate reveals the absence of federal law, which moved
President James Buchanan to dispatch troops to the Mormon territory.
It also exposes the conditions that led to the Mountain Meadows
massacre and Brigham Young's autocratic leadership.

SIX "GENTLEMEN OF GOOD ADDRESS" KNOWN AS THE AIKEN Party, rode into Salt Lake Valley from California in October 1857 and were never seen or heard from again by family members or friends. Their covert arrests and executions illustrate why James Buchanan early in his presidency ordered troops to Utah to enforce federal law and expose the conditions that led Mormons and their Indian allies that year to massacre over one hundred California-bound emigrants at Mountain Meadows.[1] The Aiken Party murders, ordered by Mormon leaders and carried out by church members in central Utah, are also a haunting reminder of the fear

---

1   For an early treatment of the Aiken story, see Harold Schindler, *Orrin Porter Rockwell: Man of God, Son of Thunder*, 2nd ed. (Salt Lake City: University of Utah Press, 1983), 268–81.

and desperation the millennialist Mormons felt, and the absolute power Brigham Young exerted over the lives of all who entered the territory.[2]

Named after brothers Thomas and John Aiken, the party knew that in May 1857, Buchanan had ordered the U.S. Army to escort a new governor to Utah to replace Brigham Young and serve as a *posse comitatus* in asserting federal law in the vast theocratic territory.[3] Members of the Aiken Party planned to meet the federal army approaching Utah and profit from some twenty-five hundred soldiers stationed in the Salt Lake Valley, but Brigham Young's explosive reaction would ignite the 1857–1858 Utah War and prevent for eight months the arrival of U.S. troops.[4]

"If they can send a force against this people, we have every Constitutional and legal right to send them to hell, and we calculate to send them there," Young thundered.[5] On September 15, 1857, acting as governor after his term had expired and before his appointed successor arrived, he proclaimed martial law. Young ordered the territorial militia, known as the Nauvoo Legion, to repel the "invasion" and shut down travel without a permit "into or through or from" a region of the American West that reached a thousand miles from the Rocky Mountains to the eastern slope of the Sierra Nevada.[6]

The immediate impact of the trails closure, which virtually cut the nation in half, fell on California. There the newly elected fifth governor,

---

2   "Alleged Murder of Five American Citizens in Utah," *San Francisco Daily Evening Bulletin*, January 18, 1858, 2.

3   Young's four-year term had expired in 1854, but a provision of the territorial organic act allowed him to serve "until his successor shall be appointed and qualified." See "An Act to Establish a Territorial Government for Utah," *Statutes at Large of the United States of America, 1789–1873* (Boston, 1851), 9:453.

4   For studies of the Utah War, see Norman F. Furniss, *The Mormon Conflict, 1850–1859* (New Haven, Conn.: Yale University Press, 1960); *The Utah Expedition, 1857–1858: A Documentary Account of the United States Military Movement under Colonel Albert Sidney Johnston, and The Resistance by Brigham Young and the Mormon Nauvoo Legion*, ed. by LeRoy R. Hafen and Ann W. Hafen (Glendale, Calif.: The Arthur H. Clark Company, 1958); William P. MacKinnon, *At Sword's Point: A Documentary History of the Utah War to 1858, Part 1* (Norman: The Arthur H. Clark Company, 2008); and David L. Bigler and Will Bagley, *The Mormon Rebellion: America's First Civil War, 1857–1858* (Norman: The University of Oklahoma Press, 2011).

5   J. V. Long, "Remarks By Pres. Brigham Young, Bowery, Sunday Afternoon, Sep. 13, 1857," *Deseret News* 7:29, September 23, 1857, 229.

6   Brigham Young, "Proclamation by the Governor," September 15, 1857, in "The Utah Expedition," House Exec. Doc. 71 (35-1), Serial 956, 34–35.

John B. Weller, expressed alarm over the effect of Mormons and Indians on immigration. "Our people are certainly entitled to protection whilst traveling through American territory," he said, "and to secure this, the whole power of the Federal Government should be invoked."[7] As he gave his inaugural address in January 1858, volunteer companies were forming in gold mining towns along the Sierra Nevada, ready to march against Utah from the west.[8]

Now largely forgotten, the 1857–1858 military confrontation was the nation's first civil war, but the third Mormon conflict in only twenty years. The Mormons and their millennialistic faith had seen little peace since Joseph Smith Jr. founded the Church of Jesus Christ of Latter-day Saints in 1830. Professing to speak for God as in the days of Moses, Smith went *"emphatically, virtuously, and humanely, for a* THEODEMOCRACY, *where God and the people hold the power to conduct the affairs of men in righteousness."*[9] But civil conflicts in Missouri and Illinois in 1838 and 1845–1846 had proved that theocratic rule by any name was incompatible with governments by the people through their elected representatives.

Knowing they could never co-exist in peace, in 1847 Brigham Young led his people west out of the United States and into the Great Basin, a vast region of interior drainage hundreds of miles from the nearest manifestation of rule by its professed owner, the Republic of Mexico. In the Great Basin, Young intended to establish God's Kingdom as a sovereign dominion to prepare for Christ's imminent return. But in February 1848, only six months after the Mormons landed in Salt Lake Valley, the United States acquired from Mexico all of the three present states of California, Utah, and Nevada, and large parts of four others. The Treaty of Guadalupe Hidalgo ended the War with Mexico, but introduced a constant struggle for control between a defiant theocracy, ruled by Brigham Young, and a parent republic, ruled by its people.

An 1849 Mormon bid for sovereignty through statehood failed when Congress, under the Compromise of 1850, created Utah and bestowed on it the name of its native inhabitants. President Millard Fillmore signed the measure on September 9, 1850, and the roots of the Utah War can be traced

---

7   "Message of Gov. Weller," *San Francisco Daily Alta California,* January 9, 1858, 4/2.

8   "More Volunteers for the Mormon War," *San Francisco Daily Evening Bulletin,* January 5, 1858, 2/1.

9   Joseph Smith, *Times and Seasons,* April 15, 1844, 5:510/1.

to that day. His appointment of Young as Utah's first governor only made the confrontation more intense. The next six years saw a continuous flight of appointed district judges, Indian agents, and other federal officials of Utah in fear or frustration at not being able to perform their duties.[10]

Since divine rule encompasses all human institutions, emptying them of purpose, the struggle was waged on all fronts. As in Missouri and Illinois, points of conflict included law and the courts, ownership of land and personal property, economic communalism, political processes, marriage practices, and others. Of these, one especially relates to the Utah War and the massacre at Mountain Meadows. It had to do with Native Americans.

Like the Mormons' first Zion in western Missouri, the Great Basin allowed immediate contact with the Indians, a "remnant of Jacob" under doctrines of the faith, who, the Mormons believed, were to hear the gospel of their ancestors and join latter-day Israel, as the Mormons called themselves, in building New Jerusalem. If seemingly harmless, this doctrine has an explosive side, long since defused by time. For when Zion was redeemed, according to the biblical prophet Micah, in language repeated in The Book of Mormon, the "remnant of Jacob" known as "Lamanites" would be among unrepentant Gentiles "as a young lion among the flocks of sheep, who, if he go through, both treadeth down and teareth in pieces."[11] From the faith's earliest days, this doctrine had generated alarm, conflict, and misunderstanding on the frontier.[12]

Such fears can be heard in California governor Weller's concern over the effect of "Mormons and Indians" on overland emigration. They could be read in orders to Mormon district military commanders in August 1857 to "instruct the Indians that our enemies are also their enemies."[13] They were reflected in the documents President Buchanan gave Congress in 1858 to show why he had ordered the U.S. Army to impose federal

---

10 See Eugene E. Campbell, *Establishing Zion: The Mormon Church in the American West, 1847–1869* (Salt Lake City: Signature Books, 1988); and David L. Bigler, *Forgotten Kingdom: The Mormon Theocracy in the American West, 1847–1896* (Spokane, Wash.: The Arthur H. Clark Company, 1998).

11 See Micah 5:8 and 3 Nephi 21:12, The Book of Mormon.

12 For examples of such fears, see Stephen C. LeSueur, *The 1838 Mormon War in Missouri* (Columbia: University of Missouri Press, 1990), 17, 18, 71–72.

13 Daniel H. Wells to William H. Dame, August 13, 1857, file 8, box 47, William R. Palmer Collection, Sherrat Library, Southern Utah University, Cedar City.

authority in Utah.[14] They also seemed confirmed by the massacre at Mountain Meadows and attacks on small emigrant trains on the California Trail along the Humboldt River in present Nevada.

By 1856 Brigham Young knew that his vision of God's Kingdom as a universal dominion could never be fulfilled under a territorial system. That year he inaugurated a campaign to throw off that "colonial" yoke and move up to a sovereign standing through statehood. The crusade was well coordinated, but badly timed. The new Republican Party had won control of Congress on the promise to abolish slavery and polygamy. Even more alarming to Young, Utah's delegate in Washington told him an effort had begun "to procure [his] removal."[15]

Young received the bad news in late August 1856, and from then on he defied the federal government. "As the Lord lives," he told his followers, "we are bound to become a sovereign State in the Union, or an independent nation by ourselves."[16] Three weeks later, he ignited a fiery revival to cleanse the Mormons, spiritually and physically; "this has got to be done that the Gentile bands may be broken," settlement leaders were told.[17] The reform movement featured an intrusive interrogation, called the catechism, to probe for immoral conduct. It also introduced the fearful doctrine that some sins could only be atoned by human blood.[18]

In a burst of religious zeal, Utah lawmakers in December 1856 drew up and sent to President-elect Buchanan a series of resolutions vowing to resist any effort by federal officials to ignore territorial laws or impose federal laws "which [were] inapplicable and of right not in force in this territory."[19] Buchanan received the defiant decrees soon after his inau-

---

14   "The Utah Expedition," House Exec. Doc. 71 (35-1), 126–215.

15   John M. Bernhisel to Young, Brigham Young Papers, July 17, 1856, LDS Archives.

16   G. D. Watt, "Sermon by President Brigham Young, Bowery," August 31, 1856, *Deseret News* 6:28, September 17, 1856, 220.

17   Jacob G. Bigler to John Pyper, David Webb, and counselors, December 23, 1856, Record of the Mass Quorum of Seventies, MSS SC 3244, BYU Library.

18   For more on blood atonement, see D. Michael Quinn, *The Mormon Hierarchy: Extensions of Power* (Salt Lake City: Signature Books, 1997), 243–261, 273; Gene A. Sessions, *Mormon Thunder: A Documentary History of Jedediah Morgan Grant* (Urbana: University of Illinois Press, 1982), 125–129, 130; Bigler, *Forgotten Kingdom*, 123–124.

19   Memorial & Resolutions to the President of the United States, 1856–58, General Assembly, Utah Territory, 1852–59, MIC 3150, reel 3, Utah State Archives, Salt Lake City.

guration in March 1857 and referred them to Interior secretary Jacob Thompson. Thompson stamped the Mormon doctrine of nullification "a declaration of war."[20]

From January 1857 to June the following year, the territory no longer recognized federal law, but obeyed only professed divine rule through Brigham Young. It was a violent period that saw the murder of "apostates" as they tried to escape and included the Mountain Meadows massacre, a horrific act of vengeance for the 1844 assassinations of Mormon prophets Joseph and Hyrum Smith in Illinois, as well as the May 1857 murder of Apostle Parley P. Pratt in Arkansas. The atrocity occurred in September 1857, when Mormon militiamen and their allies massacred some 120 men, women, and children from Arkansas at a rest stop on the Spanish Trail known as Mountain Meadows, near Cedar City, Utah.[21]

Even before then, federal officials had sounded the alarm in Washington. Utah surveyor general David H. Burr reported, "*These people repudiate the authority of the United States in this country and are in open rebellion against the general government.*"[22] The urgency his words conveyed moved Buchanan to adopt the earlier example of Missouri and Illinois governors and order troops to put down a Mormon rebellion. But it also led him to ignore U.S. Army commander in chief General Winfield Scott's advice that it was too late in the season to mount such an expedition.

Bureaucratic foul-ups added urgency to Scott's warning. It was mid-July before the Tenth U.S. Infantry marched west. Other units took the Oregon Trail separately as they arrived at Fort Leavenworth. The expedition's first commander, General William S. Harney, and its dragoon component had been detached to serve in "bloody Kansas." By the time

20   Bernhisel to Young, April 2, 1857, Brigham Young Papers, LDS Archives.

21   For Brigham Young's admissions that vengeance was the motive for the massacre, see Will Bagley, *Blood of the Prophets: Brigham Young and the Massacre at Mountain Meadows* (Norman: University of Oklahoma Press, 2002), 246–247. For other unpunished crimes during the Utah War period, see Polly Aird, "'You Nasty Apostates, Clear Out': Reasons for Disaffection in the late 1850s," *Journal of Mormon History* 30 (Fall 2004), 129–207, and Ardis Parshall, "'Pursue, Retake & Punish': The 1857 Santa Clara Ambush," *Utah Historical Quarterly* 73 (Winter 2005), 64–86.

22   David H. Burr to Thomas A. Hendricks, February 5, 1857, "The Utah Expedition," House Exec. Doc. 71 (35-1), 118. Emphasis in original.

Second U.S. Cavalry colonel Albert S. Johnston replaced Harney, he found himself in mid-September leading an army that stretched for a thousand miles from the Missouri River to Fort Bridger, with its supply wagons and infantry in front and its cavalry and commander at the rear. It was an inviting target.

There was no such bungling in the theocratic command structure. As many as four thousand Nauvoo Legion soldiers under Brigham Young's second counselor, Lieutenant General Daniel H. Wells, quickly mobilized and operated efficiently to stop the invader. Mormon troops fortified the narrow Echo Canyon entry to Salt Lake Valley while fast-moving mounted companies burned grass and rustled the federal expedition's cattle. On October 4, Major Lot Smith's horse soldiers burned three of the army's supply trains on the Green and Big Sandy rivers.

Brigham Young drew the line at shedding the invaders' blood at Fort Bridger. He ordered Mormon officers to attack U.S. soldiers if they pushed beyond that point or tried to enter Salt Lake Valley from the north.[23] That was as close as the Utah War came to a pitched battle. As early blizzards swept the high plains, it was all that Colonel Johnston could do to collect his scattered command and reach Jim Bridger's sheltered trading post, where it would stay until spring opened the trail. Mistakes, early winter, and unexpected Mormon resistance stopped his expedition over a hundred miles from its objective. These factors also sealed the fate of the Aiken Party.

The half-dozen "gentlemen of good address" may have disappeared forever from humankind's annals if early California newspapers had not taken such a lively interest in the huge Mormon territory on their eastern border. "Alleged Murder of Five American Citizens in Utah," proclaimed the *San Francisco Daily Evening Bulletin* on January 18, 1858, over a story taken from the *Placerville Argus* a few days before. The article cited a "Mr. Cowan," who said the murdered Americans traveled with his eastbound company of Mormon families in October 1857 from Carson Valley on the California Trail along the Humboldt River on the line of

---

23   See Daniel H. Wells to Lot Smith, October 17, 1857, Lot Smith Collection, University of Arizona Library, Tucson.

today's Interstate 80.[24] As ordered by Brigham Young, Mormon settlers from across the Intermountain West were returning to Salt Lake Valley to defend Zion against the oncoming U.S. Army.[25]

Cowan said the Indians later killed the interlopers between Salt Creek, location of Nephi, Utah, and the Sevier River. But the *Placerville Argus* thought otherwise. It reacted in the same way California newspapers had greeted Mormon reports that the Indians had massacred the California-bound emigrants from Arkansas at Mountain Meadows. "We incline to the belief that they have been butchered by the Mormons themselves, or if by the savages, at least by their instigation."[26]

Carson City founder William M. Ormsby, who ran the store in Carson Valley at Genoa, remembered the Californians because they were a cut above "the ordinary character of the traveling horsemen." They had a "considerable amount" of cash, he said, were "well armed and equipped," and owned "excellent riding and pack animals." On hearing that a Mormon wagon train had left several days before, they settled up their bills and left to overtake and travel with it for protection against the Indians. Ormsby promised to forward their names to Placerville from records at his store, but he apparently never did before 1860, when Northern Paiutes killed him at Pyramid Lake.[27]

On February 1 the San Francisco paper identified two members of the party as the Aiken brothers and reported they had "from $4,000 to $6,000 in gold" when they left Los Angeles. They had been held at Salt Lake, the story said, "where they had been robbed of all their funds," and afterward murdered. If they had tried to inform a friend of what had happened, it went on, "owing to the strict espionage exercised over the Post Office in the revolted Territory, such a letter would never have been permitted to reach California."[28]

24   *San Francisco Daily Evening Bulletin,* January 18, 1858, 2.

25   The story's source was Alexander Cowan, who moved in 1855 to Carson Valley. For the abandonment of outlying Mormon colonies, see Kenneth N. Owens, *Gold Rush Saints: California Mormons and the Great Rush for Riches* (Spokane, Wash.: The Arthur H. Clark Company, 2004), 299–352; and Bagley, *Blood of the Prophets,* 191–194.

26   *San Francisco Daily Evening Bulletin,* January 18, 1858, 2.

27   Ibid.

28   "As to the Murder Story of Five Americans in Utah," *San Francisco Daily Evening Bulletin,* February 1, 1858, 3.

Another Placerville paper, the *Index*, soon after ran a story from a "correspondent in Mariposa" that was also reprinted in San Francisco.[29] It said that Thomas and John Aiken were members of the party that included a "Mr. Eichard," who had kept a livery stable at nearby Aqua Fria, and an "Honesty" Jones, a former Mariposa lawman. They left about 1 October, the story said, to purchase cattle for California or to supply "Col. Johnston's command with beef and other supplies," but had been arrested on allegations they were "spies for the Federal Government." The story said they were murdered "on the principle that 'dead men tell no tales.'" John Boling, the former sheriff of Mariposa County, was raising a company to assist "in bringing Utah to account," it added.[30]

The Mariposa "correspondent" may have been John I. Ginn, a young journalist who sojourned in Salt Lake City for a few days in November 1857 before getting a pass and taking the southern trail to California. There he landed in the gold mining town east of Merced, where he became the co-publisher of *The Mariposa Star*.[31] If it was Ginn, his report spread word of the Aiken Party in northern California, but it also displayed the imaginative reporting that renders some of his writing of questionable value. It is now known that the Aiken brothers and John Eichard, or Achard, came from Los Angeles, not Mariposa. On word of their death, the *Los Angeles Star* said, "The Aiken boys were well known in this city, and very much respected."[32]

The identity of a fifth member of the Aiken Party came from members of a forty-two-man company "composed of desperate fellows," who swore to escape from Utah "or die in the attempt" and almost did both before reaching California in May 1858. Members of the company said he was "a young man named Chapman," who fled to Genoa.[33] D. W. Taylor, a

29   "Further particulars of the Alleged Mormon Murders of Five Americans," *San Francisco Daily Evening Bulletin*, February 16, 1858, 2. Copied from the *Placerville Index*.

30   Ibid.

31   The earliest surviving issue of the weekly *Mariposa Star*, February 1, 1859, lists John I. Ginn as co-publisher with the paper's founder, James H. Lawrence, in 1858. McClatchy Collection, Sacramento Archives & Museum Collection Center.

32   "The Murder of a Party of Americans," *San Francisco Daily Evening Bulletin*, February 5, 1858. Copied from *Los Angeles Star*, January 30, 1858, 2/2.

33   "The Hegira of the Mormons—Further News from Salt Lake," *San Francisco Daily Evening Bulletin*, May 14, 1858, 2. Copied from the *Placerville Index*.

former wagon master for the U.S. Army who arrived in California in June 1858 after Mormon leaders accepted President Buchanan's offer of a pardon for "seditions and treasons" and peace had been restored, provided additional information.[34] Among other things, the *Los Angeles Star* reported: "Mr. Taylor confirms the report of the death of the Aiken boys, Thomas and John—their horses are in the Valley, at a place called Springville, also, their revolvers, one an ivory handled pistol, with a gold-mounted belt, well known to have belonged to Thomas Aiken. They were killed at Chicken Creek, eighteen miles south of Salt Creek, and were sacrificed by the infamous band headed by Porter Rockwell."[35]

California newspapers were not always accurate, but they did give enough reliable information to identify the five original Aiken Party members. They also made it possible to track them to the end of their travels in Utah Territory and present a reasonably factual account of how and where, if not why, each of them was killed.

Given the accuracy of the 1852 census, the three from Los Angeles were John Achard, age thirty-three, known as the "colonel," and Thomas and John Aiken, ages twenty-seven and twenty-five. All were natives of Tennessee. The Aiken brothers had gone to California from Arkansas. Los Angeles County Probate Court records in January 1859 show Thomas Aiken's middle initial as "L" and state he was "killed murdered" in Utah Territory in late 1857. The attorney for his unnamed father filed a petition claiming that he left "valuable personal property" in Los Angeles.[36]

One and possibly both of the two remaining original party members were from Mariposa. Andrew Jackson Jones, better known as "Honesty," hailed from Pennsylvania, where his wife resided at the time of his death. There is no evidence that he ever served as a lawman in Mariposa, but county records show that in 1854 he sold property on the stage road from Mariposa to Stockton for one hundred dollars.[37]

34   See "Proclamation of James Buchanan," House Exec. Doc. 2 (35-2), 1858, Vol. 1, Serial 997, 69–72.

35   "From Utah," *Los Angeles Star*, July 10, 1858, 2/2.

36   Los Angeles Area Court Records, Probate, Case No. 121, Estate of Thomas L. Aiken, Huntington Library. The records spell his name both as Aiken and Aikin.

37   Index to Deeds, Vol. 1, Grantors, Mariposa County, January 26, 1854, p. 1, book B, folder 65, Mariposa Hall of Vital Records, Mariposa, California.

ORRIN PORTER ROCKWELL
As biographer Harold Schindler's
"Man of God, Son of Thunder,"
Orrin Porter Rockwell's carried out
various assignments for Brigham
Young. Despite accusations that
he was involved in various acts
of mayhem, murder, and robbery,
Rockwell maintained, "I never killed
any one but needed killing." COURTESY
OF THE UTAH STATE HISTORICAL
SOCIETY.

From Mariposa the superbly mounted and equipped pack party probably crossed the Sierra Nevada by the Big Tree Road, opened the year
before, which ran to the south of the Carson Pass Trail on the line of
today's State Route 4 from Angels Camp to Hope Valley.[38] There they
met the Carson Pass Trail and went to Genoa, former Mormon Station,
near Carson City, where they bought supplies at William Ormsby's store.
Their choice of the northern trail along the Humboldt River indicates they
chose the most direct route to meet the U. S. Army's Utah Expedition.

At Genoa they heard that a large wagon party of Mormon settlers
had left there on September 25 to return to Salt Lake Valley and defend
against oncoming U.S. troops. The Aiken Party fatefully decided to
overtake and travel with the Mormon camp for safety against the Indians, who had frequently attacked small emigrant parties that year at
Stony Point (today's Battle Mountain, Nevada) and Gravelly Ford, near
Beowawe. Unhindered by wagons, they rode along the Carson River to

---

38   See Frank Tortorich and James M. Carman, "The Big Tree–Carson Valley Wagon
     Road, A Branch of the Carson River Route," *Overland Journal* 22:3 (Fall 2004), 90–107.

present Ragtown, then northward over the Carson Pass leg of the "forty-mile desert" toward the main California Trail.

At the Humboldt Sink, west of today's Lovelock, Nevada, they met the men who became the party's fifth and sixth members. The first was Horace Bucklin, known as "Buck," identified here for the first time. He had sailed from Boston for California in March 1849 at the start of the Gold Rush.[39] On finding that trading with emigrants offered greater reward than panning for gold in cold mountain waters, he located a ranch and inn on the trail across the Sierra Nevada, north of Donner Pass, opened by James Beckwourth in 1851.[40] By early 1857, apparently Bucklin had drifted north to the mining boomtown of Richmond in Honey Lake Valley, where Thomas N. Long recalled he went to Salt Lake City with a much more colorful character, "Big John" Chapman. A large, powerful man from Arkansas, Chapman was remembered as being "a fist fighter, quarrelsome, always looking for trouble and often finding it," who some considered a desperate man.[41] The two may have decided to go Salt Lake City to purchase livestock, but if Bucklin and Chapman came to the Humboldt Sink trail junction to trade, they found business slow in the wake of Brigham Young's shutdown of overland travel. They decided to join the Aiken Party.

Now six strong, the party overtook the Mormon wagons on the California Trail along the Humboldt River and traveled with the company to Blue Spring on the Salt Lake Cutoff, now Interstate 84, to enter Salt Lake Valley from the north. The Aiken Party came to the wrong place at the wrong time. Mormon forces had stopped the American Army near Fort Bridger and fortified the winding Echo Canyon corridor through the Wasatch Mountains. Brigham Young and the Nauvoo Legion, not the U.S. Army, controlled Salt Lake Valley.

---

39 See Charles Warren Haskins, *The Argonauts of California, Being the Reminiscences of Scenes and Incidents that Occurred in California in Early Mining Days by a Pioneer* (New York, 1890), 457.

40 *Illustrated History of Plumas, Lassen & Sierra Counties with California from 1513–1850* (San Francisco, 1882), 235.

41 Asa Merrill Fairfield, *Fairfield's Pioneer History of Lassen County California Containing Everything That Can Be Learned About It From the Beginning of the World to the Year of Our Lord 1870* (San Francisco: H. S. Crocker Company, 1916), 122, 235.

On October 31 a member of the Mormon wagon company rode ahead to alert Fort Box Elder (now Brigham City) of the Californians' coming. The rest of the party from Genoa camped on Bear River with Nauvoo Legion troops returning from a forced march north. Mormon general Daniel Wells had ordered troops from Weber and Box Elder counties to block a possible attempt by Colonel Edmund Alexander, the acting Utah Expedition commander, to flank Echo Canyon defenses, and to enter Salt Lake Valley from the north, via Soda Springs. Wells's quick response confounded his U.S. Army opponent, but left the fortified settlement on Box Elder Creek shorthanded for a time.[42]

So it was that Nauvoo Legion major Samuel Smith was the only officer on duty when word of the newcomers arrived at the fort, followed soon after by the Californians themselves. In a previously unpublished document, the thirty-nine-year-old Englishman reported to Brigham Young on November 2, 1857, how he had coolly disarmed and captured the impressive intruders.

"About 9 AM A man from Carson vally informed me that 6 suspicious men had followed there train from Carson," he said. "He thought they would pass through about noon." The outsiders rode "very fast" and met Thomas Grover at the city's south wall, Smith said. Grover "saw they was well armed" and told them "they had Better go to Major Smith and get A Pass or they might be taken Prisoners as we was under marshal Law." He took them to the Mormon officer who asked them a series of questions. Their evasive answers invited suspicion in a place filled with rumors and paranoia: "W[h]ere are you going? Don't know. Are you going to the States? Don't know. Where Do you think of wintering? Don't know. How Long do you intend to stay in these valleys? Me and my Bro think of going to the States in the Spring as we have Relations there. Have any of you any here? No. Do you intend to work for your living here? No. Wages is to[o] low here. Is times bad in Calaforni made you Leave there? No. Well what induced you to come to this Place? O we wanted to see the country."

Smith concluded "they had no busnes here" and told them they must surrender their arms and leave them with him. He then promised to "give

---

42   For more on the Nauvoo Legion's move north, see Autobiography and Journals of B. F. Cummings, October 20 to November 1, 1857, BX 8670.1.C912, BYU Library.

them a pass to any city they wished to go to." The Californians talked among themselves. "I did not hurry them," Smith said. "They then swore they had never given up there Revolvers to any living white man but they supossed they must this time." The officer "told them Calmly they must." They then handed him "seven Revolvers 4 Guns and there Bowie knives."

The captain of the Carson Valley wagon train later reported "he thought these men [were] A party concerned in sending an Express to Calaforni to take the Powder &c" and had a "bad opinion of them."[43] In the short time they spent under arrest at Fort Box Elder, "they frequently wished they was Back in calaforni or in the States," Smith told Young. They "said they was caught very slick &c. [and] if they got out of this scrape they would never be caught again." Said the major: "I wish all wicked men to be trapd as Easey."[44]

Despite his promise, Smith did not hand the men a pass to the city of their choice, once they had given up their weapons. Instead he turned them over to Colonel Chauncey W. West, commander of northern Utah Nauvoo Legion forces, for delivery under guard to Salt Lake City. There Hosea Stout, former police chief at Nauvoo, Illinois, said the "six Cal prisoners taken at Box Elder supposed spies."[45] Journalist John I. Ginn, then in the city, later confirmed the ominous implications of Stout's opinion in a letter to Kirk Anderson, the editor of *The Valley Tan*, Utah's first independent newspaper. Ginn's memoirs of these events, written years later, are mainly fictional. But his appeal in March 1859 on behalf of "Honesty" Jones's widow offers a more reliable, if not entirely factual, source of information.[46]

---

43   A reference to gunpowder that the Carson Valley Mormons had acquired in California for Nauvoo Legion forces. There is no evidence the Aiken Party tried to stop the delivery.

44   All quotes in the above four paragraphs are from Smith to Young, November 2, 1857, Brigham Young Papers, LDS Archives.

45   Juanita Brooks, ed., *On the Mormon Frontier: The Diary of Hosea Stout, 1844–1861*, 2 vols. (Salt Lake City: University of Utah Press, 1964), 2:644.

46   John I. Ginn to Kirk Anderson, March 26, 1859, in *The Valley Tan*, 1:26, April 26, 1859, 2/4. William P. MacKinnon republished Ginn's letter to Anderson for the first time in "'Unquestionably Authentic and Correct in Every Detail': Probing John I. Ginn and His Remarkable Utah War Story," *Utah Historical Quarterly* 72:4 (Fall 2004), 322–342.

Ginn correctly named three Aiken Party members as Thomas and John Aiken and A. J. Jones. He said the men were kept "in the house next above Townsend's Hotel," then called the Salt Lake House, on East Temple (now Main Street) on the location of the present Tribune Building. Ginn said an unnamed Mormon told him "those men would be murdered." When asked why, his informant said "they have got $8,000 in money, and several first-rate animals, all of which we stand very much in need of right now."[47] Years later, Ginn named Joseph Hunt, the twenty-year-old son of the renowned Mormon Battalion captain Jefferson Hunt, as source of this information.[48]

Even so, such talk unsettled Horace Bucklin. He had joined the Aiken Party after it had left Carson Valley and understandably began to wonder what he had gotten himself into. On about November 15, he went right to the top and penned an appeal for mercy to Brigham Young:

Gov Yo[u]ng

Sir

I wish to state to you some of the facts of myself alone. I left California some five weeks previous to my starting for this place. I was stopping at the sink of Humbolt when these men came along on their way (so they told me) for the States, with the intention of spending the winter in this city, and going on in the spring and they asked me if I would not go along with them, for they said their party was so small they were afraid of the Indians.

I thought of the matter a while, and then told them nothing would suit me better, and so we started and here I am.

What theire [sic] business was, or their profession either I knew nothing of, untill [sic] I reached this City.

I have been told by some of your Officers of some things found with them, that I do as sincerely condem[n] as this people do.[49] Doubtless you are aware what I allude to, but to myself, I wish (with your consent) to stay here this winter, and go on through in the spring, if I do not conclude to make this place my future home, that as yet I cannot say, but this much I do say that I find this

---

47   Ibid.

48   Ginn mentioned Joseph Hunt in his rambling unpublished memoir, Mormons and Indian Wars, typescript, Ms. A 77-1, USHS. Jefferson Hunt was senior Mormon Battalion captain during the War with Mexico and a founder of San Bernardino, California.

49   This may confirm reports that the Aikens planned to start a gambling operation or allude to papers that linked them to the U.S. Army and implicated them as spies.

people very different from what they have been represented to me heretofore. I have been learned to believe that this people were no better than so many savages, but I find it very different. I find they are as smart, inteligant, and as sociable (and much more moral) a people as I ever met, and [I would] as soon live here as any place I ever saw.

When I starte[d] for this place, I knew nothing of the difficulty between this people and the Gover[n]ment nor of the Territory being under Martial law.

I have been a prisoner now some fifteen days, but have no reason to complain hoping soon to be at Liberty.

I remain your most Obdt.

Horace Bucklin[50]

In his letter to Anderson, Ginn said he left Salt Lake with a party of merchants on November 7 and learned even before he reached San Bernardino that all six Aiken party members had been "killed by the Indians."[51] But two days after Ginn left, Stout said he was still "guarding the prisoners from Ca." Not until November 20 did he record that "O. P. Rockwell with 3 or four others started with 4 of the prisoners, which we have been guarding for some days, South to escort them through the settlements to Cal via South route." He then revealed the success of Bucklin's plea for mercy. "The other two are going to be permitted to go at large till spring."[52]

By this calendar, John Ginn should have been nearly halfway to San Bernardino before the doomed party and its escort under the noted Mormon gunman Orrin Porter Rockwell left Great Salt Lake. Moreover, it is now known that two of the four men were killed on November 25 and the other two on November 28, not "about the 16th," as Ginn claimed, which would have placed the fanciful journalist almost on the outskirts of the Mormon settlement near Los Angeles.

So Ginn heard about the murders later, perhaps from Alexander Cowan, referred to above. Ginn's report the Indians killed the men is strikingly similar to the one Cowan told in Placerville in January 1858, which was republished by other northern California papers. It even suggests why Cowan, one of the returning Mormons from Carson Valley,

50   Bucklin to Young, November 1857, Brigham Young Papers, LDS Archives.
51   Ginn to Anderson, *The Valley Tan*, April 26, 1859, 2/4.
52   Brooks, *On the Mormon Frontier*, 2:645.

returned to California by the southern trail only weeks after arriving in Utah and spread the falsehood that the Indians had killed the men. Mormon messengers were the first to carry news of the Mountain Meadows massacre to southern California and proclaim the Indians alone did it.[53] Like the *Placerville Argus*, Los Angeles papers did not believe that either.

Ironically, a story meant to cover up Mormon involvement produced the opposite effect. Based on Ginn's 1859 letter in *The Valley Tan* and the testimony of teenager Alice Lamb, District Judge John Cradlebaugh later that year issued warrants for the arrest of Bishop Jacob G. Bigler and others at Nephi, Utah, for the Aiken Party murders, and of a number accused of the massacre at Mountain Meadows and other crimes.[54] Anxious to avoid trouble, Governor Alfred Cumming, who replaced Young, denied the use of U.S. troops to serve the warrants, which ended the judge's investigation of Utah War period crimes. A twenty-year veil of silence fell over the Aiken Party murders.

For good reason U.S. marshals, attorneys, and district judges failed to investigate or prosecute crimes during this period. In establishing Utah Territory in 1850, Congress created three district courts under judges appointed by the president and allowed probate courts to settle estates. To control the judicial system, Utah legislators vested the probate courts in each county with original civil and criminal jurisdiction, which emptied district courts of purpose and placed Brigham Young in control. Not for twenty years did Congress strip Utah's probate courts of their powers, so generously bestowed by Mormon lawmakers, and restore the judicial system it meant to create in the beginning. In breaking the gridlock, the 1874 Poland Act introduced some sensational trials for crimes committed years before.[55] Best known were the trials of John D.

53   Bagley, *Blood of the Prophets*, 175–178, 188–190.

54   For Alice Lamb's affidavit and testimony about other crimes, see John Cradlebaugh, *Utah and the Mormons: Speech of Hon. John Cradlebaugh of Nevada, on the Admission of Utah as a State. Delivered in the House of Representatives, February 7, 1863* (Washington, D.C., 1863), 63–66.

55   For conditions prior to the Poland Act, see R. N. Baskin, *Reminiscences of Early Utah* (Salt Lake City: By the Author, 1914), 59–60. The Poland Act returned exclusive original civil and criminal jurisdiction to the three district courts. Other provisions gave U.S. marshals and attorneys sole authority to serve writs and process and act as prosecuting officers.

NEPHI, UTAH TERRITORY, 1858

U.S. Army Mounted Rifleman's Joseph Heger sketched this Mormon settlement on Salt Creek in the shadow of Mount Nebo the summer after the community's central role in the Aiken party murders. COURTESY YALE COLLECTION OF WESTERN AMERICANA, BEINECKE RARE BOOK AND MANUSCRIPT LIBRARY.

Lee for the Mountain Meadows massacre. Less famous was the 1878 trial of Sylvanus Collett for the 1857 murder of John Aiken.[56] Rockwell had died earlier that year, as had Brigham Young the year before. Two other alleged members of the escort, John S. Lott and John R. Murdock, could not be found.

The trial of the forty-one-year-old Englishman opened October 8 at Provo before a mixed jury of Mormons and non-Mormons under a Poland Act formula for selecting balanced panels. Over the next ten days, U. S. Attorney Philip T. Van Zile called to the stand a number of witnesses who told what happened to four of the six Californians after they left Salt Lake on November 20. Their testimony twenty-one years after the crime is now corroborated by the newly discovered journal of Homer Brown.

---

56   For daily trial coverage, see *Daily Tribune, Deseret Evening News,* and *Salt Lake Herald,* all Salt Lake City, October 8 to 19, 1878.

bar of iron each from his sleeve and struck his victim on the head. Col-let did not stun his man and was getting worsted. Rockwell fired across the camp fire and wounded the man in the back. Two escaped and got back to Salt Creek."[65]

Homer Brown attended to his "business" and returned home late November 26 to find great excitement in Nephi because "two of the gentiles that stopped here night before last" had come back "badly wounded." Brown claimed the injured men said it was their own fault, that they had failed to put out a guard, and Indians were "right upon them before they knew it while they were sitting around the fire." He wrote, "The one that was wounded in the head threw away his coat and boots, and hat, and came in his shirt sleeves and bare foot."[66]

Reuben Down saw the wounded men at Timothy Foote's place.[67] One was "sitting in the corner," he said, "his head was bloody and he looked exhausted." The other struggled in later, "coatless, bareheaded and bare-foot," his head covered with "clotted blood." He had been shot from behind "under the left shoulder" and looked "fatigued and hurried."[68]

According to Brown, four men were sent out from Nephi "to look after Porter and men to see if they could find what had become of them."[69] If true, the searchers would not have had far to go. Frances Cazier testified she saw "Rockwell and his party in the tithing office" the morning after Brown came home. She overheard someone say, "Boys, you've made a bad job of it; Nephi won't be trusted with another job," but she could not recall whether it was Bigler or Bryan who said it.[70]

The settlement medical practitioner, W. A. C. Bryan, removed the bullet from one man's shoulder and rendered first aid to both. To settle up their second bill for lodging at Timothy Foote's, all they now had between them was a pistol and a gold watch. All else—animals, baggage, money, and other property—had been stolen. Aiken offered the watch

65   William Skeen Testimony, *Daily Tribune*, October 11, 1878, 2/4.
66   Homer Brown Journal, November 26, 1857, LDS Archives.
67   One of the men was John Aiken. In his testimony, Timothy Foote wrongly named the other man Tuck Wright. He was probably John Achard or A. J. Jones
68   Reuben Down Testimony, *Daily Tribune*, October 11, 1878, 2/2.
69   Homer Brown Journal, November 26, 1857, LDS Archives.
70   Frances Cazier Testimony, *Daily Tribune*, October 11, 1878, 2/2.

in pawn, but Foote said he was willing to take the less costly pistol.[71] Others said Foote forced Aiken to surrender their only means of defense.

On November 28 the doomed men boarded a buggy driven by two youths from Nephi and headed north. William Skeen told what happened to them as he concluded his account of Collett's alleged confession. A plot was drawn up "to send the two wounded men in a wagon to Willow Creek," eight miles north of Nephi, he went on. "Collett and his companions took possession of the herder's house; the wagon was driven down and the horses unhitched under pretence of watering them," he said. "Then we stepped out," Collett allegedly told Skeen, "and turned loose our double-barreled shotguns on them. We put their bodies in the springs (known as Deep or Bottomless springs)."[72]

Once again, Homer Brown's record placed him at the crime scene. In a second noteworthy coincidence, he "started with Absalom [Woolf] this morning to go to willow creek after the herd as there was an express came from the City for beef cattle," he wrote. "The two wounded men started for the City this morning as they seem very anxious to get to Salt Lake."[73] Again he left off without describing what he likely encountered at the nearby Deep Springs.

All this Sylvanus Collett flatly denied doing or telling William Skeen. Taking the stand in his own defense, he testified that on October 28, 1857, he had left the Salmon River Indian Mission, nearly four hundred miles to the north, with a party delivering pickled salmon to Utah. He arrived in Salt Lake "about the last of November," he said, and went home to Lehi.[74] "Collett could not possibly have been there with Rockwell," defense attorney Frank Tilford said, "for Collet was not there; he was hundreds of miles away."[75]

Thomas S. Smith, respected former president of the Indian mission at Fort Limhi, near present Salmon, Idaho, backed up the Englishman's story. He said Collett was at the fort when he arrived there on October

71   Ibid., Timothy Foote Testimony, October 10, 1878, 2/3.
72   William Skeen Testimony, October 11, 1878, 2/4.
73   Homer Brown Journal, November 28, 1857, LDS Archives.
74   Sylvanus Collett Testimony, "The Aiken Murder Trial," Daily Tribune, October 15, 1878, 1/2.
75   Ibid., Frank Tilford, closing argument, "The Collett Trial," October 16, 1878, 4/5.

22 with a party of new and returning missionaries. He also identified him as one of the eleven men who left the mission on Salmon River's east fork on October 28 with ox teams and wagons loaded with fish.[76] Joseph Harker, the captain of the fish-hauling expedition, "could not exactly say when they reached Salt Lake," but figured it was about "the latter end of December." Another former missionary to the Indians, Richard Bishop Margetts, also swore to this story.[77]

The prosecutor's case was credible, but Collett's testimony was unbreakable and convincing. The mixed panel of Mormons and non-Mormons found Collett not guilty. "No other conclusion could be arrived at by an impartial jury," said the Deseret Evening News, "guided only by the law and the evidence produced at the trial."[78] The noted Mormon historian Orson F. Whitney was so convinced of Collett's innocence, he even questioned "if such a murder ever occurred."[79]

Contrary to the church-owned paper's opinion, however, evidence now shows that Collett's defense rested on false testimony, deliberately given. The original journal of the Salmon River Mission, long unavailable to most historians, reports that Collett did not go with the slow ox train that left Fort Limhi on October 28. He and the mail rider Abraham Zundel instead took off with four horses between them on October 16, twelve days before the fish-hauling party left.[80] On October 18, they met Thomas S. Smith and his returning company at Market Lake, near present Idaho Falls, where three members of Smith's party recorded their arrival.[81] The mission president gave them "lief" [leave] to continue on to Salt Lake Valley.[82]

76   Ibid., Thomas S. Smith Testimony, "The Collett Case," October 13, 1878, 2/3–4.

77   Ibid., Joseph Harker and Richard B. Margetts Testimony.

78   "The Collett Trial," Deseret Evening News, October 17, 1878, 2.

79   Orson F. Whitney, History of Utah: Comprising Preliminary Chapters on the Previous History of Her Founders Accounts, 4 vols. (Salt Lake City, 1892–1904), 3:27.

80   Salmon River Mission Journal, October 28–29, 1857, 16. A photocopy of the original is in the Leonard J. Arrington Collection, folder 2, box 27, series IX, LJAHA-1, Merrill-Cazier Library, Utah State University. An edited version is in the Bancroft Library

81   See entries on October 18, 1857, in Journals of Milton D. Hammond, PAM 2068, USHS; James Miller, folder 1, box 1, MS 111, Marriott Library; and Charles F. Middleton, LDS Archives. Author's transcriptions in his possession.

82   Salmon River Mission Journal, October 22, 1857.

At their rate of travel on horseback from Fort Limhi to the early mountain men's "market," at the big Snake River bend, Collett would have passed Fort Box Elder before the Aiken Party arrived there on October 31 and reached Salt Lake over a month before the Aiken Party and its escort left the city on November 20. Moreover, if Collett had gone with the fish-hauling wagon party under Joseph Harker, he still would have reached Salt Lake in time to go with Rockwell. The ox train captain's own journal reveals this fact and puts the lie to his testimony.[83]

The evidence now demonstrates beyond reasonable doubt that two members of the Aiken Party, possibly John Achard and Thomas L. Aiken, were murdered November 25, 1857, at the crossing of the Sevier River, and two others, John Aiken and A. J. Jones, were killed three days later at Willow Creek, eight miles north of Nephi, Utah. Of the original half dozen, this left only Horace Bucklin and John Chapman. In his confession, Mormon gunman William A. Hickman matter-of-factly described what happened to the man called "Buck."

According to Hickman, Brigham Young called him to his office about that time and said: "The boys have made a bad job of trying to put a man out of the way." It was up to the feared Mormon executioner, Young allegedly said, "to get him out of the way, and use him up." Plans were laid for George Dalton, who had befriended Bucklin, to contact "this man (whose name I never heard, only he was called 'Buck') and take him home, for he had confidence in Dalton," Hickman said. He told Dalton to go past "the Hot Springs, three miles north of the city, and take the lower road, on which there was not much travel, and I was to meet him."[84]

Soon after dark, Dalton's wagon came along and Hickman told the driver to halt. "The man Buck, got a shot through the head, and was put across the fence in a ditch," he said. "A rag was hung on a brush to know the place." The one for whom today's scenic Bucks Lake and Bucks Valley

83   Joseph Harker History, October 28 to November 17, 1857, BX 8670.1 .H226, BYU Library.

84   William A. Hickman, *Brigham's Destroying Angel: Being the Life, Confession, and Startling Disclosures of the Notorious Bill Hickman, The Danite Chief of Utah* (New York: Geo. A. Crofutt, 1872. Reprinted Salt Lake City, Utah: Shepard Publishing Company, 1904). Also see R. N. Baskin, *Reminiscences of Early Utah* (Salt Lake City: By the author, 1914), 150–151.

in Plumas County, California, are named was planted in a ditch, near Bountiful, Utah. "Buck was the last one of the Aiken's party," Hickman said, "I never saw any of them but this man, and him I never saw until I saw him in the wagon that evening."[85] In this, Hickman was wrong, for John Chapman still lived.

According to a report published in the *Red Bluff Beacon* and reprinted in San Francisco, "Big John" Chapman, now the Aiken Party's lone survivor, arrived from Salt Lake with six other men at California's Honey Lake Valley about the middle of May 1858. The notice said Chapman went to Salt Lake City "last fall for the purpose of purchasing stock." There he and his companions "were taken and thrown into prison, where they remained all winter." He escaped and was pursued some thirty miles, when he "fell in with a party of forty-two teamsters from Col. Johnston's command."[86]

Ironically, saloonkeeper Thomas N. Long recalled that one Horace "Buckley" went to Salt Lake "with the Chapman crowd. He never came back with them and some thought that Chapman, who was a little afraid of him because he was so wild and reckless, had killed him while they were gone." Long speculated that Bucklin "was with Chapman when the latter made his escape from the Mormons." Lassen County chronicler Asa Merrill Fairfield indicates Long was right. Fairfield told how the Destroying Angels drove Bucklin and Chapman "out of the city in a wagon to kill them, as they supposed." As it got dark the two "made a break for liberty" and jumped from the wagon, but Bucklin's clothes caught on a single tree as Chapman ran into the brush and hid. The Mormons hunted for him, but when he could no longer hear his pursuers, Chapman "struck out regardless of the direction he took, and kept going" until he reached California. "Big John" Chapman met the fate Brigham Young had pronounced on him when Albert A. Smith (not a Mormon) shot him to death on March 7, 1860, in a dispute over a woman. "He was shot four times, through the breast, in the jaw, in the wrist, and in the back." But the story of how Chapman fled from Utah confirms Hickman's account of how he murdered Horace Bucklin.[87]

---

85   Hickman, *Brigham's Destroying Angel*, 129–130.
86   "Another Account of the Indian Battle Honey Lake," *Daily Alta California*, May 29, 1858, 1/1.
87   Fairfield, *Fairfield's Pioneer History of Lassen County California*, 235–236.

Unanswered questions remain. Why did the six men go to meet the U.S. Army's Utah Expedition? Mormon sources branded them spies, an interpretation possibly fueled by paranoia. People whose destiny was, to their mind, to establish the sovereign Kingdom of God would find it easy to believe the government had dispatched covert agents to find out what they were up to. But Washington's failure to anticipate opposition and the bureaucratic blunders surrounding the army's mobilization make it highly improbable it enlisted them to perform such a service.

A more likely reason is that they came, as some at the time reported, to establish a gambling operation and brothel at what became the U.S. Army's largest post. While California papers fail to mention any involvement in gaming and prostitution, the cash they carried and the quality of their animals and outfit indicates that they were not just travelers in search of scenery. But if gamblers, their luck ran out when the army failed to reach Salt Lake Valley that fall.

In the end, the reason they entered the "Lion of the Lord's" den may be as simple as the answer they gave William Ormsby. They had a curiosity to "take a look at the famous city of Salt Lake, and from thence would push on to see if they could make anything from our troops in the way of furnishing them with animals or other supplies," Ormsby remembered. Failing in that, Ormsby said, "They were to proceed direct to the States."[88]

As happened to the victims at Mountain Meadows, all of their property—estimated from $6,000 to $25,000—was stolen. Another common feature of crimes during this period was Governor Young's failure to recover stolen property or investigate and punish those who committed the crimes. The party's executioners got some of their clothing and animals, but the gold coins they carried may have seemed heaven-sent to finance the Mormon war with the United States.

In her classic work on the massacre at Mountain Meadows, Juanita Brooks argued that more than fifty southern Utah settlers became so emotionally unhinged by war fever and the Reformation that they were driven on their own to murder sixty or more women and children. However unconvincing this idea may be, it tells little about the Aiken Party murders, which reflect a calculated decision, reached over three weeks

---

88   "Murder of Five Americans in Utah," *Sacramento Daily Union*, January 18, 1858, 2/3.

of interrogation, to execute four of the intruders and allow the other two to remain at large over the winter.

Nor can it be said, as it often is of the Mountain Meadows atrocity, that Brigham Young knew nothing about the Aiken Party executions. Horace Bucklin wrote his petition for mercy directly to Young and his letter can be found in the Mormon leader's papers. It is also most unlikely that the notorious assassin, William A. Hickman, who did not know his victim, murdered the unfortunate "Buck" for reasons of his own. To the contrary, the episode and other crimes during this time, cited above, reflect Young's leadership style.

Brigham Young never followed Jethro's advice to Moses. He told followers who asked pointed questions to mind their own business, while he tried to manage every aspect of theirs, and he never delegated decision-making authority if he could help it. Twenty years later, Apostle George Q. Cannon eulogized Young as "the brain, the eye, the ear, the mouth and hand for the entire people of the Church." From the establishment of territorial government to the curvature of the seats the congregation sat on, the apostle said, "Nothing was too small for his mind; nothing was too large."[89] If anything, Young's personal involvement in the Aiken Party murders weakens the argument that he had no prior knowledge of Mormon participation in the attack on the emigrants at Mountain Meadows and did not learn about it afterward, as soon as it would take for an express rider to cover the 250-mile distance from Cedar City to Great Salt Lake. It also weighs against any belief that as many as seventy southern Utah settlers murdered women and children in cold blood, unless they at least thought Young wanted them to do it. If local leaders misled them on this score, the notion was at least believable at that time, and understandable as such today.

Like the Arkansas emigrants, the Aiken Party arrived in a place unlike any other they had known, a place of unbridled religious zeal, war fever, and defiance toward the United States. The arbitrary murder of both parties and other crimes at this time reveal a territory outside the rule

---

89   Exodus 18:1–26 and B. H. Roberts, *A Comprehensive History of the Church of Jesus Christ of Latter-day Saints* (Salt Lake City: LDS Church and Deseret News Press, 1930), 5:517–518.

of federal law and confirm the action by President Buchanan to restore it by military force. It also demonstrates the autocratic leadership of a man whose authority was perceived as divinely bestowed and therefore absolute among his followers.

The Utah War ended peacefully in June 1858, when Young and other Mormon leaders accepted the president's offer of a pardon to all Utah citizens who would submit to the laws. But the nation's longest struggle between church and state would not end at that; it would go on in the courts and legislative arenas for another thirty years. Its legacy can now be seen in the exclusive nature of Mormon culture and the distrustful attitude toward the federal government that makes Utah one of the country's most conservative states. And as for the Aiken Party, time alone, that revealer of crimes, must unravel the mystery which now surrounds their sad fate.[90]

---

90   "Murder of Five Americans in Utah," *Sacramento Daily Union*, January 18, 1858, 2/3.

⚜

The Crisis at Fort Limhi
1858

This is an edited version of Mr. Bigler's first published historical article,
which appeared in Utah Historical Quarterly *35:2 (Spring 1967), 121–136.*

THE MILD SOUTH WIND ON MONDAY, MARCH 8, 1858, BEGAN to blow the moisture from the communal "big fields" alongside Mormon settlements on the western slope of the Wasatch Mountains in Utah Territory. It warned of possible changes in the weather: possibly an unwelcome end to winter, or an onset of new snow to snap a short string of balmy days. About to open was the eleventh spring since the arrival of the Mormons in the Rocky Mountains. But this was the first season on their frontier that men had looked to such promising fields of tender winter wheat, planted the fall before, without an inner flush of gladness. By March, the instinctive responses of born farmers had vanished, smothered under a blanket of late winter reflection. Gone, too, on this day was the spiritual outpouring, the boastful defiance, of the previous year.

Instead, the chosen people of God cast more heavily than ever their fears and hopes for the future on the Lord—and Brigham Young. Emotionally emptied and sullen toward their American enemies, the people of the Kingdom of God got ready to plow their lands for planting, looking up uneasily at times toward the white wall of mountains on the northeast.

Out of sight, if not of mind, the reason for their apprehension was on the other side of the high peaks and ridges, near Fort Bridger. There, less than a dozen marching days away, an American army was poised like a

FORT LIMHI

Mormon Indian missionaries built Fort Limhi in 1855 on the east fork of the Salmon River, now known as the Lemhi River. The site appears on the center left of the image, which Steve Berlin captured on the Utah Westerners 2001 field trip.

frozen dagger, nearly two thousand strong, welded by its commander into a purposeful force that somehow had survived both winter and the punitive hand of God. Ice-bound and angry, the officers and men of Albert Sidney Johnston, newly promoted brigadier general, stamped the frozen ground to fight off frostbite, sharpened their fighting edge, and waited impatiently for supplies, reinforcements, and the snow to melt. Eager now were the soldiers of the Republic for a frontal assault on the Mormon stronghold.

At their backs, an aroused American government finally moved with decision to support its isolated force in the mountains by starting to mobilize more than enough manpower and materiel to put down promptly the rebellion by a new territory.

The temper of the nation also supplied good reason for Mormon leaders at Great Salt Lake City by March 8 to face realistically the deadly seriousness of a confrontation, wrought by faith and eloquence. Silent this day were the emotion-filled voices of short months before that cried for the hosts of Zion to dispatch a so-called mob of armed gentiles "to hell cross lots." With time and the weather now favoring their enemies, the heads of Israel in the Last Days bent soberly, instead, over plans to evacuate the "valleys of the mountains" their followers had learned to love so deeply in only a decade. As they had done before departing from Nauvoo, the Mormon hierarchy screened the projected movement, this time behind a curtain of warnings and false clues that the exodus would head south.

But they planned to move the other way.

Meanwhile, at the Council House at Great Salt Lake, the shifting wind from the south outside and the serious faces inside were not the only omens on March 8 of change to come for the Kingdom of God in western America. Early that morning, an intense figure on a splendid horse had galloped out of the Mormon capital toward the eastern mountains, flanked by the trusted Orrin Porter Rockwell and other chosen Mormon scouts. This mysterious newcomer, first introduced by Mormon leaders as "Dr. Osborne," a pseudonym, was in fact thirty-five-year-old Thomas L. Kane, the psychosomatic son of a prominent Philadelphia barrister. Kane also was a past benefactor of the Saints during the Nauvoo exodus and an ardent defender of the weak and oppressed everywhere.

Arriving on the stage of crisis two weeks before, via California, this self-appointed mediator had urged Brigham Young and his council to hold out an olive branch to the United States by authorizing him to offer food for the nation's hungry soldiers in the mountains. But the black-bearded peacemaker finally had ridden off to seek talks with the federals at Camp Scott, headquarters for the Utah Expedition, with little indication that Mormon leaders had approved his design, despite their warm reception for an old friend.

This was the way Monday, March 8, 1858, had opened in the Great Basin, a mild, windy day, seemingly like the others before it, yet somehow stirring with subtle omens for the future. Then, without warning, change—drastic and everlasting—came to the projected Mormon state in western America like an icy gale from out of the north.

And the door to independence banged suddenly shut.

The rolling drumbeat early on March 9 from the main gate of the square, adobe fort named Lehi, located at the north end of Utah Valley, snapped heads up to listen from fields, hills, and canyons nearby. The traditional alert of the Nauvoo Legion ordered the men of that settlement to put aside their plows and hammers—and harness up for war. After weeks of uncertainty and waiting, the call to action was almost a welcome sound.

Not long before, an express wagon from Legion headquarters at Great Salt Lake, some twenty muddy miles to the north, had rolled past the Jordan narrows that joined the two valleys, rumbled over the bridge, and into the Spanish-style fort on Dry Creek. The express bore shocking, unexpected news and military orders: "from Fort Limhi on Salmon River . . . Indains [sic] heded by some mountaineers attacted the bretheren . . . killed 2 also wounded 5 . . . stole most of their cattle."[1]

The steady drum roll touched off by this report at Lehi sounded an unintentional salute to the riders who formed the settlement's mounted company of the Nauvoo Legion, or volunteer militia of Utah Territory. These rugged horsemen had met and defeated the best warriors of a proud Indian nation, the Utah tribe, in 1850, again in 1853–1854 against the fearsome war chief, Walker, and a third time almost on their own doorstep against Chief Tintic's warriors in 1856. The Lehi cavalry had upheld its reputation in the fall of 1857 in raids on federal supply trains on Green River under the able Mormon commander Major Lot Smith. Afterward they patrolled the ramparts of the Kingdom in the mountains until late December.

So it was not by chance that Mormon general Daniel H. Wells in March 1858 ordered up his reliable veterans from the north end of Utah Lake instead of other forces at hand that were closer to the scene of trouble. In any Indian fight the seasoned horsemen from Lehi could be counted on to steady the two additional companies of fifty called out from Salt Lake Valley and settlements north of the capital.

---

1   Diary of Samuel Pitchforth, Nephi, March 10, 1858, typescript, BYU Library.

While Saints on Dry Creek gathered at their new adobe meetinghouse, the express carrying the news of the Fort Limhi massacre rolled south on a muddy wagon road that loosely beaded, for nearly fifty miles, the Mormon settlements in Utah Valley—a crescent of fertile land framed by the fresh waters of Utah Lake on the west and a sudden, seven-thousand-foot uplift of Wasatch Mountains a few miles opposite.

Spreading by the fastest means of the day was an alarm set off some forty-eight hours earlier by two Mormon missionaries to the tribes of Oregon Territory, twenty-two-year-old Baldwin Harvey Watts and a former trader on the trail to California named Ezra J. W. Barnard. On March 6, exhausted and half-frozen, Watts and Barnard had arrived at Barnard's Fort, a Mormon outpost near present Malad, Idaho, with a demand more desperate than their own survival—fresh horses to go on. In the heroics of a bloodless war, mainly fought by both sides against the common enemy of winter, the Mormon pair had turned in the most courageous feat of the Utah Rebellion.

On the night of February 28, after selecting and re-shoeing the two best horses in the besieged Limhi corral, Watts and Barnard had slipped out of the stockade on horseback to ride three hundred miles or more for help. While the Fort Limhi settlers feared every moment to hear the darkness torn by gunfire, the pair had threaded silently past the Indian camps along the river, then galloped for the nearest Mormon settlement, closely pursued the first part of the way. They covered the frozen wilderness at an average of fifty miles a day to reach Barnard's Fort in only six days. For the last forty-eight hours, they had pushed ahead without food and only one surviving horse between them.

Stitched into Barnard's coat lining by one of the women at Fort Limhi was a dispatch to Brigham Young from Colonel Thomas S. Smith, the grizzled president of the Salmon River colony in Oregon Territory. It described a fateful turn of events.

Virtually without warning, on the morning of February 25, 1858, about 250 hostile Bannock and Shoshone warriors had attacked the Mormon outpost located just west of the pass over the Beaverhead Mountains, now named Lemhi, near present Salmon, Idaho. Surprised at work on a clear day and heavily outnumbered, the Mormons of the Northern

Indian Mission saw two men killed and five others wounded in sharp, scattered fighting before they could pull back to the safety of their stockade. Among the wounded was the forty-year-old Colonel Smith, luckily only grazed on the arm during a burst of fire that had shot off his hat and cut loose his suspenders. Lost by the settlers was the raiders' primary target: almost the entire mission herd, numbering well over two hundred cattle and thirty or more horses and other animals.

But these losses, serious enough, paled alongside the heavier stroke delivered to Mormon plans to move the chosen people of the Almighty out of the path of the United States Army. For unexpectedly eliminated by the raid was the critical halfway base of supply and refitting in a projected movement north over the mountains to the Beaverhead region of western Montana on the headwaters of the Missouri River, then on to Bitterroot Valley, and, if necessary, into Canada.

Another disturbing factor in the report was that nearly all of the attackers were Mormons, baptized into the faith by Salmon River missionaries during the previous three years. In a revealing test of influence, gentile mountain men, a troublesome crew for the saints in the past, apparently had talked their Indian friends out of their new religion and into a raid on the fort. The outcome was a cruel setback at a crucial hour. But, for Mormon children of Israel in the nineteenth century, there was rarely an hour for healing lamentation.

Now calling for instant action was the emergency facing at least seventy Mormon settlers in Oregon Territory, thirty of them women and children, who were cut off and faced with sudden death nearly four hundred miles north of Great Salt Lake City. When last seen alive over a week before, the Saints on Salmon River, hammering their scythes into spears at the blacksmith shop to impale attackers coming over the stockade, were stiffening their courage and defenses for a hopeless last stand. The men then able to resist were outnumbered by as much as ten to one. On March 8, however, these unequal odds began to change, counterbalanced by the actions of those who also took up the contest.

Of these Mormon leaders, one of the least likely to be impressed by such one-sided opposition was David Evans, fifty-three-year-old bishop of Lehi and veteran of Zion's Camp in Missouri. His earlier experience fighting mobs in that state and Illinois also served him well in his position as bishop of the settlement. This high calling in the Mormon Kingdom also encompassed the lesser offices of mayor, representative to the territorial legislature, local commander of the Nauvoo Legion, election judge, probate judge, postmaster, and sundry other posts.

In keeping with his authority was the appearance of David Evans. The bishop's bulldog face, wide open eyes, set jaw, and flat nose announced a servant of God who was unadjusted to enduring slackers or bodily tabernacles that housed apostate spirits. And while the years had loosened gently his waistline, his advancing age had touched the opposite way a mind and will that were unbending to start with.

Finally, one thing was certain. Whenever Bishop Evans called for volunteers, the response was nearly always the same. Everybody volunteered. The unanimous showing of uplifted hands, however, demonstrated not so much fear of the bishop, as it reflected the understanding of his people that obedience to him was a condition of exaltation and fellowship among God's elect by the injunction: "I say unto you, be one; and if ye are not one, ye are not mine."[2]

At the same time, in calling the men of Lehi to a hazardous winter expedition into Oregon Territory, there was little need for Bishop Evans to whip a few laggards with his practiced tongue. Almost every man well enough to saddle and stay on a horse was ready to go.

Meanwhile, named by Mormon general Wells to command the 140-man force to Salmon River was a forty-one-year-old Virginian, Colonel Andrew Cunningham, also a leader in Zion's cause in prior months. In January, while Mormon leaders still labored with words to win their quarrel with the United States, Cunningham and four others had been chosen to sign "An Address from the people of Great Salt Lake City to the Honorable the Senate and House of Representatives, in Congress assembled." This defiant document had rehashed real and imagined Mormon grievances over the years and concluded that "we will no longer

2   A Book of Commandments, for the Government of the Church of Christ. Organized According to Law, on the 6th of April 1830 (Zion [Independence, Missouri], 1833), chap. XL, vs. 22.

wear your cursed yoke of unconstitutional requirements."[3] Of the United States, it said: "The young Hercules has found an adder in his path, his once manly fame is feeble and emaciated; he sickens, pales and falters."[4]

More significant, however, had been Cunningham's mission the fall before in the stepped-up Mormon undertaking to string way stations northward along the projected evacuation route should all else fail. Then he had led a chosen company of fifty to the crossing of Snake River, near the mouth of the Blackfoot River tributary, roughly midway between Great Salt Lake and Fort Limhi, close to the present location of Idaho Falls. There, near the intersection of the Mormon wagon road to Salmon River and the Oregon Trail, his party erected a settlement, located an improved crossing of Snake River, reportedly put up a saw mill, cached food, and planted winter wheat before returning to the valley.

While Cunningham was thus engaged, the second ranking officer in the mobilizing Fort Limhi expedition, Major Marcellus Monroe, had set out in fall 1857 with a small party to deliver to Indian chiefs along Bear River what he later called in his report the "necessary instructions."[5] Similar orders, to at least one other Mormon officer at that time, were to tell the Indians that "our enemies, are also their enemies."[6] Finally, in addition to the Lehi volunteers commanded by a Nauvoo Legion veteran, Captain Abram Hatch, age twenty-eight, military leaders of the Kingdom ordered to Fort Limhi two full companies of fifty men each to fill out the mounted force under Cunningham.

Of these, the unit best outfitted and the first ready to ride announced somewhat prematurely the birth in January of a new American military force—the Standing Army of the Kingdom of God. The commander of this detachment of regular Mormon soldiers from the Fourth Battalion, First Regiment, First Brigade, Standing Army, was Captain Christopher

3   *Deseret News* (Great Salt Lake City, U.T.), January 27, 1858.
4   A possible reference to the secret Mormon order of the Missouri period, known as the Sons of Dan, or Danites. See Gen. 49:17: "Dan shall be a serpent by the way, an adder in the path, that biteth the horse heels."
5   "Report of a Party of Observation," Military Records Section, Utah State Archives, Salt Lake City.
6   Adjutant General [James Ferguson], Nauvoo Legion, to Colonel W. B. Pace, August 13, 1857, Military Records Section, Utah State Archives.

Layton, a thirty-seven-year-old Englishman from the settlement of Kaysville. The second company, mobilized under the Nauvoo Legion military organization, was commanded by Captain Joseph Grover of Farmington. Under each company leader were five lieutenants, so-called captains of ten, completing an organization patterned after the desert tribes of ancient Israel.[7] The Mormon soldiers supplied their own weapons—usually a rifle and revolver—from forty to one hundred rounds of ammunition, personal gear, and at least three bushels of grain per man. Planning to ride one animal while breathing the other, most men also reported with two mounts.

Regular or volunteer, the Mormon companies more resembled large posses than formal military outfits, largely because of the lack of uniforms. Instead, troopers dressed for warmth with too little to keep them warm. They wore endlessly patched clothes—some buckskin shirts or pants, and boots that were mainly handmade or repaired. After ten years, store clothing had grown dear in the Great Basin where people were instructed to make their own.

In weapons, there were almost as many kinds as there were soldiers, although most men boasted rifles instead of muskets, even a few early repeaters like the one they called a "15-shooter." Some carried revolvers manufactured at a new Great Salt Lake arsenal. Many of these weapons, like everything else, were borrowed from somebody else.

But drawbacks like these were more than compensated by the raw caliber of the Mormon troops. They were youthful, adapted to the wilderness, and as strong as the horses they rode. Despite their close organization and conditioned obedience, the troops exhibited a distinct lack of piety, especially among their Numic-speaking native allies, in speech and manners. An old echo from the Missouri-Illinois period was their belief in roundly cursing the enemies of Zion, a rare avenue for creative expression that also opened too easily in moments of exasperation with balky oxen, straying horses, or stuck wagons. Still, every morning and again at night, they would gather shoulder-to-shoulder on the trail in a strong bond of common faith, heads bowed and bared to the wind, while one among them committed

---

7   Muster rolls and inventories of arms and provisions for the Salmon River Expedition, March 1858, are located in the Military Records Section, Utah State Archives.

aloud their mission and safekeeping to an Almighty God, who seemed Himself to ride in the midst of them, more rough and ready than the rest.

Meanwhile, in advance of the main column, an experienced commander and ten picked men rode north from Ogden. The survival of this company depended alone on speed and surprise. Their orders were to break through to Fort Limhi with a dispatch that help was coming.

By nightfall on Tuesday, March 9, a rapid mobilization of the Mormon forces already was underway to save, if possible, the Saints in peril far to the north. Only then did a proud, self-disciplined man turn to meet his sternest test of leadership. At 8 p.m. that night Brigham Young swallowed the gall in his throat to dictate a letter to Colonel Thomas Kane, dispatched "by my son, Joseph A." and a companion, who overtook the peacemaker before he reached the federals at Camp Scott. "We have just learned . . . that the troops are very destitute of provisions," his note started out.[8] Only for the sake of his people did Brigham Young go on to offer the enemy in the mountains something to eat.

Lieutenant Colonel Benjamin Franklin Cummings of the Nauvoo Legion had just celebrated his thirty-seventh birthday at Ogden when the express rode up from Great Salt Lake on Tuesday, March 9. Before noon the next day, Cummings swung into his saddle to lead ten men north to the stricken fort on Salmon River. His orders: "go through as quick as we could."[9]

For the dependable native of Maine, command of the fast-moving advance force to Fort Limhi climaxed three exhausting years of service to the Kingdom of God. Called among the first missionaries to the Indians of Oregon Territory, Cummings had played a major role in locating Fort Limhi, a few miles west of the pass over the Continental Divide in the Beaverhead Mountains that Meriwether Lewis and William Clark had crossed fifty years before. The site on the east branch of Salmon River, now named Lemhi River, also was near the birthplace of Sacagawea, the Hidatsa captive and Shoshone translator who in August 1805 arranged for the expedition to acquire horses from her native band,

---

8   Young to Kane, Senate Doc. 1 (35-2), 1858–1859, 87–88.

9   Benjamin Franklin Cummings, "Biography and Journals of Benjamin Franklin Cummings, Ogden, 1821–1878," March 10, 1858, typescript, BYU Library.

BENJAMIN FRANKLIN CUMMINGS
As a Salmon River Indian missionary,
explorer, and commander of the 1858
advance rescue mission to Fort Limhi,
few could match B. F. Cummings's devotion
to his community and faith. AUTHOR'S
COLLECTION.

the Agaidika (or Salmon Eaters). Her devotion to the American explorers became a legend in Western history.

In November 1856 Cummings and two others from Fort Limhi had crossed the Lewis and Clark gateway over the Continental Divide to the Beaverhead and Big Hole headwaters of the Missouri River and ridden north to Bitterroot Valley, now in southeastern Montana. Their mission, they had said, was to enter Brigham Young's bid to purchase Fort Hall with Neil McArthur, northwest agent for the Hudson's Bay Company. Along the way, the Ogden officer had mapped and noted carefully the advantages of that region as a future gathering place for his people. His report had prompted Brigham Young the next spring to journey into Oregon Territory to see for himself. By such meritorious service, Cummings had won "permission to stay at home for a season."[10]

Hardly had he returned to Ogden, however, before he again was ordered north, this time to lead a battalion of Mormon troops to Soda Springs on the Oregon Trail to halt a half-hearted move by "Buchanan's Army" to enter Salt Lake Valley from that direction.

---

10   Ibid., June 1857.

Past performance on the Kingdom's northern ramparts had earned Cummings the most dangerous assignment of all. Riding with him were the ten men he had chosen, four of them former Indian missionaries on Salmon River. The latter were: Baldwin Harvey Watts, called "B. H." or "Baldy" despite his wavy hair, one of the youthful couriers who rode from Fort Limhi for help two weeks earlier; George Washington Hill, an irrepressible, thirty-six-year-old Ohioan, whose good-natured bravado was like catnip to Indians; Thomas Bingham, a sturdy veteran of the Mormon Battalion; and William Bailey Lake, a stocky optimist of thirty-two, who was always looked to for cheering words by disheartened companions.[11]

Following the road to Fort Hall, the little command on March 10 and 11 rode north through Brigham City; crossed Bear River near present Collinston, Utah; and headed up the valley of the Malad River, a sweep of sagebrush between the Bannock Range on the east and barren hills on the other side.

As they urged their horses up the open valley, the mild gusts from the south suddenly reversed with chilling effect to a cold wind from the northwest. Lowering skies warned of the heavy storm front moving in. Ignoring the omen, the riders pushed steadily ahead and gained by Thursday night, March 11, a camp on Henderson Creek, some seventy miles north of Ogden near present Woodruff, Idaho. There, pinned down by a fall of snow heavy enough to blot out trail and landmarks, they fretted the next, precious day away.

In his own language, the Mormon colonel jotted down a terse account of the journey north as they went: "Crossed over the east mt and camped on a small creek about 2 miles from Marsh Creek. Severe snow storm traveled down Marsh crossed over and continued on down a few miles and struck up on to the bench and down on to Portniff and crossed over about 7 miles above the mouth of Marsh creek. Traveled down about 5 miles and camped. Stormy all day and cold."

Saturday dawned late with no sign of clearing weather. Unwilling to delay longer, Cummings decided to go on. But instead of continuing on

---

11   Others in the party were Benjamin Cutler, Thomas Bloxham, Thomas Workman, J. Hammer, and John Munson. A tenth unnamed man may have been Sylvanus Collett or George Barber, both of Lehi, or Fort Limhi's seldom-spoken mail rider, Abraham Zundel, age twenty-two, of Willard.

the main road along Little Malad Creek, he gambled to make up lost time by risking a little-traveled shortcut north over a low divide in the Bannock Range to Marsh Creek.[12] Men and horses drove into the mountains on risky footing with their heads down and shrouded with snow; their visibility was cut almost to zero by a descending blanket of white. They rolled up at night in their buffalo robes for a few sleepless hours in the open.

Sunday, March 14, opened cold and grey on the Mormon horsemen pushing slower through deep powder snow. Without pause or much conversation, they advanced down Marsh Creek to pick up and follow Portneuf River, and camped for the night a few miles south of present Pocatello:

> Mon. 15th. Start 8 am continue on down the Canyon about 10 miles and came out into an arm of the valley about 8 miles and stoped for noon 12½ pm Start at 2 pm and camp at the Black Foot creek mission.

The gamble had paid off. Cummings and his half-frozen company at last descended from the mountains into the milder climate of Snake River Valley. Heading now to the northeast, the force rested at midday near the intersection of the Oregon Trail, then rode on to camp in the comfort of the cabins built at Blackfoot Fork by Andrew Cunningham's pioneer party late in 1857. At this point they had covered about 180 miles, or about half of their journey. If they knew where to find the food cached by Cunningham a few months before, they also ate their first full meal in nearly a week. And they would benefit from the new Snake River crossing located by the earlier Mormon company.

> Tues. 16th Cross the river and travel up about 35 miles and camped.

On the seventh day the riders crossed Snake River and headed northeast at a faster pace along the north bank on the Flathead Indian Trail from Fort Hall to Bitterroot Valley. On their right the river curled its way along the valley. On the other hand a waterless carpet of crumbling lava and sagebrush, some fifty miles across, discouraged a direct approach to the mountains beyond.

> Wed. 17th. Continue on left Snake river at the Big Slough stoped at the mouth of Carmash creek 2 PM to let our horses eat found the tracks of a number of

---

12   Their trail generally followed today's Interstate 15, which superceded U.S. Highway 191 from Malad to Downey, Idaho, and then U.S. 91 to Pocatello.

ponies and mules in the road near the place where we stopped. Supposed to the Indians who had pursued the Brethern who came in with the express. 4 PM start on for Spring Creek where we arrived about 1 o'clock at night.

Near the big, marshy loop in Snake River about twenty miles north of present Idaho Falls, the Mormon party turned sharply away from the river on a new bearing northwest toward Mud Lake, then an aptly named, milky body in a barren region. They halted in the early afternoon to rest and graze their mounts on the grass along Camas Creek near the parting of the route to Fort Limhi from the Flathead Trail. Here, Watts pointed to tracks in the mud perhaps made by the war party that had pursued the twenty-two-year-old and his companion less than three weeks before. As the hoof prints verified, Cummings and his men had traveled some 240 miles to pause at the very brink of peril.

Prior to Indian hostilities, the distance from this point to the Lewis and Clark pass over the Continental Divide near Fort Limhi had looked to Mormons like a divinely planned corridor of escape from the U.S. Army, a covered route through the mountains to fertile lands beyond.

> Bro Brigham said look to the west ... and on the west side was high mountains ... do you see where that creek comes out [?] there is room for one man to pass in at a time let us go in ... and there was a beautiful valley.[13]

This dream of an envisioned gateway to paradise by one Mormon leader had been drastically changed by the Indian attack on Fort Limhi to a trail of sudden death through a valley apparently designed by a bronze creator as an ideal setting for his favorite war tactic—ambush.

The first leg, about thirty-five miles from Camas Creek to Spring Creek[14] at the narrow entry in the mountains, was an invitation to a massacre. This naked approach to the mountains led the unwary across a sloping tableland of low brush and lava gravel unbroken by a shred of cover or protecting ravine. Any lookout in the mountains could see for miles anyone coming on this flat wasteland. The rest of the way was an eighty-mile gauntlet up a narrow, barren valley, ranging in width from a few thousand feet to eight miles and hemmed on both sides for the

---

13   Diary of Samuel Pitchforth, February 19, 1858.
14   Today named Birch Creek.

entire distance by impassable mountains.[15] The Lemhi Range on the west soared over ten thousand feet. Only a shade less rugged, the Beaverhead Mountains blocked any exit to the east. Between the imposing barriers, the wagon road northwest wound along birch-lined creeks, over broken benches of sagebrush, and through a maze of brush, side canyons, and dry creek beds. For Cummings and his men, Fort Limhi was no haven of rest in a covered alley to freedom. Instead, the outpost was a compelling piece of live bait at the far end of a bushwacker's heaven.[16]

To escape detection from the mountains, Cummings timed the start of his exposed approach for late afternoon. He pushed his command across most of the flat tableland under cover of night. By the first hour of morning, the party reached the cover of the birch willows and brush near the sink of Spring Creek, still a few miles short of their entry point into the mountains.

Stiff and cold from riding into a hard, freezing wind that blew up shortly after dark, the men worked their horses down into the heavy cover along the creek, where a small fire would be unseen for more than a few hundred feet. In this shelter, they thawed out and napped until earliest dawn, when they moved on.

> Thur. 18th Wind continues very strong from the north which we had to face Started about 6½ AM and traveled 14 miles up the creek and turned into a small Kanyon on the right opposite the first crossing [of] the creek about 10 AM found good feed and little wind.

After bucking ahead into a driving wind and blowing snow, the riders by midmorning that day passed the narrow entrance between the mountain ranges. From here on they would stay away from the exposed trail in the lower valley, favor the protective benches that hugged the east mountain, and travel mainly at night and early morning.

> Fri. 19th wind continue[s] very high Start 9 AM Travel up to the mouth of Bear Creek Kanyon[17] and camp. wind blow hard all day but ceased about Sunset considerable snow.

---

15 Today this route roughly follows Idaho State Highway 28 from Mud Lake to Salmon.

16 Brigham Young, who had an instinctive eye for military terrain, made a similar comment on his first visit to the region in May 1857.

17 Properly named Bare Creek Canyon, east of present Kaufman, Idaho.

The Mormon horsemen girded now for a final push of about sixty miles, with brief stops only to breathe their mounts. The last leg of their journey led over a low divide between the Snake River Basin and Eighteenmile Creek, a headwater of Salmon River, along the latter stream to the east fork of Salmon River, and another two dozen miles down river to their destination near present Tendoy, Idaho.

> Sat. 20th Start 7 A M crossed the divide. Snow very bad crusted in many places so as to bear the horses.

From the snowbound pass, their target came within striking distance, downhill all the way. With restored spirit the men urged their tired horses forward, kept their rifles checked and ready, and scanned carefully every hill and ravine for any sign of Indians. It was after dark that day when the trouble Cummings so long had expected at last came.

The eleven horsemen reined up sharply at the glow of Indian sentinel fires on high ground that commanded a narrowing in the trail ahead. After a whispered counsel the Mormon colonel again elected to gamble, this time on the odds that his hard-riding company had reached this point undetected and that he would not lead his men into a whole Indian camp on the far side of the flickering beacons.

Throwing caution away, they spurred their horses and drove straight into and past the threat, while surprised lookouts tried in vain to stir up a sleeping Indian encampment. Speed and decision delivered the hardy force when the moment of danger finally arrived.

Shortly after 1 A.M. on Sunday, March 21, near the end of the eleventh day, Lieutenant Colonel Benjamin Franklin Cummings and his jubilant company of ten rode up to the log stockade on the east bank of the river. Shouting to the guard to hold his fire and open the gate, they charged inside the fort to cries of joy and tears of welcome and were pulled from their horses by the arms of those they had saved—all of them still alive.

Three days later, Captain Abram Hatch and the veteran Indian fighters from Lehi rode up as ordered by Bishop Evans. They arrived in company with the Standing Army regulars under Captain Layton, a total of nearly a hundred troopers, all of them spoiling for a fight. The last company of fifty from Davis County reached the spot soon after to bring up the rearguard of Colonel Andrew Cunningham's force.

Even before the militia arrived, according to orders carried by Cummings, Mormon settlers on Salmon River had begun packing to evacuate their outpost in the northwest and bring to a close a significant episode on the Mormon frontier that had lasted less than three years.

As the colonists for the Kingdom of God loaded their wagons for the long journey home, Colonel Cummings and nine men, seven of these from his earlier company, saddled up and rode out ahead of the rest on Friday, March 26, with news of the rescue.[18] On the ride north the Mormon officer from New England at least twice had studied unfavorable odds, then chosen to gamble. Both times his luck held. But this good fortune and the size of friendly forces now between his small command and the former point of danger apparently offered too much temptation to overconfidence.

For on the return trip, with no need to, Cummings took another chance. But this time his luck ran out.[19]

The outcome was a bloody footnote to a crisis that altered the course of the Kingdom of God in western America and to the heroic action in March 1858 to rescue the saints in distress on Salmon River in Oregon Territory.

---

18   Besides Cummings, the return express included George W. Hill, Baldwin H. Watts, Thomas Bingham, William Bailey Lake, Benjamin Cutler, George W. Barber, Thomas Bloxham, John Blanchard Jr., and Thomas Workman.

19   Cummings and his men seized three Indian horses near Mud Lake. In the running gunfight that followed, Bannock warriors shot and killed William Bailey Lake and killed or captured seventeen of Cummings command's horses. The rest of the Mormons escaped, most of them on foot. See Bigler, ed., *Fort Limhi*, 271–274.

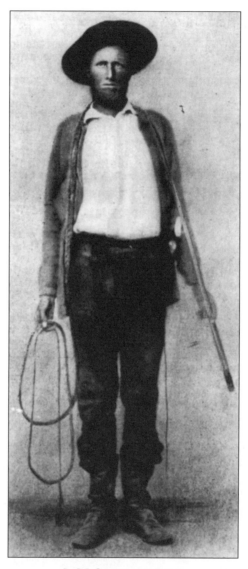

L. W. SHURTLIFF, 1855

Lewis Warren Shurtliff holds a whip in what may be the greatest picture ever taken of a Mormon cowboy. After his tumultuous romances at Fort Limhi, Shurtliff became one of the most respected citizens of northern Utah. AUTHOR'S COLLECTION.

⚜

One of Nature's Ladies: The Life and Loves of Lewis Warren Shurtliff

This essay is an edited version of a chapter in David L. Bigler,
Fort Limhi: The Mormon Adventure in Oregon Territory, 1855–1858
(Spokane, Wash.: The Arthur H. Clark Company, 2004), 161–175.

WHEN MORMON MISSIONARIES FIRST CAME TO SALMON RIVER in June 1855, the natives "received their company with the best of feelings, yet they were not asleep for they had already undertaken to prove the chastity of the men by offering them their females," wrote clerk David Moore, "but in this they failed to bring any into transgression."[1] As Thomas Smith later admitted to Brigham Young, the missionaries had not realized at the time that one of their responsibilities, as emissaries to the "remnants of the House of Jacob," was to marry Indian wives, a policy made possible by the practice of polygamy. After Young's visit in 1857, they attempted to correct this misunderstanding. Recalled Pleasant Green Taylor:

> President Young had told us to go and identify ourselves with the Indians or Lamanites. The following day after our arrival at [Salmon River] some 500 Lamanites came to our camp and were very friendly. Many fathers among them brought their daughters and desired us to marry them but not understanding the meaning of the term identify as used by President Young, he

---

1   David Moore and Jacob Miller, Salmon River Mission Journal, June 23, 1855, LDS Archives.

knowing that if we should take this course it would have the effect of uniting us and causing them to remain our friends. When they found that we would not take their daughters they departed.[2]

As the mountain men understood, native peoples regarded an invitation to marry their daughters as an expression of tribal acceptance and friendship, which the Mormon newcomers mistook as a test of their morality. By rejecting the offer, they set themselves apart from their native cousins to the benefit of their mountaineer adversaries, as later events would point up. In the meantime, the oldest missionary wasted little time in showing that there was at least one member of the company who welcomed the opportunity to form an alliance with their new neighbors.

Forty-eight-year-old Isaac Shepard from Farmington "has been trying to get a squaw to live with ever since we have been on Salmon River," reported Charles Dalton on June 24, 1855. Later that year, Shepard "took one into his house to keep unbenouns [unbeknown] to the President or to any one else of the mission until in the afternoon he then told of it and on the 25th the president made him turn her away," Dalton said. The wayward missionary further "had a Spaniard and his family living in his house with him at the same time the squaw went away and stayed two days, returned, and lived with the spaniard until the 17th of November when the Brethern returned from Salt Lake," Dalton went on. "Manuel also said that Shepard is sleep[ing] with his squaw."[3]

With only this known exception, prior to Brigham Young's visit in May 1857 the missionaries maintained a deliberate distance from native women. At that time, Young asked the mission president "why we had

---

2   Pleasant Green Taylor Autobiography and Family Record, typescript in author's possession.

3   Charles Dalton Journal, LDS Archives, entries in June, October, and November 1855. Manuel may have a Mexican trader who came to Bitterroot Valley as early as 1852 to make adobes for John Owen's fort. Frederick Burr purchased ammunition and tobacco from him in 1857. Frank Woody spoke of "an old Mexican trapper named Emanuel Martin, generally known as and called 'Old Manwell, the Spaniard.'" See Seymour Dunbar and Paul C. Phillips, *The Journals and Letters of Major John C. Owen, 1850–1871* (New York: Edward Eberstadt, 1927), 1:45, 46; Journal of Frederick H. Burr, 1857–58, Beinecke Library; and Frank H. Woody, "How an Early Pioneer Came to Montana," *Contributions to the Historical Society of Montana* 7 (1910), 161.

told him that he had escorted the intruders after they were turned over "to Rockwell, Lott, Murdock and himself, with the order to make away with them." The four assassins were afraid to tackle their prisoners by themselves, Collett allegedly said, because they were "large, strong men," so a party was raised at Nephi and sent ahead to the Sevier River to camp and wait for them.[60]

Guy Foote remembered the departure of the reinforcements from Nephi. While the doomed men slept the night of their arrival, Foote testified that he hitched up a wagon and "drove to the tithing office." It was "quite dark," he said, but he recognized the voice of John Kienke "who stood on the tithing house steps with three others." They all climbed in the wagon and "drove off south."[61]

Homer Brown was also among the group—one of the four Bishop Jacob G. Bigler sent from Nephi to make the odds eight to four.[62] "I was called up between ten and eleven o'clock last night to go out to the Sevier river on business," Brown wrote the next day. He failed to say what "business" needed doing at the lonely Sevier River crossing, some twenty-five miles south of Nephi, but it would take four men to do it, he said: Absalom Woolf, Miles Miller, John Kienke, and himself. They left before daylight, "arrived at the Sevier a little after noon, and camped for the night."[63]

As Brown and his companions waited, the Californians paid for their lodging the next day at Timothy B. Foote's house. "They all seemed to have plenty of money," his son Guy Foote remembered. Thomas Aiken's belt was made to carry twenty-dollar gold pieces six deep, he said, and it was "full of money." Young Foote saw the men start south that morning from his father's house.[64]

Continuing his testimony, William Skeen said Collett told him that the two parties met at the Sevier River and camped together as planned. After supper, the newcomers sat around the fire singing. "Each assassin had selected his man. At a signal from Rockwell, [the] four men drew a

60 William Skeen Testimony, "The Aiken Massacre," *Daily Tribune*, October 11, 1878, 2/4.

61 Ibid., Guy Foote Testimony, October 10, 1878, 2/2.

62 For the record, Jacob G. Bigler is the author's great-great-grandfather.

63 Homer Brown Journal, November 25, 1857, LDS Archives.

64 Guy Foote Testimony, *Daily Tribune*, October 10, 1878, 2/3.

According to trial witnesses, five Aiken Party members and their four-man escort under Rockwell traveled south some twenty-five miles to Lehi, where Thomas Singleton remembered they were "well dressed and a fine looking party of men." One was named John Chapman, he said, who decided to stay there over the winter. As the others left, one of them turned to him and said, "Goodbye, John. If you come this way and see our bones bleaching on the plains, bury them."[57] Horace Bucklin, the other member of the Aiken Party allowed to remain in Utah over the winter, stayed in Salt Lake.

The other four and their escort rode south on the same trail the Fancher Party followed to their death at Mountain Meadows two months before. At Nephi, eighty-five miles south of Salt Lake, twenty-seven-year-old Homer Brown left the only known contemporary record of the combined party's arrival on November 24 at the settlement on Salt Creek. "There were four men came in this evening that are gentiles," he wrote. "They are going to Callifornia [sic] the South route. They have lately come from Callifornia the North route and were going East, but were stopped in the City and sent to Callifornia escorted by O. P. Roc[k]well, John Lot, and John Murdock."[58]

Brown next revealed why the four Californians would never reach Los Angeles. "One of the men had a letter of recommendation from a commander of a U.S. Station in Callifornia to Col. Johns[t]on stating that the bearer was a man that could be trusted and was capable of performing any scheme that he might undertake etc.," he said. "This letter fell into Brighams hands, and thus he found out who they were."[59] The rest of Homer Brown's journal places him at the scene of all four murders.

At the trial, William Skeen, a key prosecution witness, accurately described the part that Brown and three others would be called on to play. A longtime friend of Collett, Skeen testified that the Englishman

57   Thomas Singleton Testimony, "Collett Murder Case," *Daily Tribune*, October 10, 1878,

58   Homer Brown Journal, November 24, 1857, Keith Franklin Larson transcription, Film 2/2.
#MS 2181 1, LDS Archives.

59   Ibid. Given the paranoia current in Utah, a character reference may have been misunderstood, or it may have been a legitimate offer of the Aiken Party's services should Johnston see the need.

not identified ourselves with Israel," according to Pleasant Green Taylor, and a puzzled Thomas Smith answered, "he did not understand what he meant by that term." So Young's first counselor spelled out what it meant for the seed of Abraham "to be grafted in."[4] Apostle Heber C. Kimball "told us to go now and take their daughters to wife," Taylor said, "to which President Young replied that Brother Kimball says for you to 'go and get wives from among the daughters of the Lamanites,' but I do not say for you to marry them but I say for you to go and try for I think the time is past, it is now too late."[5]

Having been told to "go and try," Taylor that same day "took eight of my brethern with me and went out among the Indians and we tried hard to get them to marry us but they said no."[6] As Young had predicted, the natives rebuffed their overtures, which may have been a blessing for the thirty-year-old Kentuckian. For "Green" Taylor already had three wives in Utah, including two sisters of Lewis Warren Shurtliff, plus seven children: five by his first wife and two, plus one on the way, by the second. Just before leaving Ogden with Brigham Young's company to Fort Limhi, he had married Shurtliff's younger sister, Jane Narcissus, age sixteen.

Acting mission head Thomas Bingham on July 19, 1857, advised the missionaries to go slow when it came to marriage with the local inhabitants.[7] "Pres Bingham gave us some advice as to trying to get wives from among the Natives," said Jacob Miller, acting as the mission recorder in place of the absent David Moore. "They have refused to let thier [sic] daughters go or at least seem not willing and said the Pres [Bingham] it is enough for the present let it rest say nothing more about it."[8]

---

4   Cummings, Travel of President Brigham Young to Oregon 1857, LDS Archives, May 10, 1857.

5   Pleasant Green Taylor Autobiography and Family Record.

6   Ibid. Eventually at least three missionaries did marry Indian women. Englishman Thomas Day Jr. at age forty-three married a Bannock woman on December 22, 1857; twenty-seven-year-old Ezra Barnard took a native wife on December 28, 1857; and Richard Bishop Margetts, also from England, at age forty-three married an Indian woman. All three had other wives in Utah. As far as it is known, these unions produced no offspring.

7   On June 18 Thomas Smith left with a party of fifteen to bring their families in Utah to the fort.

8   Salmon River Mission Journal, July 19, 1857.

At the same time, there were two schools of thought on this question. Forty-year-old New Yorker Crandall Dunn from Ogden brought it up before the Sunday meeting on August 30. "Br. Dunn in his remarks seemed to be very pointed upon the subject of our not having done any thing for which we were sent out here referring to remarks of Pres. Kimbal[l] when he was here," Miller recorded.[9]

Most of the missionaries, however, shared the feelings of twenty-three-year-old Charles Franklin Middleton about the duty to forge marital ties with the natives. "As far as us marr[y]ing squaws is concerned I can say that if that is [the] only way of bring[ing] them about to what the Lord wants of them I am afraid the thing will be prolonged some time yet from the fact that the natives are not that way inclined at all, neather do I believe that there are but few of the Mormon boys in this place that are very keen to perform that part of their religion," he wrote his wife, Martha Browning. "I can say for one that if it should be made known to me that it was the only way for me to secure my salvation I mite go forward in the performense of that duty though with a degree [of] reluctence."[10] When Middleton went to Fort Limhi in October 1857, he left behind his wife and their two sons, the youngest less than three months old, at Ogden.

Of all the missionaries, perhaps the one least interested in the idea of "grafting" with the seed of Abraham in the wilderness, formally or otherwise, was twenty-one-year-old Lewis Warren Shurtliff. Being the only male out of eight children born to his father, Luman A. Shurtliff, and Eunice Gaylord, the first of his five wives, the young missionary had already learned much about the opposite sex from his seven sisters. But he still found it difficult to establish a lasting relationship with one of its members.[11]

In Iowa he had "formed an acquaintance with a young Lady whose name was Eliza Hadden." They became "intimate friends and passed many happy hours together," he said. But after his family left for Utah in 1851, "we never met but once; and that was on the plains in Eighteen

9   Ibid., August 30, 1857.
10   C. F. Middleton to Martha Middleton, November 27, 1857, Charles F. Middleton Journal, LDS Archives.
11   All Shurtliff quotations, unless otherwise indicated, are from Life and Travels of Lewis Warren Shurtliff, Idaho State Historical Society, copy in author's possession.

Sixty three." By then "she had been twice married and was then a widow," he later remembered.

His family moved into Bingham's Fort in 1854, established three years earlier by Vermont native Erastus Bingham and guarded by a redoubt of mud and adobe within the present limits of today's Ogden City. Boasting a population that year of more than seven hundred, the settlement offered ample opportunities for a young man to form "acquaintance with many fine young men and women or girls." The first young woman Shurtliff "kept company with" was a "girl of no learning, or refinement, and this I could not endure," he said. "I could tolerate, and even associate with men who were uncouth, but could (not) endure such rudeness in the op[p]osite sec [sic]."

"To the fair daughters of Eve" Lewis Shurtliff had little to say over the following year. He built a house and "kept company" with several young women. "The last of this number was Jane Fay," he said, but then added, "We fell out." Discouraged and unhappy, he hired himself out to Nathaniel Leavitt as a proxy to go to Salmon River in his place for six months at twenty-five dollars a month. It was then that his fortune changed. As he left Ogden on October 19 with a party bound for Fort Limhi, "I first saw She [sic] who after ward became my wife, and made the remark that such would be the case," he said. "She like myself was on her way to Salmon River." Among this company were the first white females to settle in present Idaho, including the subject of Shurtliff's attention, a young woman who turned thirteen on the day they arrived at the mission, November 17, 1855.

Louisa Catherine Smith was the daughter of Addison and Laura Bentley Smith of Vermont, who adopted Mormonism and gathered in 1843 with latter-day Israel to its new city-state of Nauvoo on the Mississippi River. Soon after their arrival, her mother became ill and died, leaving four children, ranging in age from eight to the youngest, Louisa, less than one year old. Her father "was also sick and destitute of means," so the children were "scattered to different places." Asked to "take a little girl," David and Susan Moore, a childless couple, went to see Smith about "taking Louisa" and he "gave me the child as my own," the Canadian said. She was a "little over a year old when we took her."[12]

---

12 Compiled Writings and Life History of David Moore, BYU Library, 19.

For Lewis Shurtliff the winter of 1855–1856 at Fort Limhi "wore away almost impreceiptibly." He broke the boredom by hunting and "put myself assiduously to the task of learning the Indian Language or Dielect [*sic*]," both with success. He spent holidays "in dancing and social entertainments where I formed an acqua[i]ntance with Miss Louisa C. Smith, an adopted child of David and Susan Moore." Otherwise, "the winter wore on and we were constantly studying and attending to our daily avocations." Finally spring came and "put on her richest foliage and the wildnes[s] of the Mountain scenery delighted and pleased me":

> Our Summer labours now began to bear heavily upon our men, and it seemed a treat when Sunday came. July fifteenth I attended meeting, or services after Worship. Feeling somewhat lonely I sauntered out for a walk bending my steps towards the River. After crossing a fine streach [stretch] of butiful meadows covered with fine wild flowers, as I wandered alone, along the River I saw a butifull vision near the stream. She was warbling some little song.
>
> I stood fixed to the spot, not knowing whether to approach her or not, fearing the fair creature should leave me and all become an illusion.
>
> I approached and said fair Maiden, you have wandered far from your cottage? Are you not fearfull that some young Bannock Chief will become Enchanted or enamored with one so young and butifull and spirit you away to his rude Lodge there to bask in the light of thy smile.
>
> Oh, no kind Sir. I have no fear of those red men, there is a power that binds them in my presence. I am not alone as you suppose, there is one near who is ever watchfull for my saf[e]ty and will protect the Lonely Wanderer.
>
> We sat down together on the green sward in order to arrange a boquet of wild flowers which we had gathered from the Meadows. I was no longer my own master. I was enslaved by this young Maiden. She had won my heart.
>
> After a pleasant walk we returned to our home which stood a short distance from the River. Surrounded in the distance by Mountains covered with perpetual snow.

Soon after this idyllic interlude, Shurtliff took off on horseback with Nathaniel Leavitt, riding fifty miles a day, to obtain a load of salt from Mormon settlements so that the mission could begin to ship pickled fish to Utah. Before leaving, he saw Louisa again and apparently allowed his religious zeal to gather Israel's remnants in the wilderness to overwhelm the desires of his heart. It was a mistake he would quickly regret.

> I one evening took a walk and met Louisa Moore on the road to the field. We sat down together on the hillside and chatted. I knew she loved me and I told

her (although contrary to my feelings) that we never could be else but Brother and Sister. This was like a dagger to her heart, the color left her butiful cheeks, and she seemed perfectly lost. After a short time in silence she arose. Standing there in all the dignity of her sec [sex]. She stooped down and imprinted a kiss upon my cheek, and was gone before I could rally. When I did come to, I was alone. Long I sat in meditation and wished that I could recall those bitter words that I had spoken. But alas it was to[o] late.

Shurtliff soon became "a lonely wanderer" while Louisa Moore "found the society of others that seemed to suit her." The two did not meet again before the young woman left Salmon River later that year "to finish her education" in Utah. Shurtliff rode alongside her party for a few miles, but "did not converse privitly [sic] with Miss Louisa Moore." As winter came on, Shurtliff devoted himself to "improvements of the mind" and kept himself busy at the mission where he was "installed Chief Cook," which "took most of my time." To overcome his loneliness, he "determined to make a good use of my present advantages by apropriating all of my time to useful study."

Then there came in late January an unexpected, if dangerous, opportunity to see Louisa again. Thomas Smith named Shurtliff as one of a four-man party, including Smith, Pleasant Green Taylor, and Lachoneus Barnard, to make a perilous midwinter ride to Great Salt Lake and to deliver to Brigham Young the report and map by Benjamin F. Cummings on Bitterroot Valley. To better their chances for survival, they took three horses each, but still often covered only three or four miles a day as they fought their way through heavy snow along the divides.

Reaching his father's home at Ogden in mid-February, Shurtliff greeted his family and enjoyed his full first meal in nearly a month before hurrying to David Moore's house "to see Miss Louisa." To his regret, he found that "her affections were weened from me," he said, admitting, "I had no one to blame but my own dear self." The meeting was "cool and formal; each seemed ill at ease." He left "much depressed in spirit." He tried to forget his sorrow as he prepared to return to Fort Limhi, but Louisa Moore seemed always to be on his mind. He once saw her at a public gathering and that night "dreamed that we were married." Shurtliff thought this fantasy would never come to pass, he said, "but little did I understand the providences [sic] of my Heavenly Father." Without seeking such outside help, however, he put down his stubborn spirit and humbly begged the young woman to forgive him:

Ogden City
March 6th 1857

Miss Louisa

It is with pleasure, I write a few lines to you, To inform you of my present feelings, I feel verry lonesome at present but I hope for better days. Do not be offended with me for this letter. But remember our friendship while at Fort Limhi; which I look upon as happy days, often have I been to places, where we have sat together, and talked of different subjects, Alas, those happy hours are past, and now am left alone, I want you to forgive me, if you can, for it seems as if I was deprived of my best friend, if you cannot forgive as I shall be verry unhappy, write to me the first chance, I remain, your friend, and lover.

Lewis W. Shurtliff

His letter brought no response and the young missionary's hopes seemed blasted. On March 31 he "went to see my girl," and discovered "another man there." Leaving her suitor in the house, he took Louisa Moore outside and "went out on the well curb" where he poured out his heart. "She was much affected with my confession and she wept," he said. "We parted the best of friends." Soon afterward, however, he "went to see Louisa" again. "All was now over," he said. "She treated me with the utmost coldness." Four days later he went to see her again, he said, and "she treated [me] scornfully." The day before he left to return to Fort Limhi as a member of Brigham Young's company, he addressed a final note to the young woman he loved and had seemingly lost.

Ogden City   April 24th 1857

Miss Louisa, It is with a sorrowful heart, that I take my pen in hand to write a few lines to you, not to make you unhappy (because that would make my own heart bleed) but to ask of you one small favor, to remember you by, when Sorrow and gloom shall surround me, and I shall rove over the mountains, to drive away those unhappy feelings that now fill my breast. I feel that I am despised and hated and I know not the cause. I have tried to think wherein I have hurt your feelings, but I cannot, I done as I agreed by comeing to see you, what more could I do [?] we met at Farmington you treated me coolly. I saw you at Conference [when] you still treated me the same, I went to your house your treatment was severe. Prehaps [sic] you never want to see my face again, if so your wish shall be granted although it would be hard for me if I have to stay in the mountains for years, Oh that I could call back those happy days that we have spent together, but no, they are past and gone forever, yet you have denied me the comfort of seeing you, or conversing with you whitch was my only joy. Oh my dear girl I am almost led to wish that we had never met, but it is wicked to make such a wish, when an overruling power has caused it to be so. I wish I could tell you my feelings. I am alone and am lonesome, permit me to enjoy your parting hand before I go, let me see you one moment before I go, I wish to know why you have forsaken me. I cannot write any more at present.

I remain as ever your friend, and lover
Lewis W. Shurtliff

Receiving no answer, the young missionary started the next day, April 25, 1857, "for my northern home, with a sad heart, in the Company of the President and Company," he said. "I rode as rear guard." Later, at Fort Limhi, he heard Apostle Heber C. Kimball enlighten the missionaries on their responsibility to "connect ourselves with the house of Israel," hopefully with a chief's daughter, for "when a man marries a chief's daughter," Kimball said, "he marries the whole family! Yes the whole nation."[13] That Shurtliff had a mind of his own he had already demonstrated during the great Mormon revival, known as the Reformation, when he called one church leader's sermon "the most vulgar preaching" he had ever heard. And he dismissed Kimball's instruction to marry Indian women as just "stray doctrine."

Accordingly, the young missionary did not join "Green" Taylor and the others who went out to the Indian camps over the next month to investigate the availability of Indian women they might marry. Instead he spent his time "in herding cattle and horses" and "continued to cook during the month."

Then came the fateful day. "Friday twenty fourth of July George W. Hill asked Snagg the Snake Chief, for Catherine his daughter." The Ohioan "returned to the Fort in high spirits telling all that he would soon marry the Chiefs daughter." Although tribal interest in forming marriage ties with their Mormon cousins had cooled, it did appear that there was one native maiden who seemed anxious to take this step.

She was Catherine, the daughter of Shoshone chief Ti-o-von-du-ah, better known as Old Snag, who had been baptized with other members

13 Cummings, Travel of President Brigham Young to Oregon 1857, May 10, 1857, LDS Archives.

of his large family at Fort Limhi in November 1855. Before becoming available for marriage, she had been the live-in wife of Bitterroot Valley trader Frederick H. Burr, who had started for California earlier that year, encountering Brigham Young's company to Fort Limhi on the Flathead Trail along Snake River. This was apparently unknown to the missionaries. That the Shoshone woman was comely, and that her former husband had been smitten by her, is suggested at the end of Burr's 1857 journal. Over a page listing trade goods he scrawled in large letters the name "Catharine" as if daydreaming.[14] But his departure had left her alone and ready to establish a new relationship.

When George Hill rejoiced that he had obeyed Apostle Kimball's instruction and won the hand of the chief's daughter, "Some one told him not to be two [sic] sanguine of success," Shurtliff said. "At this remark there was a thrill ran over my whole frame. What could it mean[?]" He soon answered his own question.

> The next day this fair daughter of the Rocky Mountains came to see me, returned the following day and told me plainly that it was me she wanted, this announcement was astounding, and had it not been for an open window near at hand I should have fell. I finally rallied and said I am to[o] young to marry; this she contradicted. I done all that I possibly could to dissuade her from such a rash (and I thought an imprudent) step; but all to no purpose. She said she did not want Mr. Hill that he was two [sic] old and that if she did not get me she would have no one.
>
> When this dark Damsel left me I sat down and wept. My thoughts were of Louisa. She to whom I was devoted both soul and body, [and] here I was, either must disobey the President's wish or marry this woman. I saw the sacrifice that I was now called upon to make. I must forever abandon the thoughts of marrying the girl of my choice.
>
> No sleep came to my eyelids nor food passed my lips. Often would this thought come to my mind. Shall I shrink from a duty imposed on some one, by the President of the Church to marry this particular [woman] or should I do whatever they told me and trust the event with God.
>
> Before the dawn of day my mind was made up to confer with our President,[15] over the question in regard to the matter.
>
> Morning came at last and breakfast being ready I told the President of my situation. He sympathised with me; but shook his head in silence, he called

---

14   Frederick H. Burr Journal, December 1857, Beinecke Library.

15   Mission president Thomas Smith.

the Brethern of the Mission together and after the matter was fully put before them they desided [*sic*] I should take her. This I felt was my death knel[l] sounding in my ear.

I told them of a lovely fair creatur[e] whom I loved and that I wished not to shrink from any duty but I would like to marry a white girl first.

This request being denied me I saut [sought] the solitude of the grove; where I oft had wandered, here I asked the Lord to strengthen me for the task.

The following Evening this dusky maid came to see me and asked me to go home with her, this wish I complied with; We had a long talk together and I can assure you it pertook of the romantic.

This brought to pass a dream that I had some time previous. I had an interpreter who went with me to see the girl's father and he said that she could not marry without sertain papers from the former husband. Catherine told me that Geo. W. Hill had not acted fairly with me but that he had been disseatfull and asked her father for himself instead of asking for me. All this I was prepared to endure. It mattered but little what should be my fate for all was now lost.

A few days passed by and the Old Chief moved away down the River Catherine staying untill after dark then out of galentry [gallantry] I saddled my horse and went with her and her Brother to take a ride of twelve miles in the butifull moonlight with one of Nature's Ladies. Reminds me of wandering in Berlin Museum among the statuary.[16]

Her Brother was sent ahead and we rode alone. She confessed her passion for me and at our parting said she would see me again. We parted, I to a twelve mile ride she no doubt to dreamland. But it is doubtfull whether those dreams were pure and free from sensual desires, for she was an uneducated unsafistakated [unsophisticated] Squaw—

A few days brought her back to our house. She stayed there for some days and like Patipher's she saut [sought] to ceduce [seduce] a boy.[17] I soon got clear of her and then I began to feel free again.

As if in answer to the young man's prayers, events worked together to "clear" him of Chief Snag's daughter. While there was no escape from his companions' judgment that obedience to counsel required him to marry her, the obligation rested on her desire to do so. On September 16 Thomas Harris, Dr. Monroe Atkinson, and David Pattee came from Fort

---

16   Shurtliff's offhand comment referred to a visit to Germany after he was called to the LDS British Mission in 1867.

17   Potiphar was one of the pharaoh's officers who purchased Joseph from the Midianites after his brothers had sold him into slavery. For the story of his wife's attempt to seduce the young son of Jacob, see Genesis 39:1–20.

Owen to "get some mill irons made" by the mission blacksmith. When they left two days later they "took with them Indian Snags d[a]ughter her Husband having sent for her."[18] Catherine's "husband" was Frederick Burr. He had set out that spring for California, but after meeting Brigham Young's party on Snake River and visiting his brother, David A. Burr, in Great Salt Lake City, he had decided to return to Bitterroot Valley instead. He then sent for her, and she dutifully went back to him.

At the same time, the evidence also points to the intercession of Thomas Smith, who engineered Shurtliff's release from the religious duty and opened the way for him to realize his heart's desire. In keeping with Brigham Young's promise to expand the colony in Oregon, Smith returned to Utah that July to collect a new company of settlers and lead them back to Salmon River. Events indicate that while in Utah he discussed the problem with Young and won approval to release Shurtliff from this duty. Moreover, the outcome suggests that he talked with David Moore and even Louisa herself, who appears to have concluded that she had made the young missionary suffer enough for his earlier rejection. For while Catherine left, she came of her own will.

To carry the good news, Smith left his main settlement company at Market Lake on Snake River and rode ahead with Milton D. Hammond and William Marlow to arrive on October 22 at Fort Limhi. "I listened to the reports with anxiety, in their report I should hear my destiny," Shurtliff said. "I stood in a retired corner of the house [and] at last the President said Where is Lewis I have news for him." He went on, "Miss Moore is coming in this Company, but I think she is looking in another direction." Shurtliff did not believe that. "I saddled up my horse," he said, "and rode out to meet the company."

> I met Miss Louisa. The meeting was not like some of our former associations—Spent the Evening with the Company [and] great was our joy to once again see each others faces.
>
> And now after an estrangement of years our meeting in the same place of our first acquaintance was all that our hearts could desire, we now revisited the butifull spot where we had met and there we found two rose trees had grown and twined their slender branches together. This thenomenon [sic] we looked upon as a token of our own futur[e] happiness, and here beneath the

---

18   Salmon River Mission Journal, September 16 and 18, 1857.

azure sky just as the sun had sank behind the lofty mountains casting its dim last rays of light upon our peacefull and butifull little Valley; It was here just as the stars shed their glimering light upon the scene, here we plighted our future; to love each other. There was one thing concerning this meeting that caused us to look forward to the future with some anxiety.

Those two rose bushes after they had come to perfection one of them faded and died. Not being superstitious, we tried to treat this Bad omen of our future with indifference.[19] Still there was something which would whisper your future may not allways be that perfect happiness and joy. We returned to our homes after our Stroll.

Soon after winning back Louisa's affection, Lewis Shurtliff asked David Moore for his daughter's hand, Shurtliff said, and "he gave his consent and a fathers blessing upon us." Moore's wife, Susan, who had come with the latest settlement party to Salmon River, "also gave her heartfelt blessing upon her only adopted child." The couple's "joy was now full and we only wanted the bond of Matrimony to make our happiness complete."

The fourth of January 1858 was the "Eventful Day" for twenty-two-year-old Lewis Warren Shurtliff. As the threat of Indian trouble grew around the isolated colony in Oregon, nearly four hundred miles north of main Mormon settlements, Thomas Smith married the young missionary—but not to the daughter of a Shoshone chief, as instructed by the leaders of his faith. Instead he married him to the girl of his choice. His new wife, Louisa Smith Moore Shurtliff, whose middle name was also Catherine, was fifteen years old.

---

19   This "bad omen" unfortunately proved true in October 1866, when Louisa Shurtliff died at Ogden, Utah, five months after the birth of their fourth child. The other Catherine, Chief Snag's daughter, apparently had other husbands.

Mormon Missionaries, the Utah War, and the 1858 Bannock Raid on Fort Limhi

This is an edited version of an article that first appeared in
Montana The Magazine of Western History
53:3 (Autumn 2003), 30–43.

ABOUT MIDMORNING ON FEBRUARY 25, 1858, APPROXIMATELY 250 Bannocks and a handful of Sheepeater Shoshones swept down on the Mormon settlement at Fort Limhi, some nineteen miles southeast of present-day Salmon, Idaho. In scattered attacks they killed two missionaries, wounded five others, and seized thirty or more horses and almost all of the colony's nearly three hundred cattle. The attackers met little resistance and suffered no known casualties.

Leading the Bannocks was a giant chief known as Le Grand Coquin, "the grand rogue," a name bestowed by Richard Grant, a Hudson's Bay factor at Fort Hall. Mistaking the French words for an Indian name, the Mormons had taken it down as it sounded, Grow-kre-kah or Rock-e-kay. They also called him Shou-woo-koo. By any name, the native leader was an impressive figure. He stood four or five inches above six feet in his moccasins and towered over everyone else, native or white. Riding with him was mountaineer John W. Powell, after whom Montana's Mount Powell and Powell County are named.

The Fort Limhi raid cut off sixty-nine white settlers "over 300 miles from our friends" in the Salt Lake Valley.[1] Isolated and fearful, thirty-nine men, seventeen women, and thirteen children huddled together in a log stockade built to house a third that number. The impact of the attack, however, reached far beyond the colonists' immediate well-being. At a stroke, it also eliminated the possibility of moving Mormon settlement north from the Salt Lake Valley in the event that the Great Basin theocracy failed to win the Utah War, a military confrontation with the United States that had been ongoing since 1857. No longer would the Fort Limhi serve as a strategic location in Young's plan of last resort.

In 1855, only three years before the attack, the Bannocks had welcomed the Mormons and invited them to settle in their territory. The Mormons had come as part of a great upsurge in proselyting to American Indians, known under doctrines of the faith as the "Lamanites." At the Mormon general conference that year, some 160 missionaries were called as the first of hundreds sent out over the next three years to convert the Cherokees, Choctaws, Hopis, Nez Perces, Delawares, Crows, Shoshones, Bannocks, Paiutes, Shawnees, Navajos, Utes, and other tribes. Among the missionaries were twenty-seven emissaries "to the Remnants of the House of Jacob, which inhabit the Mountain Regions Known as the Rocky Mountains." The men who formed the Salmon River Indian Mission were told "to go North as far as [the] Flathead Country if the Missionaries thought it wisdom to do so," the company's clerk, David Moore, said.[2]

The men ordered to Le Grand Coquin's territory averaged thirty-two years in age and hailed from ten states and two foreign countries. Most

---

1   Salmon River Mission Journal, February 25, 1858, LDS Archives. There is a photocopy of this document in folder 2, box 27 series IX, LJAHA-1, Merrill Library, Utah State University, Logan, and an edited version in collection P-F68, Bancroft Library.

2   *Deseret News*, May 16, 1855; *Latter-day Saints' Millennial Star*, August 25, 1855; Salmon River Mission Journal, April 6, 1855; Compiled Writings of David Moore, Journal and Life History, April 1855, BX 8670 1.M782, BYU Library. The name Lamanite is from the Book of Mormon, accepted by the faith as the scriptural account of how a Hebrew prophet, Lehi, led his family to the New World in about 600 B.C., before the fall of Jerusalem to the Babylonians. His descendants became two great peoples, the dark-skinned Lamanites and white Nephites, who waged war against each other. The Lamanites destroyed the Nephites about 400 A.D. and became today's Native Americans.

were married with families to worry about, and some were polygamists with more than one wife and family to support. At a time of drought in northern Utah, few wanted to leave their homes and take up a calling that was hard and often dangerous. None of them, including their leader, thirty-seven-year-old New Yorker Thomas S. Smith, had any knowledge or understanding of the peoples they sought to redeem. Complicating matters, Smith's ordination as president of the mission rested on such absolute authority that it emptied of substance the outwardly democratic governance observed by those under him.

In May 1855 this tightly organized company followed the Fort Hall Road north from the Salt Lake Valley to the deserted Hudson's Bay trading post near today's Pocatello, Idaho, some 180 miles from Great Salt Lake City. From there, finding the spring runoff too high to ford the Blackfoot River on the Flathead Trail, they crossed the Snake River at Ferry Butte in an abandoned boat and swam their livestock with the help of a young Bannock named Warra-hoop. They then traveled up the north bank of the Snake River to meet the Flathead Trail at a ford near present-day Blackfoot, Idaho, and followed this wagon trace along the line of today's Interstate 15. At the bend of Snake River, the party turned northwest to break a wagon road along an Indian trail that ran between the Beaverhead Mountains and the Lemhi Range, along the route of present-day Idaho Highway 28. As they went, the news of their coming flew before them.[3]

As the company neared its destination, there suddenly appeared in the distance a giant Indian, riding toward them on a powerful horse. With his wife and child, Le Grand Coquin had ridden seventy-five miles up the valley to meet the Mormon party near the head of Lemhi River. The Bannock chief told them they were very welcome, clerk Moore said, "and

---

3   For a description of the route between the Salt Lake Valley and Fort Hall, see Brigham D. Madsen, ed., *Exploring the Great Salt Lake: The Stansbury Expedition of 1849–50* (Salt Lake City: University of Utah Press, 1989), 157–188. See also Madsen's "The Bannock Mountain Road," *Idaho Yesterdays* 8 (Spring 1964), 10–15. From Fort Hall the Flathead Trail crossed the Continental Divide at Monida following the line of today's Interstate 15 and ran along the Red Rock River and through the Big Hole Valley to Gibbons Pass. There it entered Ross's Hole at the south end of Bitterroot Valley and followed the Bitterroot River to Fort Owen.

he was very glad that we had come to open up farms and show the Indians how to work, as they were in a suffering condition for want of food, the traders not being allowed to trade them any ammunition."[4] Le Grand Coquin invited the Mormon party to stay among his people and personally escorted its members to a place on Salmon River's east fork that had long been a central trade location for Great Plains and Rocky Mountain tribes.

Here, near where Sacagawea was reunited with her family in 1805, Bannocks and Sheepeaters fished the mountain stream for the Chinook salmon that filled its waters each summer. Here, too, horse trails converged from the north and the south, funneling hunting parties of Shoshones, Nez Perces, and the Bitterroot Salish, Kootenai, and Pend d'Oreilles tribes (now known as the Confederated Salish and Kootenai Tribes of the Flathead Reservation) over the Continental Divide for swift forays into the buffalo-hunting grounds along Horse Prairie Creek and other Missouri River headwaters. The location was a gathering place and a crossroads of many tribes, ones not always friendly toward each other.

Three days after the arrivals chose a spot for their cabins on the right bank of the river, Nez Perce captain Tipiyelehne Ka Awpo—Eagle from the Light—"a fine looking man of about fifty years of age," rode in from the east with over twenty lodges and camped on the meadows nearby. When the missionaries assembled for prayer, "the old chief and the Bannock chief also met with us and united their voices in keeping time with the time of the hymn sung, and during the time of prayer they observed the utmost attention and silence."[5] Among the Nez Perces was "one in Particular named Clark a half Breed son of Clark of Clark and Louis [fame] Journall with Bright red hair blue eyes as thin skin as you would see on any man," George W. Hill said. "He always called me his Little Brother because I was of the same Complection [sic] as he was and he was a little older."[6]

---

4   Salmon River Mission Journal, June 12, 1855.

5   Ibid., June 12, 1855. Thanks to Otis Halfmoon, Nez Perce National Historic Park, and Dennis Baird, University of Idaho Library, for the identity of the Nez Perce leader.

6   Incidents in the Life of George Washington Hill, 1855, LDS Archives, typed and indexed copy in author's possession. According to Flathead Reservation historian Peter Ronan, William Clark fathered a son by a Flathead woman when the explorers remained with the tribe two days and nights, September 4 and 5, 1805, at Ross's Hole on the headwaters of Bitterroot River.

At first nothing seemed to shake Le Grand Coquin's friendship. At his invitation Hill helped build a fish trap on the river while the chief's followers made the wicket work so "we would all fish together." Upon coming to the river the next morning, the missionary and a companion, Benjamin Franklin Cummings, found the Bannocks lined up waiting for them to catch the first fish. A big man himself, Hill used a pole twelve feet long with a hook four inches across, and he jerked it back with such force that it struck a native standing behind him. "The Chief sayes [sic] to me Look at that Indian you have killed," Hill said. "I Looked and saw him lying there sure enough." Cummings wanted to leave, but the Bannock chief assured Hill that it was not his fault, that "he had no business standing behind me [and] that I had no eyes in the back of my head."[7]

Nor was Bannock forbearance limited to fishing mishaps. "The Indians are very honest here or have been so far," William Burgess told church apostle George A. Smith. "Not one thing has been stolen yet," he noted, adding, "I wish Christians were this honest." An even better measure of friendship was the number of conversions. Mission records show the names of forty-eight men and thirteen women, Bannocks and Sheepeater Shoshones, baptized that fall. Most belonged to the band of the Sheepeater chief Ti-o-von-du-ah, better known as Snag, who brought his family members for "washing" the following spring. While he remained a fast friend of the Mormons even after the 1858 raid, other conversions were "not as far-reaching as [missionaries] could have wished, the Indians apparently failing to sense the nature of the covenants they were taking upon themselves."[8]

Even so, partaking in the ritual signified native acceptance, a friendliness seemingly unreciprocated by their new white neighbors. The missionaries were at work building their cabins in the shape of a hollow square, each side 231 feet long, with the cabin fronts facing an inner court of nearly four thousand square feet. As the natives looked on, they enclosed the cluster of cabins within a square palisade 264 feet long. The

7   Ibid.
8   William Burgess to George A. Smith, October 9, 1855, LDS Archives; John V. Bluth, "The Salmon River Mission: An Account of Its Origin, Purpose, Growth and Abandonment," parts 1 and 2, *Improvement Era* 3 (September–October 1900), 1:809.

log walls were twelve feet high with three feet below ground and nine above. The east gate, facing the Continental Divide, was ten feet wide and nine high and "made of timbers well fitted together and four inches thick." A smaller gate on the opposite side opened toward the river. The missionaries named the palisade Fort Limhi after King Limhi from the Book of Mormon who had preserved a colony of his people in the wilderness. Proud of it though the colonists might be, the square of upright timbers was a wall of separation that signaled distrust. Nor was it the only worrisome sign. That fall Indians watched as missionaries ploughed and fenced the fertile meadows along the river where as many as four hundred Nez Perce horses, some "very heavy and well made," had grazed.[9]

As the Mormons erected a literal fortress, they also opened a cultural divide. The Indians had received them "with the best of feelings, yet they were not asleep," clerk Moore said, "for they had already undertaken to prove the chastity of the men by offering them their females." In this, he continued, "they failed to bring any into transgression." Zion's emissaries to the tribes would later learn that their duties did indeed include marrying Indian women and having families. By then, however, they would find the opportunity virtually withdrawn. By the time Brigham Young visited Fort Limhi the next spring, Le Grand Coquin and other Bannock leaders were no longer interested in friendship and were conspicuous by their absence.[10]

Young decided to make the journey to Fort Limhi, the longest of his western career, after seeing the report of three emissaries from the settlement who had ridden to the Bitterroot Valley the previous November to deliver Young's bid to purchase Fort Hall to Hudson's Bay agent Neil McArthur. What they learned during the trip convinced them that "Bitter-Root Valley as well as other portions of the country over east of the mountains would become the abode of the saints."[11]

---

9   Salmon River Mission Journal, June 21 and July 30, 1855.
10   Ibid., June 23, 1855. Thomas Day Jr., Ezra J. W. Barnard, Richard B. Margetts, and possibly others married Indian women. As far as is known, these unions produced no children.
11   Autobiography and Journals of Benjamin Franklin Cummings, October 20 to November 1, 1857, BX 8670.1.C912, BYU Library. The meeting took place at the abandoned Cantonment Stevens twelve miles south of Fort Owen, near present-day Victor, Montana.

Young's May 1857 visit transformed the Salmon River Indian Mission into a permanent settlement of great strategic importance. The makeup of his 142-member train was a "who's who" of Utah Territory military, religious, and settlement leaders and included Arapeen, the chief of the Wasatch Utes. The half-brother of the late war chief Wakara had come to meet with the northern tribes, assure them of the Mormons' friendly intentions, and encourage them to become allies of the faith's Rocky Mountain kingdom. But the ostentatious display of interest in the upper Salmon River region served mainly to alienate the Bannocks.

Only Snag, "with his band numbering sixteen lodges," moved his camp upriver to Fort Limhi. "He came for the purpose of seeing the Big Mormon Chief and to get some presents which he had been told he would get by visiting the fort," said the clerk of Young's party. But Snag was in no humor for talk. He had shot himself in the thigh and was "peevish and fretful" from having to walk on crutches. The lame Sheepeater chief's friendship was well enough, but the good will of the Bannocks who also claimed the valley as their homeland was a condition of the missionaries' survival. Le Grand Coquin and his Bannocks pointedly ignored the meeting, and only a handful "pitched their tents adjacent to the fort."[12]

During his visit Brigham Young signaled that the establishment of Fort Limhi was just the beginning of an overall shift in Mormon colonization to the north. "I will settle in the north all the time in preference to the South," he told the missionaries. He gave them permission to bring their families and settle permanently on Salmon River's east fork. Soon after, the missionaries agreed new farms should "begin south of the fort and be laid off down the river or north as far as the bottoms would admit," Moore said, "and each of the brethren to have what land they could cultivate." There is no record of any intention to purchase the land from the valley's native inhabitants.[13]

To a member of Young's company from Parowan, Utah, on the trail to California over two hundred miles south of Great Salt Lake, the message

12   James W. Cummings, Travel of President Brigham Young to Oregon 1857, May 12, 1857, DS Archives; Albert Carrington diary, May 11, 1857, folder 7, box 1, MS 549, Marriott Library.

13   Cummings, Travel of President Brigham Young, May 10, 1857; Salmon River Mission Journal, May 23, 1857.

was clear. Said William Dame: "[The] presidency felt well toward the brethren in this place and said the settlements must go north instead of south."[14]

Rumors of the announcement rippled across the Northwest. Ordered to investigate reports that Fort Limhi was "supplying the Indians with arms and ammunition," Flathead agent R. H. Lansdale visited the Bitterroot Valley in August 1857 and concluded that such stories were groundless. However, he also found the Flatheads afraid the religionists were headed in their direction. "Leading Flathead chiefs have serious fears lest the Mormons, being driven from their present settlements by the government, should overrun and occupy their lands by force," he said.[15]

To the Fort Limhi missionaries, visiting Mormon leaders gave religious instruction that might also have eased Indian fears: "We have got to become one and connect ourselves with the House of Israel." Daniel H. Wells, Young's second counselor, took pains to spell out what this meant: "In relation to our connections with the Lamanites I would say that the marriage tie is the strongest tie that can be found," he said. "They are of the seed of Abraham," added Heber C. Kimball, the plainspoken first counselor in the faith's first presidency. "They have got to be grafted in." That same day missionary Pleasant Green Taylor "took eight of my brethern [sic] with me and we went out among the Indians and we tried hard to get them to marry us but they said no." They were no longer interested in being grafted.[16]

On returning to Great Salt Lake, Brigham Young publicly had little to say about the region he had seen. "When people are obliged to live in the north country," he told his followers on May 31, "that will be high time for them to go there." Later that year, however, knowing that an American army was marching on Utah, his message was different. Calling his inner circle's attention to Fort Limhi, Young asked: "Now do we not want a station about half way from here say near fort Hall?" According to Apostle

14   William H. Dame Journal, May 18, 1857, Vault MSS 55, BYU Library.

15   James Nesmith to James Denver, September 1, 1857, in "Annual Report of Commissioner of Indian Affairs," Sen. Doc. 11, v.2 (35-1), 1858, Serial 919, 612; R. H. Lansdale to James Nesmith, September 22, 1857, ibid., 663–669.

16   Cummings, Travel of President Brigham Young, May 10, 1857; Pleasant Green Taylor Autobiography and Family Record, May 1857, LDS Archives, typescript in author's possession.

Wilford Woodruff, Young also announced, "The North is the place for us not the South" and called the region near the upper Missouri River "the key of this continent."[17]

The development that made this decision urgent occurred during the thirty-three days of Young's northern excursion. While he was away, President James Buchanan sacked Young as governor and ordered a United States Army expedition of not less than twenty-five hundred men to escort a new governor, Alfred Cumming, to Utah and assert federal control in the territory. To justify this action, Buchanan submitted to Congress some sixty reports written by government officials over a span of seven years that charged Mormon leaders with disloyalty. Of these, more than forty came from the Office of Indian Affairs.[18]

Young's reply showed why his people called him "the Lion of the Lord." Four years before the South fired on Fort Sumter, this territorial governor whose appointment had expired threw down the gauntlet to an American president. "CITIZENS OF UTAH," he proclaimed on September, 15, 1857, "We are invaded by a hostile force." He stamped the army as "an armed mercenary mob," declared martial law, and ordered the territorial militia, the Nauvoo Legion, to repel the "threatened invasion." Before leaving for Fort Limhi, Oliver Lee Robinson heard Young go even further: "Prest. B. Young Declared our independence. He said if we would live our religion god would fight our Battles."[19]

To make good on Young's bid for sovereignty, Nauvoo Legion soldiers fortified the Echo Canyon approach to the Salt Lake Valley. Mounted

17   Brigham Young, "Remarks," May 13, 1857, *Journal of Discourses*, 4:323–327; Scott G. Kenney, ed., *Wilford Woodruff's Journal*, 10 vols. (Midvale, Utah: Signature Press, 1984), 5:90.

18   These reports are compiled in "The Utah Expedition," House Exec. Doc. 71 (35-1), 1858, Serial 956.

19   "Proclamation by the Governor," September 15, 1857, ibid., 34, 35. Printed copies of the proclamation are located at the Marriott Library, University of Utah; Oliver Lee Robinson Diary, September 13, 1857, book 1, box 1, MS 24, Marriott Library. For other reports that Young at this time declared Mormon independence from the United States, see Joseph Harker Journal, October 21, 1857, BX 8670.1.M782, BYU Library; Milton D. Hammond Journal, September 13, 1857, PAM 2068, USHS; Salmon River Mission Journal, October 22, 1857; and Juanita Brooks, ed., *On the Mormon Frontier: The Diary of Hosea Stout*, 2 vols. (Salt Lake City: University of Utah Press, 1964), 2:636.

Mormon companies torched grass on the Oregon Trail, rustled army herds some 150 miles to the east, and burned the expedition's supply trains on the Big Sandy and Green rivers. As a backup plan, Young ordered fifty men north to build cabins, plant grain, and cache food on the route to Fort Limhi, near the Snake River ford on the Flathead Trail.[20] No longer would he compromise or coexist with the "gentile" nation. As a last resort, Fort Limhi would offer a place to rest and resupply in a staged move north to the Bitterroot Valley and the upper Missouri region.

To ready the Salmon River colony for this important new role, Mormon leaders moved to enlarge it, even as they called other outlying settlements and missions to return and "stand by the kingdom."[21] From the west and south, the faithful at San Bernardino, California, and Carson Valley in present-day Nevada streamed back to Zion, while the only outbound company that fall left Ogden on October 5 and headed north to Oregon Territory. It numbered about seventy men, women, and children, including returning missionaries and their families and first-time colonizers.

At Fort Limhi their compatriots waited for the company with growing anxiety. The "news of soldiers coming" and Mormon troops "going to prevent them" had spread among the Indians, acting mission clerk Jacob Miller said. In spite of Brigham Young's hope that the Lamanites would join their cousins of Israel, Miller saw the Bannocks "becoming more impertinant [sic] and aggressive." Four months earlier, one of the northbound company, Milton D. Hammond, had left the fort and gone to Utah on leave. He returned on October 22 and saw the difference at once. "The Indians did not seem to be possessed of a very good spirit," he said.[22]

Neither would it have lifted the spirit of the tribe, whose survival depended on the river's bounty, to watch as eight wagons loaded with barrels of pickled salmon rolled out for the Salt Lake Valley the day after the new settlers arrived. In Utah the territory's dominant tribe, the Utes, had lived for centuries close by Utah Lake, then one of the most productive fisheries in western America and their primary food source. But Mormon

20   The ford was located at today's Blackfoot, Idaho, where three islands divided the river into four channels.
21   Brigham Young, "Remarks," *Deseret News*, September 23, 1857.
22   Quotes are from Jacob Miller Journal, September–October 1857, folder 1, box 1, MS 111, Marriott Library; Hammond Journal, October, 22, 1857.

use of advanced methods to net large hauls of fish for pickling and ship-
ment elsewhere had impoverished the Utes and made them resentful and
ready for war. The Bannocks could not be expected to react differently.

Nor would the tribe likely have looked with favor on the enlargement
of the settlement that took place that fall. On October 29 Thomas Smith
assigned eighteen new arrivals, some with families, to go to the site of a
second fort two miles north of the existing stockade to construct their
future homes. Marked off after Young's visit, the new fort was to be nearly a
third larger than the existing one, with north-south sides 264 feet in length
and east-west walls 403 feet long. To provide space for families, each of the
twenty-eight cabins was to be 533 square feet, nearly twice as big as in the
largest in the first fort. The land marked for development at least doubled
the three hundred acres enclosed by pole fences at the first location.

As the Fort Limhi colony grew, far to the south the unorthodox tactics
of Mormon lieutenant general Daniel Wells, who boasted a lofty rank
but no schooling in the art of warfare, were confusing the Utah Expedition's acting commander Colonel Edmund Alexander and render-
ing him ineffective. Stymied, Alexander marched up and down Hams
Fork in southwestern Wyoming as the signs of an early winter warned
of impending disaster if the hastily called force remained on the plains.
But hurrying west to take command of the endangered expedition was
Second United States Cavalry Colonel Albert S. Johnston, an energetic
officer who had left his regiment in Texas under his capable second in
command, Lieutenant Colonel Robert E. Lee.

As blizzards swept the plains, Johnston ordered the scattered forces to
concentrate at Fort Bridger, James Bridger's trading post on Blacks Fork.
With what Johnston called their "last possible step forward," the troops
covered the last thirty-five miles in fifteen days, but weather claimed the
lives of some three thousand cattle, horses, and mules. This loss would
prove critical. Later that winter the officer took steps to replace the animals
and supplies lost to Mormon raiders and weather. Unintentionally or not,
this measure would serve as a catalyst to the February raid on Fort Limhi.[23]

---

23   William Preston Johnston, *The Life of Albert Sidney Johnston, Embracing His Services in
      the Armies of the United States, the Republic of Texas, and the Confederate States* (New
      York: D. Appleton and Co., 1878), 214.

Similarly, a quarrel among the tribes, though seemingly unrelated to the Mormon settlement, had by December been festering for months, further exacerbating Bannock grievances. In June 1857 two Bannocks arrived at Fort Limhi with word that a party from the tribe was headed to the Flathead country to steal horses from the Pend d'Oreilles "as they had stolen several head from them last spring," Jacob Miller said. Soon after, "five Nez Perces rode in looking for some 60 head of horses stolen from them." Just before leaving for Utah that summer, Thomas Smith wrote Flathead agent John Owen to ask him "to use his influence to have the Bannock horses restored saying we would use ours to have the Nez Perces returned to them again." Owen seemed unaware of the problem. By the time he heard "about the Nez Perce camp in the Big Hole having lost a great many horses by the Bannacks," it was too late to act on Smith's request. The failure to settle the dispute came at a time of deteriorating relations between the Mormons and their native neighbors. The bitter wrangle over horses intensified the Bannocks' hostile attitude.[24]

In December the quarrel between the tribes almost flared into open warfare with Fort Limhi dangerously in the middle. That month "the old Nezperce chief" Tipiyelehne Ka Awpo (Eagle from the Light) and his interpreter, Alexsey, arrived at the stockade "from a chase after the Bannocks who had stolen their horses." The chief asked to remain at the fort while Alexsey and a war party searched for the horses. Smith granted the request, but his act of friendship offended local tribesmen. Tensions rose when the twenty-three-year-old mountaineer John W. Powell, a Virginian who had married a Bannock woman and reportedly exercised great influence over the tribe, arrived from a well-known wintering ground on the Beaverhead River followed by forty Bannock and Shoshone lodges.[25]

On December 26 Smith asked Powell to induce the Indians "to stop burning the fences," which he agreed to do. About noon Powell started for the upper valley, but south of the fort he ran into fifty or sixty Nez

---

24   Salmon River Mission Journal, June 10, 15, 17, 1857; Seymour Dunbar and Paul C. Phillips, eds., *The Journals and Letters of Major John C. Owen, Pioneer of the Northwest, 1850–1871*, 2 vols. (New York: Edward Eberstadt, 1927), 1:169.

25   Salmon River Mission Journal, December 17, 1857. For more on Powell, see Grace Piazzola Helming, *John W. Powell: An Historical Biography of a Notable Western Montana Mountain Man* (Wisdom, Mont.: Montana Ghost Town Preservation Society, 1993).

ALBERT SIDNEY JOHNSTON, 1858
Albert Sidney Johnston, pictured here in an
engraving from *Harper's Weekly*, commanded
the U.S. Army's Utah Expedition in 1857 and
1858 with skill and determination. AUTHOR'S
COLLECTION.

Perce warriors. They recognized him, "took him prisoner and marched
him down to the fort again, singing their war songs and yelling in a fright-
ful manner." At the fort the Nez Perces rejoiced to find Eagle from the
Light, whom they feared had been killed by the Bannocks, as a Mormon
guest and "showed much friendship towards us," clerk David Moore
said. To keep their good will, the fort made no attempt to free Powell,
who escaped anyway. Being "light and young and active," he climbed
up a travois leaning against the stockade and sprang over and into the
willows.[26]

The Mormons also fed the visiting war party, but when the local natives
found out, "quite a number of them came to the fort much excited." The
Nez Perces pretended not to notice them. They "ate their suppers and
then had a war dance" that went on until long after dark. "One of them
would go out at a time and dance around the fire, holding his tomahawk
before his bre[a]st until he got done," Moore said. "He would then raise
it over his head and give a yell which was repeated by all present, the
dancer would then leave his place for another."[27]

26   Salmon River Mission Journal, December 26, 1857; John J. Healy, "J. W. Powell and
      Fort Lemhi Told by Johnny Healy," John W. Powell folder, Biographical Vertical Files,
      Montana Historical Society Library, Helena.
27   Salmon River Mission Journal, December 26, 1857.

The next day Thomas Smith called a parley and tried to make peace, but the Nez Perce refused "to be friends until the Bannocks and Shoshones would return all the horses they had stolen." At one point the Nez Perces left the conference, "dressed themselves up and came out, formed in line, while the old chief made quite a long speech to them." After much posturing, both sides backed down. Peace seemed to prevail when the next day the Nez Perces appeared to head for home. That night, however, they slipped back and stole as many as seventy Bannock and Sheepeater horses. It was a punishing blow that would have far-reaching consequences.[28]

After that raid, the Fort Limhi settlement managed to regain the trust of a few Sheepeaters, but many others were "very much inraged [sic] at Snag." They came to the fort "all painted up and much excited." Powell was with them, "painted up like the natives," said Moore. When Smith invited all of the Indians on the river to a feast of boiled wheat and bread, most came, but "some would not eat, saying that they were not dogs," he added. The Nez Perce raid had hurt the settlement's standing with the Sheepeaters—and it put the Bannocks beyond the outstretched hand of friendship.[29]

The new year opened with increasing signs of native hostility. Amid preparations to fight the Nez Perces, Bannock chieftain Mattigan, once friendly, urged the tribe to "fight us before they go to fight the Nez Perces." At rumors the Indians intended to steal cattle, Smith sent eight men to guard the livestock. They did not lose any cattle, but they arrived too late to stop herder Ezra Barnard's Bannock wife who "left & took some things." Nor did they prevent Tingosho and two other Bannocks from making off with an ox. The Mormon party overtook the trio and seized two ponies in payment, fueling native resentment. Said Oliver Robinson: "The Devil is at work among the Lamanites."[30]

The fort's hope of peace with its Israelite cousins all but vanished on February 9 when a Bannock came from the east with alarming news. Ten soldiers were camped on the Beaverhead River, he said, and "they

28 Ibid.
29 Thomas Sasson Smith Journal, December 16, 1857, LDS Archives; Salmon River Mission Journal, December 29, 1857.
30 Salmon River Mission Journal, January 11–12, 1858; Charles F. Middleton Journal, January 12, 1858, LDS Archives; Robinson Diary, February 10, 1858.

had two Mormon prisoners." The story was partially true. There was indeed a party from Camp Scott, the army's winter post at Fort Bridger, then camped with mountaineers at the confluence of the Beaverhead and Ruby Rivers, near present-day Twin Bridges, Montana, but they were not soldiers and held no Mormons prisoner. The leader of the party, Benjamin Franklin Ficklin, has been called Montana's first cattle buyer, but he was much more than that.[31]

Ficklin was known as "a bold, imaginative, restless man, ruthless to outlaws and other evil-doers," and his reputation appears to have been honestly won. In 1857 he was directing a survey crew on the Fort Kearney, South Pass, and Honey Lake Wagon Road when the Utah War halted the project. Colonel Johnston then hired him to lead a party of ten civilian volunteers north and contract to purchase five hundred head of cattle from the mountaineers on the headwaters of the Missouri and Columbia Rivers for April 1 delivery to the army encampment. On January 10 Ficklin's party reached Robert Hereford's camp near the mouth of Big Hole River. Camped nearby were Granville and James Stuart, Jacob Meeks, Robert Dempsey, John Saunders, John W. Powell, and others. From here or from the nearby Deer Lodge Valley, Ficklin and his guide, Edward "Ned" Williamson, made two trips to Fort Owen and the Flathead Valley to carry out the mission. Ficklin failed because mountaineers such as Richard and John F. "Johnny" Grant were too afraid of the Mormons to make delivery. "He wanted me to take the cattle I was selling to him to Fort Bridger, at my own risk," said Johnny Grant. "I positively refused to do it."[32]

Just before Ficklin left the mountaineer camp on his second cattle-buying journey to the Bitterroot Valley, the Bannock arrived at Fort

---

31   Robert H. Fletcher, "The Day of the Cattlemen Dawned Early in Montana," *Montana The Magazine of Western History* 11 (Autumn 1961).

32   Dan L. Thrapp, *Encyclopedia of Frontier Biography*, 4 vols. (Glendale, Calif.: The Arthur H. Clark Company, 1988, 1994), 1:489; Granville Stuart, "A Memoir of the Life of James Stuart," in *Contributions to the Historical Society of Montana*, Vol. 1 (Helena, Mont., 1876), 38–41; Lyndel Meikle, ed., *Very Close to Trouble: The Johnny Grant Memoir* (Pullman: Washington State University Press, 1996), 67. A Virginia Military Institute graduate, Ficklin proposed the Pony Express and served as its superintendent, took up blockade running during the Civil War, and later operated the dangerous San Antonio–San Diego mail route and other Southern stage lines.

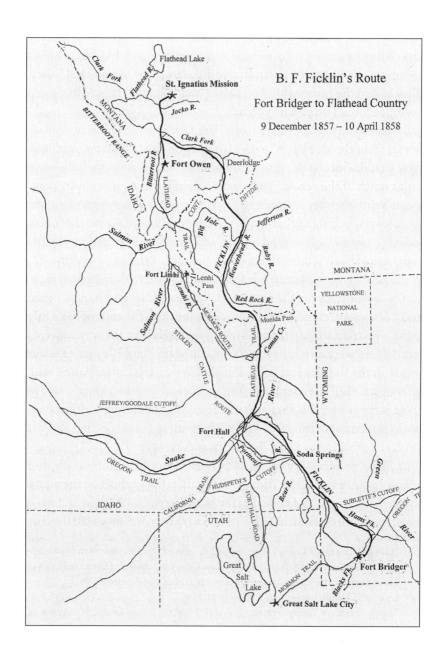

B. F. Ficklin's Route

Fort Bridger to Flathead Country

9 December 1857 – 10 April 1858

Limhi with news of his party, then returned the colony's hospitality by stealing Thomas Smith's horse out of the walled corral. Ten men from the fort rode over the divide in pursuit and caught up with him near Robert Dempsey's winter place, about twelve miles from the Beaverhead Valley. They seized the horse while the native "made off for the soldiers camp saying he would bring them on us."[33]

Seven days after the party from Fort Limhi returned with Smith's horse, "Powel come back," said Milton Hammond. The mountaineer rode past the fort to the spread of Bannock and Sheepeater lodges five miles north of the second settlement. Uneasy at the growing encampment, Smith that day ordered the remaining settlers there to move to the main stockade. On February 24 William Perry "went down to the Indian lodges" to see Powell, who advised him "to keep a good wach [sic] for the Indians had been talking of burning our stacks & taking our cattle."[34]

The next day, just after the herders had driven the livestock out to graze on the foothills east of the fort, the Bannocks, led by Le Grand Coquin and a few disaffected Sheepeaters, came for the herd and took it. Only those who tried to stop them or found themselves in the way suffered; in all, there were two killed and five wounded. "Powel a mountaineer was with the Indians and helped them drive off the cattle," Smith said, although Powell later denied it. The attackers drove the animals back to their camp where the Sheepeaters received a small number. The Bannocks took most of the cattle and thirty or more horses and left for Fort Bridger, according to Snag. But the storm was spent.[35]

Lacking the necessary horses and oxen to move sixty-nine people over a long distance in winter, Thomas Smith dictated a report on the attack to Brigham Young and appealed for help. Two of his bravest and most experienced men, Baldwin H. Watts and Ezra Barnard, mounted the only

33   "Life and Travels of Lewis Warren Shurtliff," microfilm of handwritten copy made in 1926 from original manuscript owned by Elsie Van Leuven of Emmett, Idaho, in Idaho Historical Society, Boise, photocopy in author's possession.

34   Charles F. Middleton Journal, February 24, 1858.

35   Thomas Smith to Young, February 24, 1858, Brigham Young Papers, LDS Archives. Powell said he was there but did not participate. See Sen. Doc. 1, (35-2), 1858, Serial 974, 80, 81; William Hooper to Alfred Cumming, April 13, 1858, ibid., 71, 74–76; and Thomas S. Smith affidavit, April 15, 1858, frame 274, reel 5, MS 1234, Brigham Young Collection, Marriott Library.

two horses left and took off after dark on February 28 for the 380-mile ride to Great Salt Lake. Eight days later the news they bore struck the Mormon hierarchy like a cold blast. Suddenly the option to move north was gone. The word came at a pivotal moment.

On that day, March 8, Thomas L. Kane, Young's influential friend from Philadelphia, wound up discussions with Mormon leaders at Great Salt Lake. For twelve days the self-appointed peacemaker had urged them to accept President Buchanan's unofficial offer of a pardon or to hold out an olive branch in the form of food to the hungry American soldiers. Kane had received a cordial hearing but no encouragement on either score. The following day he left the territorial capital with a Mormon escort and bedded down for the night on the Weber River route to Fort Bridger.

As he broke camp the next morning, "[w]ith great gratification," Kane "saw two horsemen come up." Brigham Young's oldest son, Joseph A. Young, age twenty-three, and George Stringham had ridden all night to overtake him before he reached the army post on Blacks Fork. The two men dismounted from their horses, "which had been badly hurt by falls on the ice," Kane reported to President Buchanan. They handed him a message from Young. "We have just learned through the southern Indians, that the troops are very destitute of provisions," it began. The Mormon leader then offered to send two hundred cattle and twenty thousand pounds of flour to his enemies in the mountains.[36]

At Camp Scott, Colonel Johnston rejected Young's offer out of hand, but Utah's new governor and President Buchanan both recognized it as a peace offering and moved to accept it. On April 5 Cumming left Fort Bridger to visit Utah settlements, where he was "universally received with such respectful attentions as are due to a representative of the executive Authority of the United States."[37] The Utah War, the first armed bid for independence by an American territory or state, had ended.

Even before Thomas Kane left Great Salt Lake on March 9, Brigham Young launched a military expedition to rescue the stranded Salmon

---

36   Thomas L. Kane to President James Buchanan, March 15, 1858, folder 13, box 14, Utah War Correspondence, Vault MSS 792, Thomas L. Kane Collection, BYU Library; Brigham Young to Thomas L. Kane, March 9, 1858, Sen. Doc. 1, (35-2), 1858, Serial 974, 87, 88.

37   Alfred Cumming to Col. Albert S. Johnston, April 15, 1858, Sen. Ex. Doc. 1 (35-2), 1858, Serial 974, 71–73.

River settlers. "We think you had better vacate the Fort and come home," Young wrote Thomas Smith. He advised "giving to the Indians such property as you cannot secure by safely cacheing or bring away."[38] Bearing this word were 150 Nauvoo Legion soldiers with wagons, oxen, and supplies to bring the Fort Limhi inhabitants safely to Utah settlements.

Their return touched off a verbal war as Mormon leaders accused federal agents and the United States Army of inciting the Fort Limhi attack. Governor Cumming, "with feelings of profound regret," sent the charges to Colonel Johnston and called for an investigation. His demand mainly produced evidence that Colonel Johnston was not only capable in the profession of arms but also skilled in defending his honor on the field of public opinion. Otherwise the investigation produced only carefully worded denials by all concerned that were more notable for what they failed to say than for any enlightenment they offered.[39] In the end, nothing came of it.

After 150 years, Snag's story, as told to Thomas Smith, squares the best with events known at the time and evidence that has since surfaced. Snag said that John Powell "instigated and took part" in the attack and directed the Bannocks "to meet him with the stolen stock at Soda Springs or Bear R. Lake and that he would conduct them into the Camp of the U.S. Troops at Ft. Bridger." Snag further stated that "a small detachment of U.S. Troops was at Beaver Head, a distance of about 100 miles from Ft. Limhi; that it was from this camp Powell came to the camp of the Indians." According to other sources, Powell returned to Ficklin's camp after the raid, then the two of them set off for Fort Bridger, where Colonel Johnston hired Ficklin as a guide at the generous rate of five dollars a day.[40]

---

38 Brigham Young to Thomas Smith, March 8, 1858, frames 4 and 81, reel 1, MS 566, Brigham Young Collection, Marriott Library.

39 For an examination of the charges and denials, see David L. Bigler, *Fort Limhi: The Mormon Adventure in Oregon Territory, 1855–1858* (Spokane, Wash.: The Arthur H. Clark Company, 2004), 281–313.

40 Smith Affidavit, Young Collection, Marriott Library; William H. Hooper to Alfred Cumming, April 13, 1858, in "Report of the Secretary of War," 1858, Sen. Exec. Doc. 1, (35-2), Serial 974, 74–76; F. J. Porter to J. H. Dickerson, April 16, 1858, Letters Sent July 16, 1857 to July 15, 1861, Department of Utah, U.S. War Department, National Archives, copy in MIC 112, USHS.

While Ficklin's involvement is problematic, Snag's story at least provided a motive for the attack, which was directed at Fort Limhi's herd, not the settlement itself. It also indicated that Powell deliberately incited the Indians to carry it out, although, to his credit, he warned the fort in an apparent attempt to avoid casualties. All that is now known about the raid is consistent with this conclusion.

But for Le Grand Coquin to lead his warriors against the settlement took more than Ficklin's desire to obtain cattle or Powell's influence over the Bannocks, however great. Contrary to Smith's claim that before the raid "the Shoshone and Banak Indians were on terms of unquestioned friendship with the settlers at Ft. Limhi," relations between them had become increasingly unstable over many months.[41] Moreover, the sources of Bannock disaffection were strikingly similar to causes of conflict between Mormons and their Indian neighbors elsewhere in the Rocky Mountains.

The Bannock change of heart likely began the first summer as the new arrivals erected walls, literal and cultural, between themselves and the natives. The stockade was a barrier of separation and distrust. Although polygamists themselves, the Mormons also displayed aloofness when they misunderstood and rejected the offer to marry Indian women and did not make reciprocal offers. Just before he led the raid, Le Grand Coquin arrived at the settlement and "complained of being angry with the Mormons for not giving him some white wives," Thomas Smith said. "He seemed in a very bad spirit."[42]

It was an especially unfavorable sign when Bannock leaders ignored the invitation to meet with Brigham Young during his visit to Fort Limhi in May 1857. Moreover, the grandiose show of Mormon interest in the tribe's homeland set off rumors throughout the Northwest that alarmed not only the Bannocks but other native peoples as well. Intensifying these sources of discontent by fall 1857 was the news that American soldiers were coming to fight the Mormons. Bannock chief Mattigan virtually gave notice of coming trouble that October when he said, "[W]hen the snow is deep Soldiers and Mormons would fight."[43]

41   Smith Affidavit, Young Collection, Marriott Library.
42   Thomas Smith to Brigham Young, February 28, 1858, LDS Archives.
43   Jacob Miller Journal, October 14, 1857.

For their part, the natives were quick to exploit differences among interlopers on tribal lands. In this, they would receive plenty of encouragement from the white mountaineers who lived apart from settled society and saw the communal-minded religionists threaten their own way of life. These men did not want the true believers, whose symbol was the beehive, swarming in their backyard. To these sources of Bannock hostility must be added the unpredictable nature of Le Grand Coquin, the man who led the attack.

Such causes of conflict were minor, however, compared with the blindness of the Mormons to differences among the natives, a common failing of Anglo-Americans. Unlike mountaineers, who learned and adopted the ways of a chosen tribe, the Mormons persisted in seeing all Indians as one people, the Lamanites, ignoring the evidence before their eyes that all Indians were not alike. The more fervent the believers, it seemed, the slower they were to be taught by experience. And in their zeal to lead the natives to baptism, the colonists overlooked an essential lesson of survival in the wilderness: "the friend of my enemy is my enemy." It was taught once more by the quarrel over horses.

Lessons unheeded often result in lasting consequences. In this case, they triggered the destruction of one of Idaho's earliest white settlements, altered the course of Mormon colonization in the West, and brought the Utah War to a sudden but peaceful resolution. Today the melting ruins of Fort Limhi's mud corral at Tendoy, Idaho, identify the northern limit of the Mormon kingdom's expansion from 1847 to 1858 and mark the end of its audacious 1857 bid for sovereignty. The colony lives on only in its misspelled name at such familiar Idaho places as Lemhi Pass, crossed by Lewis and Clark in 1805, Lemhi River, Lemhi Range, and Lemhi County. Even the former Sheepeaters are known today as the Lemhi Shoshones.

✢

James Hervey Simpson:
Exploring the Great Basin

Foreword to Jesse G. Petersen's
A Route for the Overland Stage: James H. Simpson's 1859
Trail Across the Great Basin *(Logan: Utah State University Press, 2008).*

AT THE END OF THE UTAH WAR IN JUNE 1858, GENERAL Albert S. Johnston selected Cedar Valley to establish a military post for some twenty-four hundred officers and men of the U.S. Army's Utah Expedition. The location west of Utah Lake at today's Fairfield, Utah, met the immediate needs of his command for grass for its animals and remoteness from population centers to avoid clashes between his soldiers and settlers of the territory ruled by Brigham Young.

At the same time, Johnston knew that the location for his new post, named Camp Floyd, was less than ideal when it came to its mission to support enforcement of federal law in the defiant territory. For one thing, it was some forty miles from the capital at Salt Lake City. For another, the same geographical formations that had allowed the territorial militia to block his advance the year before and force him to spend the winter of 1857–1858 at Fort Bridger made his force vulnerable in the event of renewed hostilities. The winding Echo Canyon corridor through the Wasatch Mountains ruled his line of communications on the east. And the way to northern California from Camp Floyd led through Salt Lake Valley and around the north end of Great Salt Lake, two hundred miles out of the way.

To make his army effective in relation to its duties, Johnston had to open a supply line on the east that bypassed the Mormon Trail from Fort

Bridger and the easily fortified Echo Canyon portal to Salt Lake Valley. In addition, he needed to make a wagon road to northern California that eliminated the northern loop around the Great Salt Lake. Instead it should run due west from Camp Floyd on the south side of that briny body to meet the California Trail near Genoa in today's western Nevada.

Johnston had the right man to fill these requisites in Captain James Hervey Simpson of the U.S. Army's elite Corps of Topographical Engineers, who arrived at Camp Floyd in July 1858. The forty-five-year-old engineer first surveyed a new line of supply to the east that ran up Provo Canyon to Parleys Park and down the Weber River to present Coalville. From there, it continued up Chalk Creek to bypass Echo Canyon on the south. During the 1857 conflict, Utah Territorial Militia general Hiram B. Clawson had inspected this avenue to find out if it offered a way for the U.S. Army to flank Echo Canyon defenses. He reported that, without extensive roadwork, it did not.

A fall 1858 preliminary reconnaissance of the proposed route west motivated the energetic engineer to expand the wagon road survey to Genoa. With the approval of Secretary of War John B. Floyd and Johnston, Simpson set his sights on a vast area of the American West from which no water flows to any ocean. He planned to conduct the first recorded exploration directly across the heart of the Great Basin, a region large enough to encompass New England, New York, Pennsylvania, and Ohio.

In width, the area of high-altitude desert and north-south running mountain ranges extends from central Utah's Wasatch Range to the crest of the Sierra Nevada. From north to south, it stretches more than eight hundred miles from Oregon to the Baja Peninsula in Mexico. In between, its triangular shaped rim encloses most of Nevada and parts of Utah, California, Idaho, and Oregon. As a region of interior drainage, its waters flow into briny bodies, such as the Great Salt Lake and Pyramid Lake, and desert flats, never into the sea. Its longest perennial rivers are the Bear, which flows into Great Salt Lake, and the Humboldt, followed by the California Trail and today's Interstate 80.

On May 2, 1859, the topographical engineer headed into this virtually unknown region "to explore the country between [Camp Floyd] and

JAMES HERVEY SIMPSON,
CIRCA 1864
An 1832 West Point graduate, James
Hervey Simpson explored and mapped
the Great Basin as a captain in the
Topographical Engineers. He opened
new overland roads from Fort Bridger
to Camp Floyd and across today's
Nevada. Simpson is shown here
during the Civil War as a colonel in the
Fourth New Jersey Volunteer Infantry.
COURTESY OF THE LIBRARY OF
CONGRESS PRINTS
AND PHOTOGRAPHS DIVISION.

Carson River, at the east foot of the Sierra Nevada, for a new and direct route to California." The sixty-four members of his expedition included an artist, geologist, wheelwright, blacksmith, teamsters, twenty soldiers, twelve 6-mule wagons, scientific apparatus, and one of Nevada's first citizens. John Reese in 1851 had purchased Genoa, the state's earliest settlement, when it was still a trading post named Mormon Station on the California Trail's Carson River route. Now he served, but not always to the captain's satisfaction, as Simpson's guide.

Over the next three months, Simpson traveled over eleven hundred miles across part of central Utah and virtually all of Nevada. His west-bound exploration covered 564 miles to Genoa, while his more southern return route to Camp Floyd added only eight to this number. Either way would shorten by more than two hundred miles' travel from Salt Lake City to Genoa along the Humboldt River. His report also estimated the cost to open a wagon road and included the geology, plant and animal life, and Native American tribes of the Great Basin, among other things.

As Simpson was the right one to complete this significant study and report, Jesse G. Petersen of Tooele, Utah, has proved the right man to locate his trails and evaluate his major contribution to western expansion. Since 1999, the retired police chief of Tooele, Utah, has traveled some eighteen thousand miles on all-terrain vehicles and an estimated 140 miles on foot. In his personalized narrative and seventy-two maps, he describes his search and pinpoints Simpson's routes and campsites to within a few yards, "except for about nine miles along the Carson River."

Petersen brings to his book a lifelong interest in history and overland avenues of travel and transportation. A charter member of the Lincoln Highway Association's Utah Chapter, he produced in 1997 the first study of the first transcontinental highway across the state, *The Lincoln Highway in Utah*, now in its fourth edition. In 2003, he co-authored with Gregory M. Franzwa *The Lincoln Highway: Utah*, published by The Patrice Press. When he heard it said that the coast-to-coast thoroughfare followed Simpson's path across the Great Basin, he looked into it and found there was little information on the topographical engineer's exact routes to back up that claim. Typically, Petersen decided to find out for himself.

The product of his search manifests on every page his character and background. The quality of his scholarship reflects his degrees from Brigham Young University and the University of Utah. His experience in law enforcement can be seen in his dedication to accuracy and attention to evidence on the ground. His narrative is richly detailed and incorporates interesting and accurate information on the region's history as it goes along. His writing is clear, straightforward, and trustworthy. His work makes it possible for a novice to follow Simpson without losing the trail more than a stone's throw on either side.

In normal times, Simpson's expedition would have won the acclaim Americans normally bestowed on western explorers, such as John C. Fremont, but as he prepared his detailed report, the nation was torn by the Civil War. General Johnston, who ordered the exploration, lost his life leading a Confederate army in 1862. Not until 1876 did the War Department carry out Johnston's instructions while serving as Utah Department commander and order the publication of Simpson's report.

Meanwhile, if Washington looked the other way for over ten years, Simpson's exploit won the immediate attention of the nation's emigrants and entrepreneurs. Within a year, westering American families had worn a new wagon road across the central basin. In 1860, trim young men aboard fast horses began to carry mail between Sacramento and St. Joseph, Missouri, on Simpson's route across the vast expanses of the Great Basin. The short-lived Pony Express was followed by the Pacific telegraph, Overland Stage, Lincoln Highway and U.S. 50, known today as "the loneliest highway in America." All followed the corridor Simpson opened in 1859.

To recognize James Hervey Simpson's contribution to the history of the Great Basin and western exploration, the University of Nevada Press at Reno in 1983 reprinted the topographical engineer's report as *Report of Explorations Across the Great Basin in 1859* with foreword by Steven D. Zink. Jesse Petersen's volume now makes an excellent companion to this significant work.

"A Most Bright, Earnest and Winsome Company": Christian Missionary Teachers in Utah Territory

*Presentation to the Salt Lake Theological Seminary Seminar,
July 26, 2003.*

I'D LIKE TO MAKE CLEAR AT THE OUTSET THAT MY KNOWLEDGE of history offers little hope for easy answers when it comes to models of effective missionary work among Mormons. All too often, it seems to me, the observation of Frederick E. Lockley, a *Salt Lake Tribune* editor in the 1870s, appears to be as true today as it was over a hundred years ago. He said that the testimony of someone who had left the church "bore the most weight with those still within the church." But a disenchanted former member, "who comes back to the world, returns divested of all belief in religion," he continued. "His faith has been imposed on by false priests, and when his eyes are fully opened to the imposture that has been practiced upon him, he resumes the exercise of reason without any regard for sacred things."

My own circle of friends and academic associates is not great, but many of them sadly fit that description. They no longer believe in Mormonism, but find it inconvenient for various reasons to leave the church and see no point in looking for higher ground on which to rest their faith. Skeptical of all spiritual experience or conviction, they just go along with a "fool me once, shame on you; fool me twice, shame on me" attitude. At the same time, Utah's history does hold an inspirational model of missionary work among Mormons that provides some important lessons that bear directly on the subject of our discussion. And it has a personal meaning for me.

Years ago, my mother showed me a reminiscence left by my grand-mother, Annie Watt Anderson, who lived in Sanpete. It described her early life after marrying my grandfather, William Anderson, and their struggle to survive in an area that held few opportunities. To my surprise, this handwritten document revealed someone quite different from the loving grandmother, who could bake wonderful apple pies in a wood stove, whom I had known as a child. She was also a talented writer. Her spelling and grammar were nearly perfect, her handwriting pleasing to the eye, and her descriptions clear and compelling. I asked where she had learned all this, and my mother said she received her education at Manti from a Presbyterian missionary.

That caught my interest at once and led me to one of the many under-told chapters of Utah history—the story of the Christian missionary teachers who came after the Civil War and completion of the transcon-tinental railroad. Since the purpose of our panel today is to explore his-torical models of missionary work among the Mormons, the chronicle of this remarkable endeavor strikes me as an appropriate place to begin. It also reminds us that Christians here are not strangers from another planet in a different culture. They are as much part of Utah's heritage as any member of the dominant religion. The society we know here today was largely shaped by since forgotten Christian men and women, whose contribution to life in this state is as profound as it is generally unknown and unappreciated, even by those of our faith, who should know better.

Utah's Christian tradition is actually older than the Mormon if we go back to Fathers Francisco Atanasio Domìnguez and Silvestre Vélez de Escalante and the famed explorer, Jedediah Smith, a devout Christian who called Salt Lake Valley "my home in the wilderness." But not until completion of the transcontinental railroad in 1869 did many evangeli-cal Protestant churches mount a full-scale effort to take the gospel of Jesus Christ to Mormons. They came, first, because they saw this place as a mission field, as it should be viewed today, and they recognized an opportunity to harvest it. "Primitive schools were built in pioneer times and children sometimes attended," historian Charles S. Peterson observed, "but schooling was a hit or miss affair that had only fleeting influence on the lives of many." Mormon communities offered so little support that a "splendid teacher, Gentile Harry Haines," traded his position as an educator in a Salt Lake Mormon ward's one-room school for the "more lucrative business of bartending" in the Murray saloon of "apostate bishop" Andrew Cahoon.[1]

Yet one of the many enduring myths of Utah history is that early Mormon leaders gave education the highest priority. In fact, however, Brigham Young spent only eleven days in a classroom, and his views on education may have reflected his own lack of it. The day he laid out Salt Lake in July 1847, he said, "I shall have a School for my own children & the people on a block can choose a School for themselves." It took Young thirteen years to build his children a school, and he adamantly opposed public education. "Would I encourage free schools by taxation? No!" roared the Lion of the Lord. "That is not in keeping with the nature of our work."

When handcart-veteran John Chislett called for public schools in 1873, Young attacked him in conference as "a man who talks about free schools and would have all the people taxed to support them." Chislett shot back that he did not expect a man "who cannot write a correct sentence in his mother tongue, and hardly spell half-a-dozen consecutive words correctly" to support public education.

For more than thirty years, every Utah governor after Young had called on Mormon lawmakers to establish tax-supported, so-called "free schools," to replace the controlled fee system centered in ward houses. And for that long, territorial lawmakers had ignored their appeals. The consequence was uneven standards, mediocre teachers, a school year of three months or less, and average attendance levels below 50 percent of enrollment.

It is hardly a surprise that average attendance in the territory's community schools was only 31 percent in 1862. It shot up to 44 percent in 1876 and dropped back to 36 percent by 1889, but by then private Protestant

---

1   Charles S. Peterson, "The Limits of Learning in Pioneer Utah," *Journal of Mormon History* 10 (1983), 67, 69.

mission schools were educating almost ten thousand students, most of them Mormons. Historically, believers who expect Christ to come at almost any moment, perhaps tomorrow, or next week at the latest, do not give high priority to such long-term concerns as education. And the leaders of the ardently millennial Mormon movement, from Young to the end of the century, did not.

Congregational evangelist Norman McLeod was among the first to recognize the opportunity this inadequacy offered. He decided that the most promising way to carry the gospel to Mormons would be "through the operation of free schools, conducted by the mission boards of the churches, in which to educate the young people of the L.D.S. faith." He was not alone in perceiving education as a great opportunity. Episcopal bishop Daniel S. Tuttle founded St. Mark's grammar school in 1867. Gustave Pierce opened the Rocky Mountain Seminary in 1871 to initiate a quarter-century Methodist commitment that included forty-five grade schools, five seminaries, and three academies. Baptists, Lutherans, and other denominations also took part in the mission-school effort.

Known to place a high value on education, Presbyterians made, in terms of quality and expenditure, the greatest contribution. Led by Sheldon Jackson, this reformed body from 1870 to 1890 opened more than fifty grade schools, the forerunner of Westminster College, and four academies, including one for women.

To open a school outside of Salt Lake Valley took dedication and courage. Given my Sanpete family background, my favorite missionary teacher is Duncan J. McMillan, a former Illinois school superintendent who came to Utah for his health, but found it sorely threatened after he opened Wasatch Academy at Mount Pleasant in 1875. The following year, Brigham Young came to Sanpete and scored the brash educator twice—on his way to Manti and on his return to Salt Lake. According to McMillan, Young "took two turns at abusing me, pronouncing me a vile, godless man." If allowed to stay here, the Mormon chief reportedly warned, he would "send sorrow and distress into many a mother's heart, and rob many a home of its virtue." McMillan was described as a "disseminator of false doctrine, and a man so corrupt in his conversation and deportment, that no young person placed under his tuition could escape pollution."

For a while the barrage emptied the missionary's classrooms. "Some of the parents of his former scholars admitted they had found his conduct irreproachable, and their children progressing well under his instruction; but they durst not fly in the face of their spiritual masters," said Lockley. But the missionary educator "stood his ground, and the force of this crusade expended itself, and his school again did good service, he said."

As this example illustrates, most Mormon parents did not share the views of their strong-minded leader on education. They would pull their children out of the missionary schools and wait until their religious authorities were looking the other way, then send them right back. Opposition seemed only to spread the word and promote the demand for more schools. In 1880 McMillan became mission superintendent and developed a plan to start up primary schools in every part of the territory.

In the meantime he and the missionaries followed the frequent biblical injunction: Be not afraid. Nor were the arriving volunteers, mostly women, easily frightened. "Night before last fourteen young ladies reached Salt Lake from the East," announced the *Salt Lake Tribune* in 1880. Calling them "a most bright, earnest and winsome company," the paper said the newcomers would go to their assigned locations across the territory, "and ten new schools will at once be opened." Many of them came from the desire to minister to polygamous families. One of them may have taught my grandmother.

A respected Mormon historian has said that "there is frequent reference to bishops inviting the evangelical teachers or missionaries to speak to their Sunday congregations" and several instances "in which the Mormon meeting house was rented during the week for an evangelical school." Such cases "tend to indicate that the antagonism was not too great," he wrote. But a leader of the mission school movement disputed this. Rev. Robert McNiece said the schools were bitterly opposed. "In Mormon towns it is no uncommon thing for these school buildings to be stoned and besmeared with filth," he said. If half of what he said was true, it took remarkable courage for young women to leave comfortable homes in the east to become missionary teachers in frontier towns where they were not wanted. But come they did, despite opposition.

By 1885, there were 31 Presbyterian schools here with 53 teachers and about 900 students, 28 Congregational schools with attendance of over

1,900, 13 Methodist institutions with 865 enrolled, 5 Episcopal schools with 795 students, and 2 Baptist schools with 205 scholars.

The magnitude of the Christian commitment to education, prior to establishment of public schools in 1890, is shown by the estimate that some fifty thousand children, or nearly one-fourth of Utah's population that year, mostly from Mormon families, received some education in mission schools. Mormon historian Thomas Edgar Lyon estimates that six Protestant denominations spent nearly three million dollars on this endeavor. According to Bancroft, the schools "received so much of patronage that it became necessary for the Mormons to bestir themselves in the matter . . . private institutions being also founded by the saints, among them the academy at Provo, and the Brigham Young college at Logan." Not by accident did academies named after Young start up in Provo and Logan right after Duncan McMillan founded Mount Pleasant Academy.

If beneficial in many ways, the twenty-five-year crusade produced a disappointing harvest when measured by conversions. The report by the moderator of the Presbyterian school system to the territorial governor in 1885 may offer at least one reason for this. Rev. Dr. R. G. McNiece, the Presbyterian patriarch of Utah, said: "The Presbyterian denomination is now carrying on thirty-one day schools in Utah, in which about nine hundred children and youth are being educated, 75 per cent. of them being of Mormon parentage. These schools are practically free, since the buildings and teachers cost the patrons nothing in most cases. With one exception, the local receipts are not sufficient to pay for the fuel and annual repairs. In these schools fifty-three teachers are employed, most of them experienced teachers from the East. Nothing of a denominational character is taught; they are simply American schools."

The end of the evangelical Protestant campaign, based on education, essentially came in 1890 when Utah became the last state or territory to establish tax-supported free elementary schools. In yet another irony, Christian leaders of the education effort actively supported this legislative package and thereby eliminated the need for their own schools. The Christian sponsor of the legislation told Mormon lawmakers that they could pass the bills and take credit for them, or "you can take the same legislation from the hands of the United States." They passed the measures.

Thomas Edgar Lyon further credits evangelical Christian leaders with insisting there could be "no political freedom in Utah, no protection of minorities or participation of minorities in politics" under one political party ruled by the Mormon church. They charged "there could be no true political freedom in Utah, as long as the Mormon church, which controlled the elections, could check the ballots and determine how each person voted," Lyon said. Thanks to these unknown forbears, all citizens now vote in secret.

What can we learn from the brothers and sisters in Christ who came to Utah more than a century ago as missionary teachers? You no doubt have your own thoughts on this, but for what they are worth, here are a few of mine.

As they demonstrated, evangelism to Mormons, in Utah and elsewhere, requires more than just lip service. It takes real commitment, a level of dedication one seldom sees today. When we returned to Utah some years ago and joined a mainline Christian church, we were surprised to find that mission was the least of its priorities, well below political activity, social causes, and fellowship. The denomination's missionary teachers apparently were made of sterner stuff than today's members. At times I found myself reminding the pastor that we were Republicans and hoped there was room in the church for conservative members.

Real commitment begets opportunity. Over a century ago, the Christian churches rightly saw education as an opening to effective missionary work and moved to make the most of it. This opportunity is gone, but others, at least as promising, have opened up in our own time. Today's new honesty in Mormon history and doctrine, for example, largely pioneered by Sandra and Jerald Tanner, represents an important avenue to mission. The work of historians, archaeologists, medical researchers, and anthropologists refutes the old nineteenth-century myths on which Mormon scripture and doctrine are based and reveals the relatively rapid transformation of the faith from what it was in the beginning to what it is now. If advances in knowledge lead some to become indifferent toward all religion, who will tell them otherwise? Who will be not afraid, or ashamed, but keep on speaking, and not be silent? Who will step up and fulfill this vital calling?

What I've seen among many Christians in Utah today is a somewhat patronizing wish to understand what makes their Mormon neighbors tick in order better to get along with them. The upshot is that, as their neighbors send young men and women out into the world to make Mormons out of Christians, be they Baptists, Methodists or Episcopalian, here at home Christians worry about how to get along. But truth does not just get along. Truth prevails. The difference between getting along and prevailing is commitment, the kind of commitment that motivated the Christian missionaries who came here a century ago. Where are the men and women today who will take their example?

As they step up, they could also learn from their predecessors that missionary work among the Mormons takes more than good intentions and dedication, however important. The Christian teachers somewhat naively believed that a raise in educational level here would point the Latter-day Saints to higher spiritual light. But we know from their experience over twenty-five years that effective evangelism requires more than that. It takes knowledge of Mormon doctrine, including changes that have taken place over the years, and the history of this millennial movement. Even more important, effective mission work must be grounded on scripture and a solid grasp of basic Christian theology. The growth of Mormonism for nearly two hundred years shows that it is highly competitive within a Protestant Christian context. It should never be underestimated.

In addition, Christians with a heart for a mission today might take another lesson from the earliest crusade here, which, I believe, would enhance the effectiveness of their efforts. To me, the story of the mission educators clearly illustrates the need for greater cooperation among the Protestant denominations in taking the historic gospel of Jesus Christ to Mormons. While there was some mutual support in that time, the campaign was essentially denominational in orientation. Each church basically went ahead on its own—Methodists to make Mormons into Methodists, Presbyterians to spread Presbyterianism, Baptists as opposed to Mormons, and so on. The differences among the denominations, so important then, are taken less seriously today. They allow greater cooperation and call for a new orientation—*Christians* to make *Christians* out of *un*Christians.

In all of these areas, it should have occurred to you, as it did to me in preparing this presentation, what a great asset and opportunity the Salt Lake Theological Seminary represents in making the most of all we can learn from the missionaries who have gone before us. There is no better way to support missionary work among the Mormons today than to support, to the best of our ability, this excellent and growing center of Christian preparation to carry the gospel throughout this entire region and beyond.

For those who think of evangelism as hundreds coming forward at a Billy Graham Crusade, a final lesson from the nineteenth-century missionary crusade in Utah. It is this: we should not expect to accomplish miracles overnight. So the Biblical injunction to be not afraid or ashamed should include: be not discouraged. To be an ambassador of Christ to Mormons is not for the lukewarm—not for the fainthearted—not for the uninformed—and finally, not for the impatient.

A final thought in closing: Each of us should remember the men and women who came here before our time and understand that they lifted the cross of Jesus Christ in this place trusting that you and I would follow and carry it forward. To fulfill this obligation and follow in their footsteps takes a level of commitment, perhaps beyond what we may imagine, as well as perspective. For the seeds we plant in Mormon soil may take longer to grow than in other fields of mission.

When I faced the need the surrender my life to Jesus Christ, I knew where to go because a Christian missionary teacher taught my grandmother in Sanpete how to read and write. So I turned myself in at the nearest church of her faith. It took time for the seed she sowed to grow, but grow it did, and grow they will, as we take the example and make our own contribution.

The Coast-to-Coast Rock Road: The Lincoln Highway in Utah

Foreword to Gregory M. Franzwa and Jesse G. Petersen,
The Lincoln Highway: Utah (Tucson, Ariz.: The Patrice Press, 2003).

WHEN THE FIRST WAGON PARTY TO TRAVEL ACROSS UTAH TO
northern California came down Bear River in 1841, its members faced
the same question that confronted leaders of the newly created Lincoln
Highway Association seventy-two years later. Squarely in their path was
Great Salt Lake, the Great Basin's most distinctive geographical feature, a
briny body seventy miles long and fifty wide, with mud and salt flats along
its south shore that reached in places another forty miles or so. Which
way should they go to get around it, they wondered, to the north or south?

The Bidwell-Bartleson Party, thirty-two men and one woman, nineteen-year-old Nancy Kelsey, had left the Oregon Trail's emerging trace
at Soda Springs to look for a way to California. They had "no guide, no
compass, nothing but the sun to guide them," said a member, but they
fortunately took the firmer ground to circle the lake on the north. Not
so lucky were the three hundred or so emigrants to California in 1846
that followed promoter Lansford W. Hastings from Fort Bridger over
an alleged "shortcut" across the south end of the lake. They barely made
the eighty-mile *jornada* over the salt flats to the spring at Pilot Peak on
today's Utah-Nevada border. The last to try it that year was the Donner
Party, usually referred to as "ill-fated."

After that tragedy, most travelers avoided Hastings Cutoff around the Great Salt Lake's southern shore. Instead they went from Utah's capital over the Salt Lake Cutoff, skirting the lake's northern coast to join the California Trail in southern Idaho. But after U.S. Army captain James Simpson in 1859 explored a more direct route to Carson Valley, commercial interests moved fast to exploit the new avenue that ran far to the south of the Salt Desert.

A year later, eighteen-year-old Richard "Ras" Egan, son of Mormon plainsman Howard Egan, was the first to ride the seventy-five-mile leg of the Pony Express Trail west from Salt Lake City. Mail carrier George Chorpenning and the Overland Mail and Stage lines also followed portions of the central Utah-Nevada route.

The way west changed once more with the arrival of the steam locomotive. In 1868, Union Pacific engineers, like most emigrants and contrary to Brigham Young's wishes, decided to build the transcontinental railroad on high ground to the north rather than cross the mud flats that stretched for miles to the south. Bypassing Salt Lake City, the new rails followed Echo and Weber canyons to Ogden, then went north on the line of today's Utah highway 83 to Promontory Summit and around the north shore of the lake. The joining of the rails at Promontory in 1869 bestowed on Ogden the title of "Junction City," a coveted distinction the new transportation center would not easily surrender, as Lincoln Highway leaders would later discover.

The coming of the automobile at the turn of the century found Utah, like the rest of the nation, unready for the new revolution. Roads made for wagons and horse-drawn carriages were unsuitable for the increasingly popular new form of transportation. As the need grew, Utah became a leader in road improvement. In 1909 newly elected Governor William Spry spearheaded creation of the state road commission.

Elsewhere, about this time, entrepreneur Carl Fisher, founder of the Indianapolis Motor Speedway, began to see in his mind a thoroughfare that ran across the continent in an unbroken line from New York to San Francisco. He called this vision the "Coast-to-Coast Rock Highway." In 1912 he unveiled it before automobile-industry executives and invited them to help bring it to pass. They incorporated the Lincoln Highway

Association in July 1913 and announced its purpose was to establish the nation's first transcontinental highway.

In a bid for support, association president Henry Joy a month later described the venture and the route it would take before the Western Governors' Conference, attended by Governor Spry. Joy pointed out that the association's aim was to define and work to improve the chosen route, not build the highway itself. The support of the states would be needed, he made clear, and the western governors without exception endorsed the undertaking and its projected track.

Two weeks later, the association publicly announced the Lincoln Highway route through Utah. It was to enter from Evanston, go down historic Echo Canyon to its mouth on the line of the Mormon Trail, turn south through Coalville and Wanship, up Silver Creek to Parley P. Pratt's old Golden Pass Road through Parley's Park and Canyon to Salt Lake City. From Utah's largest city the original 1913 route would run south of Great Salt Lake through Grantsville to Timpie at the north end of Skull Valley, then south up the valley, via Orr's Ranch, some sixty miles to the Pony Express and Stage route, and follow this historic trail to Fish Springs, Callao, Ibapah, and Ely, Nevada.

Within two days, Governor Spry surprised association leaders with notice that he would not approve the announced route because it did not include Ogden City and Utah's northern Weber and Davis counties. Spry claimed to have understood at the meeting that it would do so, but no one recalled giving him that impression. Caught in the old struggle for dominance between Utah's largest cities, the governor gave the association no choice but to change its route and add unwanted mileage. From the mouth of Echo Canyon, the new course went down Weber River through Henefer and Morgan to the mouth of Weber Canyon, near Ogden, then south through the Davis County towns of Layton, Farmington, and Bountiful to Utah's capital. But differences remained over the way the road would go after reaching either Salt Lake City or Ogden.

About this time, businessmen and politicians from the two cities met to reach a solution pleasing to both. By joint resolution they called for the new highway to run from Echo to Salt Lake, via Parley's Canyon, then go north to Ogden and around the north end of the lake. At this agreement, William D. Rishel, manager of the Utah Automobile Club, drew himself up to his full six feet, three inches. Said this early champion of Utah automobile travel: "I promise you there will be a direct route through Salt Lake City, and it will go south of Great Salt Lake and west by the way of Wendover." At this, Matthew Browning, director of Ogden's Browning Arms Company, jumped up. "As sure as my name is Matt Browning there will never be a route built south of the lake," he vowed. "Such a route will be built," Rishel fired back.

Heartened by Salt Lake support, the association in 1915 restored its first Parley's Canyon route and improved the road south of Great Salt Lake. But even as now-antique automobiles bounced over the 1913 route in Skull Valley and sank in Fish Springs mud, opposition came from another quarter, led by the influential Rishel and his Automobile Club. A decade-long fight had already begun as early as September 1914, when Salt Lake businessmen and state officials resolved to back a road directly west across the salt flats to Wendover on the line of present Interstate 80 and proposed to call it the Lincoln Highway. The following January the state legislature voted thirty thousand dollars for the route and work began in the spring.

Stung by these developments and looking to improve the 1913 road, the Lincoln Highway Association in 1915 took up Nevada's suggestions to shorten the miles required to drive across western Utah to Ely. Proposed shortcuts called for improving an existing wagon road over Johnson's Pass at the southern end of the Stansbury Range and building an eighteen-mile causeway across a deep southern loop of the Great Salt Lake mud flats. To encourage Utah support, association director Frank Seiberling, president of Goodyear Tire and Rubber Company, promised some seventy-five thousand dollars to construct the causeway, and Carl Fisher put up twenty-five thousand dollars to widen Johnson's Pass. But the generous offer, as measured by the dollar's value at that time, failed to win approval of Governor Spry and the state road commission. They had their eye on Wendover instead. Spry's opposition to the Lincoln Highway ended in 1916 when Simon Bamberger won election as the state's fourth governor. The association promptly dusted off its earlier proposal to shorten the western Utah road by bypassing to the north the 1913 route along the Pony Express Trail. In 1918 its directors and the Utah Road Commission reached agreement. As offered before, Fisher and Seiberling committed twenty-five thousand dollars and one hundred thousand dollars, respectively. In return, the state agreed to widen the Johnson's Pass road and construct a causeway, known as the Seiberling Section, across the deep loop of the mud flats. The state further agreed at its own expense to build two additional short cuts, one between Johnson's Pass and Granite Mountain, the other from the Seiberling Section to the 1913 route at Overland Canyon. The latter commitments were never met.

Perhaps most important, the state road commission agreed to designate the new route as a state highway, thereby making it officially a part of the Utah road network.

By mid-1919 crews had finished the Johnson's Pass project, known as the Fisher Section. At this time, the Lincoln Highway Association terminated its 1913 Grantsville–Skull Valley–Pony Express Trail segment and pointed automobiles instead over the new Goodyear Cutoff that now ran through Tooele, across the U.S. Army's present Dugway Proving Grounds, and on to Gold Hill. The 1919 road across the U.S. Army's top-secret test range is closed to visitors without permission, but it holds many remnants of the highway, including remains of an early bridge.

Workmen that year also finished a bed of rock and dirt on the Seiberling Section and surfaced seven of its eighteen miles with gravel. But, if passable for automobiles, the new section was unready for the U.S. Army to test its new heavy trucks that summer by driving a convoy over the Lincoln Highway's entire length from coast to coast. The test went as scheduled until the parade of trucks arrived at the unfinished Seiberling segment. Rishel described how the road across the mud flat appeared after that. It "looked like a plowed field," he said. "There were almost enough new planks buried in the mud to build a bridge." Lieutenant Colonel Dwight Eisenhower, a convoy member, never forgot the debacle. The Goodyear Cutoff may have inspired him to build the interstate highway system.

In the meantime, the roadbed could be repaired to allow automobiles to roll over it, but nothing could overcome a lack of funds after association and state money had been expended. As work stopped on all sections, an increasingly powerful three-state coalition called for completion of the highway to Wendover. In 1918 supporters of the more direct road over the salt flats organized the Nevada-Utah-California Automobile Associations to promote and raise money for the route. San Francisco business interests actively backed the project, as did towns along the Humboldt River on the old California Trail in northern Nevada. As the momentum grew, 1919 saw creation of the Victory Highway, a coast-to-coast project to memorialize the nation's success in the First World War. When asked to propose the highway's route west of Salt Lake, William Rishel and his Utah Automobile Club pointed due west to Wendover.

The final blow fell in 1921. That year Congress provided money to improve the nation's roads under new federal highway legislation. Later, the state road commission named the Wendover route among Utah highways eligible for such funds, but refused to include the Goodyear Cutoff to Ely, even though it bore official designation as a state highway. According to Jesse Petersen, the foremost authority on the first coast-to-coast highway in Utah, business and civic interests in Salt Lake City exerted pressure on state officials to force the decision. Efforts on local, state, and national fronts failed to reverse it. The eventual end of the 1919 segment was now in sight.

The new highway to Wendover opened in 1925 when the first automobile rolled over it, following the dedication ceremonies. Now Interstate 80, it ran as true as an arrow across the mud flats that still bore faint traces on the salt-encrusted surface made by the Donner Party wagons seventy-nine years before. Far to the south, the Goodyear Cutoff continued to deteriorate and was eventually removed from the Utah Highway network.

Looking back, one can see that Lincoln Highway Association directors, if well intentioned, were mistaken in the belief that their route across western Utah was best for all concerned. Moreover, time has shown that they were wrong to stubbornly defend this position in the face of western opinion to the contrary and repeated invitations to add the association's famous name to the Wendover route. Not until 1927 did they designate the latter as part of the Lincoln Highway in order to restore the great highway in an unbroken line across the country. In so doing, they made the original road to Grantsville again part of the highway and eliminated the 1919 section through Tooele, Gold Hill, and Ibapah. So it is today that motorists crossing the Great Salt Lake Desert to Wendover are actually following the last designation of the Lincoln Highway in Utah, Petersen is quick to point out.

If Lincoln Highway leaders were not always right, even William Rishel would probably admit that their vision made a historic contribution to overland travel in Utah. The chronicle of their early automobile highway is as deserving of remembrance in state annals as the story of the Bidwell-Bartleson Party, bravely following the sun to California in 1841; the driving of the gold spike in 1869 at Promontory; young "Ras" Egan aboard his prized mare, "Miss Lightning," riding the first leg of the Pony Express west from Salt Lake City; and the overland stage. To the traces on the ground that mark the passing of many forms of transportation and make Utah widely known as America's "Crossroads of the West," they added the nation's first coast-to-coast highway.

Finally, when it came to the question of which way to go, north of Great Salt Lake or south of it, leaders of the Lincoln Highway Association to their credit stood firm. Their decision to pass on the south clearly contributed to construction of today's highway from Salt Lake City to Wendover, latest of the Lincoln Highway's several routes across Utah.

Today members of the Lincoln Highway Association's Utah Chapter preserve the heritage of the nation's first coast-to-coast highway in the state by placing its distinctive marker along the original and subsequent routes, protecting the road itself from needless damage, and undertaking educational activities, including tours over these historic avenues.

⚜

More Than a Beacon:
A Tribute to
Jerald and Sandra Tanner

ON THE BICENTENNIAL OF BRIGHAM YOUNG'S BIRTHDAY, a Salt Lake City newspaper in 2001 asked a well-known local historian to describe the legacy of the Mormon leader. To see Young's legacy, the noted authority on Utah's past said, "All you need to do is look around you."

Yet if one looks beyond Temple Square, he discovers a more meaningful legacy, not of Brigham Young, but a bequest of forgotten Christian men and women who came over a century ago to labor on what they called "the picket line of civilization." Their gift to modern Utah is as profound as it is largely unknown. It cannot be seen in granite walls, but mainly found in freedoms that Utahans of all faiths now often take for granted. They include the right to live where one wishes, to own property, to equal protection under the law, to vote in secret, to come and go as one chooses, to make the economic choices that decide the quality of life, to normal family relationships, and to worship as one chooses.

If commonly assumed as an American birthright, these freedoms speak of a heritage whose roots predate Utah's earliest settlement. One of its truest manifestations in the state today is the Utah Lighthouse Ministry, a unique missionary outreach in the Intermountain West. Some have seen it as an untypical beacon of light in a predominantly Mormon community. For more than twenty-five years, the work of Jerald and Sandra Tanner has been more than a lone source of enlightenment in the society it serves. It rests on a missionary tradition that began with the coming of the earliest Christians to the Great Basin.

The first Christian missionaries came to Utah in 1776, the year of American independence, looking for a route from Santa Fé to the six new missions of their faith in Alta California. Franciscans Francisco Atanasio Domìnguez and Francisco Silvestre Vélez de Escalante entered the Great Basin at the head of Strawberry River and followed Diamond Fork. At the mouth of Spanish Fork Canyon, there now stands a tall slender cross on the hill from which they first beheld Utah Valley. Missionaries and traders came after them from New Mexico to the Utah Indians.

In the 1820s Jedediah Smith "entered the West owning his rifle, his Bible, the clothes on his back and very little else," but as Dale L. Morgan noted, "He took his religion with him into the wilderness and let nothing corrode it." As one of Utah's earliest Christian inhabitants, the great explorer and devout follower of Jesus Christ called Salt Lake Valley "my home in the wilderness."[1] Nancy Kelsey, the only woman in a party of thirty-two men, came to Utah in 1841 with the first wagon train following the sun west to California. Barely eighteen and barefooted, she carried a baby with one hand, led a horse with the other, and kept a precious Bible in her few belongings, which she read every day of her long life. She was the first white woman to see the Great Salt Lake.

Utah's Christian legacy was already a rich tradition by 1865, when Rev. Norman McLeod, a spirited Congregationalist preacher, came to Salt Lake to build a new church and school on Third South, west of Main Street. Finished in 1866, his new meeting place was known as Independence Hall. The gifted evangelist was one of the first to recognize the opportunity "to educate the young people of the L.D.S. faith" through operation of free schools, "conducted by the mission boards of the churches."[2] Daniel S. Tuttle came to the same conclusion. The young Episcopal missionary bishop decided in 1867 that "our great work in this Territory is with the young" and founded St. Mark's grammar school.[3]

---

1   Dale L. Morgan, *Jedediah Smith and the Opening of the West*, 8; and *The Great Salt Lake* (Indianapolis & New York: Bobbs-Merrill Company, 1947 and 1953), 88.

2   Thomas Edgar Lyon, "Evangelical Protestant Missionary Activities in Mormon Dominated Areas: 1865–1900," Ph.D. diss., University of Utah, 1962.

3   James W. Beless, Jr., "Daniel S. Tuttle, Missionary Bishop of Utah," *Utah Historical Quarterly*, 27:4, 1959.

This word quickly spread. With completion of the transcontinental railroad in 1869, evangelical Protestant churches mounted a decades-long crusade to take the gospel of Jesus Christ to Mormon youngsters, many of them from polygamous families, through free education. The missionary teachers came, first, because they saw Utah as a mission field, as it should always be seen, and they recognized an opportunity to harvest it. Frederick Lockley, editor of the *Salt Lake Tribune*, described the opportunity they set out to fulfill: "The Mormon school system being so miserably inefficient, the churches of the United States came in with missionary schools," he recalled.[4]

One of the many myths of Utah history is that the early Mormons made schooling a primary concern. Yet Brigham Young's views on education, resting on just eleven days in the classroom, likely reflected his own lack of it. "We should never croud [crowd] and force the minds of our children beyond what they are able to bear," he instructed Apostle Wilford Woodruff. "If we do we ruin them for life."[5] Historically, those who look for the Lord's imminent arrival, tend not to assign a high priority to long-term purposes, such as education. Leaders of the fervently millennial Mormon movement during the nineteenth century generally did not.

Territorial governors who followed Brigham Young after 1857 repeatedly called on Mormon lawmakers to establish tax-supported education, then called "free schools," to replace the fee system centered in ward houses. And from then until 1890, territorial legislators ignored them. The consequence was uneven standards, mediocre teachers, a school year of three months or less, and average attendance levels below 50 percent of enrollment. But a steam-powered portent of change was on the way.

As iron rails neared Utah in 1868, Young moved to save Zion from the coming invasion of Christian teachers. His first line of defense was to renew the demand for his followers to adopt the Deseret Alphabet, introduced in 1854, a new method to write the English language. It consisted of thirty-eight characters designed to represent the sounds of spoken English. For more than a dozen years, normally obedient church members

---

4   Frederick E. Lockley Remembrances, 1869–1904, Huntington Library.
5   Scott G. Kenney, ed., *Wilford Woodruff's Journal*, 10 vols. (Midvale, Utah: Signature Books, 1983), 5:605, 536.

had quietly ignored his directive to replace the English alphabet with the queer-looking symbols.

Mormon parents would continue to keep their backs turned on the radical system as Christian teachers stepped off the train at Corinne, a new northern Utah railroad town, then known as the "Gentile capital" of the territory. In 1871 Rev. Gustave Pierce arrived to establish the Rocky Mountain Seminary and open a Methodist dedication to education that spanned a quarter-century, numbering forty-five grade schools, five seminaries and three academies in Utah. The Methodist Women's Home Missionary Society, founded in July 1880, within six years sent missionaries and teachers to Salt Lake City, Ogden, Moroni, Spanish Fork, Richfield, Elsinore, Grantsville, Ephraim, Mount Pleasant, and Spring City.[6] Presbyterians, Baptists, Lutherans, and other Protestant denominations also performed active roles in the mission school movement.

Duncan J. McMillan, a former school superintendent in Illinois, came to Utah for his health, but found it seriously endangered after he opened Wasatch Academy at Mt. Pleasant in 1875. The Mormon chief allegedly described him as a "disseminator of false doctrine, and a man so corrupt in his conversation and deportment, that no young person placed under his tuition could escape pollution."

The irony of the mission school movement is that its success "spelled its own doom," says Christian educator Kenneth Mulholland.[7] While Utah's missionary teachers are little remembered today, their legacy lives on in many of the rights informed citizens exercise and too often take for granted today. For this bequest, a celestial company of young women, who left secure homes to teach children in the outlying settlements of a frontier territory, deserves to take a bow. To make it, they came to Utah trusting others would follow and carry forward the work they had begun. True to their confidence, ambassadors of Jesus Christ from many faiths now build on the foundation they passed on. In a number of ways, the work of Jerald and Sandra Tanner stands as a notable reflection of the example they left to all Christians. The first has to do with commitment.

6   Connie Fife, "Methodists in Utah," *Utah History Encyclopedia*, ed. by Allen Kent Powell (Salt Lake City: University of Utah Press, 1994), 361–363.

7   Kenneth R. Mulholland, "Robert G. McNiece," 6, paper in author's possession.

Some in Utah and around the world think the sole purpose of their work is simply to disseminate unfavorable information about Mormonism. But it is much more than that. Utah Lighthouse Ministry is a mission in the best sense of the word, whose founders have seen this region as a mission field and dedicated themselves to harvest it. As missionaries their commitment matches the faithfulness shown by the mission teachers. For more than three decades their dedication has never wavered.

As they and their predecessors demonstrate, commitment begets opportunity. The mission teachers saw the state of education as a promising avenue to carry the gospel of Jesus Christ to Utah. In pioneering today's new honesty in Mormon history and theology, the Tanners saw opportunity in the changing nature of a faith that claims eternal truth, the same yesterday, today, and tomorrow, and opened another important mission front. Often based on information from Utah Lighthouse Ministry is the work of researchers in many disciplines that now refute old nineteenth-century myths. And Christian missionary work worldwide benefits from their labors.

A hallmark of both mission endeavors is integrity. The mission teachers did not preach in their classrooms; they exemplified their faith by personal example and spotless lives. Nothing of a denominational character was taught, Rev. Robert McNiece told Uah Governor Murray. "They are simply American schools," he said.[8] They won acceptance because they were trusted.

Equally trustworthy has been the work of the Tanners whose dedication to truth is legendary. When forger Mark Hofmann allegedly found a Martin Harris letter professing Joseph Smith had said that when he went to get the gold plates for the Book of Mormon, a "white salamander" in the hole turned into a spirit and hit him several times, he fooled just about everybody, church officials, handwriting specialists, and old document experts. But not Jerald Tanner. He "would never be satisfied if my case against Mormonism was based on fraudulent material," he said.[9]

---

8   "Annual Report of the Governor of Utah, 1885," in Annual Report of the Department of the Interior, 1885, House Exec. Doc. 1 (49-1), 1885, Serial 2379, 1043.

9   Jerald and Sandra Tanner, *Tracking the White Salamander: The Story of Mark Hofmann, Murder and Forged Mormon Documents* (Salt Lake City: Utah Lighthouse Ministry, 1986), 6.

In 1984, a year before the forger-turned-bomber murdered two people, the Tanners exposed Hoffman's fakes and won national recognition and the respect of all for their integrity.

As their experience demonstrates, a mission to Mormons takes more than good intentions. It demands knowledge, not only of Mormon doctrine and history, but even more important, a firm understanding of Christian theology, based on the inspired word of God, personal integrity, and above all, commitment.

Finally, like the missionary teachers, the founders of Utah Lighthouse Ministry have suffered persecution, relentless opposition, and misrepresentation. True to the legacy they personify so well, they consistently meet each affront with courage, patience, and Christian kindness. They never respond in kind and cannot be provoked by unkind behavior.

As Christian emissaries demonstrated over a century ago, to be an ambassador of Christ within a Mormon culture is not for the lukewarm, the uninformed, the fearful, the unimaginative—or those easily discouraged. They lifted the cross of Jesus Christ in Utah trusting that others would follow and carry it forward. In an exemplary way, Sandra and Jerald Tanner have upheld their trust. Over the years their ministry has been more than a beacon in an unbelieving place. It is an inherent part of an inspirational Christian heritage that calls the followers of Jesus Christ today to go forward and do likewise.

In Memory of Harold Schindler

Tribute at the Funeral of Harold Schindler,
Salt Lake City, January 2, 1999.

PERHAPS THE TRUEST MEASURE OF A MAN IS GIVEN TO US BY the 24th Psalm:

> Who has the right to climb the mountain of Yahweh,
> who the right to stand in his holy place?
> He whose hands are clean, whose heart is pure,
> whose soul does not pay homage to worthless things
> and who never swears to a lie.

These words offer a perfect definition of integrity. And integrity is the single word that best describes the dear friend whose memory we honor here today. In him could be found no hypocrisy or deceit. With him, one never needed to wonder what the meaning of is is. He used words to define the truth precisely, not conceal it or mislead others for some imagined higher end. The life of Harold Schindler was a true reflection of what he believed and who he was.

Who Harold Schindler was, above all, was a man deeply devoted to his wife and family. He wore his love for Bonnie and his pride in their children on his sleeve. So well I remember how pleased he was when he told me about Carolyn's accomplishments as a librarian and how his face lighted up at the sight of one of his sons. He was faithful and true to those he loved and he gave freely to them without thought or concern for his own welfare.

Who Harold Schindler was, also, was a true son of Utah and the American West. He was born in Chicago and lived for a time in New York, but it is impossible to think of him apart from these mountains and valleys. He was more a native child of Utah, devoted to all this state stands for, than any fourth-generation descendant of the first pioneer party. For him heaven would be here. It is hard to imagine his soul living in peace in any other place. One must look for him here.

Who Harold Schindler was, quite simply, was Utah's premier journalist-historian. He combined the best of both of these great professions. Like the late Dale Morgan, the friend he most admired, his knowledge of the history of the West was unsurpassed. Also like Morgan was his willingness to share what he knew with others. To have lunch with him was to receive at no cost a lesson in Western history. It has been a great blessing for this community, if one too seldom recognized, that James Shelledy and other associates of the *Salt Lake Tribune* recognized Harold's abilities and gave him the opportunity in recent years to share what he knew on the pages of this great newspaper.

To his work in journalism, a profession often forced by time to focus on the here and now, Harold Schindler brought the perspective of a historian, the awareness that the world wasn't made when we were born, some baby boomers and generation Xers to the contrary notwithstanding. His respect for the experience, wisdom, and example of those who had gone before him, including his own father, was deeply held in his bones. And it gave depth and maturity to his productive career over a remarkable span of fifty years as a newspaperman—a profession he was proud of.

To his work as a historian, he brought his exceptional gifts as a writer and the dedication of an old-fashioned journalist to accuracy. He knew that the credibility of one's work depended on the details—spelling, punctuation, getting every fact right. I thought I was pretty good on this myself until he reviewed the manuscript of my first book. It was a humbling but instructive experience. He was a good teacher, and the lessons he taught about the quality and integrity of one's work apply to every field of human endeavor.

To his dedication to accuracy he added the perception that history, like news, is about people, not dates or events. He made history come alive because he filled his work with real men and women, like the ones you and I know, who overcame obstacles not all that different from the ones we face.

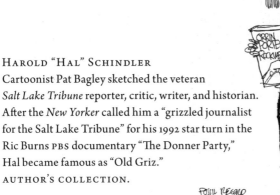

HAROLD "HAL" SCHINDLER
Cartoonist Pat Bagley sketched the veteran
Salt Lake Tribune reporter, critic, writer, and historian.
After the *New Yorker* called him a "grizzled journalist
for the Salt Lake Tribune" for his 1992 star turn in the
Ric Burns PBS documentary "The Donner Party,"
Hal became famous as "Old Griz."
AUTHOR'S COLLECTION.

And his writings are richly detailed. If you followed his day-to-day story of the 1847 pioneer company, you learned about more than hardy Mormon pioneers. You also received an education on western snakes, vegetation, fish, mountain men, birds, and historic sites along the trail. His works are true gems of Western history—timeless, alive, informative, and a pleasure at any age to read. They will live on after you and I have been long forgotten.

Who Harold Schindler was, too, was a man who was fiercely loyal to his friends and the secular organization he loved most, Utah Westerners. In 1968 Harold and a select company, including Bud Rusho, Sam Weller, Carl Woolsey, Msgr. Jerry Stoffel, Hugh Garner, Bill McCaffrey, Blaine Simons, and others who have since passed on, joined to create this somewhat exclusive fellowship. We came from many walks of life and almost every faith and background. But we were united by a common love for the history of Utah and the heritage of the American West and the desire to get the story right.

Over the years, the name of Harold Schindler became virtually synonymous with Utah Westerners. One cannot think of one without the other. For nearly thirty years he served as an officer and director. Out of some 350 dinner meetings held in that time, he missed only two because he was too ill to attend. Honesty was the only standard he lived by, and the FBI might have relished, as we did, his interrogation of speakers at the end of their papers. He made anyone who was less knowledgeable or devoted to the truth than he was squirm under his relentless questioning.

For Harold, joy was a four-day Westerners field trip with his son Jeff and his friends on the trail, an event he looked forward to and planned on for months. For the rest of us, his company was pleasure enough. He was ever a valued friend and an inexhaustible source of fascinating information about the historic places that we visited.

Who Harold Schindler was, finally, was a generous, kind-hearted man who was uniformly considerate and thoughtful toward others on whatever rung of life's ladder they stood. His convictions were strongly held and forthrightly expressed, but he was never mean-spirited, discourteous, or condescending. In his relations with friends or strangers, the hands of Harold Schindler were honest and clean, as the psalmist said, and his heart was pure. He was a good man whose integrity will stand as a treasured example for his children and for all of us who loved him.

It is my prayer, and I know you share it, that our gracious Heavenly Father will receive Harold into His Kingdom, that He will fill the hearts of Bonnie and their children with His comfort and love, and that He will grant them the assurance that in Jesus Christ lies our hope of eternal life with those we love.

A Few More Good Men

Remarks Before the 150th Anniversary Commemoration,
The Mountain Meadows Association, September 8, 2007, St. George, Utah.

PRESIDENT JOHN F. KENNEDY SAID: "THE GREAT ENEMY OF the truth is very often not the lie—deliberate, contrived and dishonest—but the myth—persistent, persuasive, and unrealistic." He might have added that myths can be a great barrier to the reconciliation and fellowship we seek tonight, as we come together to commemorate an event in which none of us was involved and all of us deeply wish had never happened.

What myths am I talking about?

James H. Berry, the U.S. senator from Arkansas, referred to them in 1907. Reared in Carroll County, he knew many of the men and women who left there for California in 1857 and now lie in unmarked graves in southern Utah. He said they numbered from 140 to 150. And he emphasized: "They consisted of the best citizens of that county."[1]

The people he mentioned surely needed *someone* to speak on their behalf, as Barry did. For more than a century, the stories told about them have been, as President Kennedy said, persistent, persuasive and, above all, "unrealistic." They tell us that 140, half of them women and children, were not just passing through Utah, but came here for the sole purpose of mistreating forty thousand of their fellow Americans for their religious beliefs.

My late friend Harold Schindler referred to this implausible idea in his *Salt Lake Tribune* series for the statehood centennial. He rehearsed these

---

1   Berry, "Speech of Senator from Arkansas," *Congressional Record*, February 11, 1907.

tales and wrote the emigrants "reportedly left in their wake a seething string of settlements," a myth he justified repeating by using the word "reportedly.[2] For their passage was notable for the *absence* of evidence of harm to persons or property or contemporary notice by journal-keeping Latter-day Saints, known as Mormons.

So how can we explain these myths of misconduct?

First, what occurred here is completely out of harmony with what many of us have learned from childhood. It doesn't belong with the image of pioneer ancestors we hold in honorable remembrance. It doesn't fit. It rudely violates our comfort zone. For the historian, it is a black hole that swallows up and distorts much that is praiseworthy in early Utah history. Rather than face it, some have faulted the dead for what took place. They brought it on themselves, they imply. But make no mistake. This implication conflicts with the idea of fellowship.

In addition, the myths live on today because, as Schindler said, they cannot be proved or disproved. There was not one left to defend against such defamation. Humans are not easily killed. And to slay so many, without leaving even one to contradict such stories, speaks of a conscious effort to make certain everyone old enough to remember was dead indeed—and not just "reportedly."

Now it is good to join hands on occasions like this. But there is a more practical way for us to serve the purpose we share tonight of reconciliation and fellowship. This would be for you and me to make a personal commitment to ensure the story is a faithful rendition of what happened, not one based on myths that do injustice to the memories of those who perished here. For much too long, we have allowed this impediment to stand in the way of mutual respect and understanding. It is time to remove it.

As we do, we should remember the wisdom of one of our greatest historians. Nobody ever lived in the past, David McCullough said. Our ancestors didn't go around saying, "Isn't this fascinating, living in the past?" They lived in the present, just as we do, only it was *their* present, not *ours*. Just as we don't know how things are going to turn out, they didn't either. The author of *1776* said it's easy to find fault with people

---

2   Harold Schindler, *In Another Time: Sketches of Utah History* (Logan: Utah State University Press, 1998), 72

for why they did this, or didn't do that, "because we're not involved in it, we're not inside it, we're not confronting what we don't know, as everyone who preceded us always was."[3] If memory serves me correctly, then LDS president Gordon B. Hinckley said essentially the same thing at the dedication of a new monument at Mountain Meadows eight years ago.

The emigrants who left Arkansas in spring 1857 for California surely had no idea of what lay ahead. Some think they were going to look for gold. Some no doubt were. But hydraulic mining machines by that year were rapidly bringing to a close the days of the placer miner, panning for shining flakes of the root of all evil. By that time, powerful streams of water were reducing Sierra Nevada foothills to mud and rocks, leaving scars still visible today but producing more gold with fewer men. By 1857, both methods had yielded some five hundred million dollars in gold, and none of it went to the government. Instead, it generated a level of prosperity that made California attractive as a place to live for people who produce the goods and services others want to buy—like beef.

To get there from Arkansas, the best way was the Cherokee Trail, opened in 1849 by a party of Indians and whites. A feeder line from Fayetteville joined the main trail at Tahlequah, Oklahoma, then ran north to meet the Santa Fe Trail near McPherson, Kansas. From here, it followed the northern leg of this historic trade route along the Arkansas River to Pueblo in today's Colorado, then ran north along the Rocky Mountains to Fort Collins, northwest to the Laramie Plain, and west between the Colorado border and Interstate 80 to Fort Bridger. From Bridger's trading post, it followed the Mormon Trail to Salt Lake Valley.

In those days, it was common for westering emigrants to leave one party and join another, or travel at different speeds and become separated at least for a time. But this company appeared more settled in its makeup than most.

Malinda Cameron Thurston later testified that their train arrived at Great Salt Lake City on August 3 and numbered about one hundred. At Salt Lake, members had a choice. They could go to northern California by the trail along the Humboldt River and over Donner Pass, on the

---

3   David McCullough, "Knowing History and Knowing Who We Are," *Imprimis* 34:4, April 2005.

line of today's Interstate 80, or go to southern California along the line of Interstate 15 to Los Angeles. Malinda lived to pass on such important information because her husband decided to take the northern route.[4]

Thurston also testified that the main party—including the rest of her family—heeded Mormon advice and went south. She further said other people with wagons joined the larger group at Salt Lake, but did not say who they were or how many. A later report claimed they were Arkansas families, but some may have been Mormon dissenters, who wanted to leave but feared to try it on their own. At least one runaway joined at Provo; others may have done so along the way.

The main party followed—but at a slower rate—LDS apostle George A. Smith, who took off in a mule-drawn carriage the day they arrived, August 3, on a flying visit to the settlements along the corridor south to the Spanish Trail.

Largely thanks to the work of Roger Logan and Ron Loving, we can draw an informed picture of the people who traveled south from Salt Lake. Their research and contemporary newspaper reports give us valuable information about who they were and why they had undertaken the journey.

First, this company was unlike the parties of young men during the Gold Rush period that quickly splintered in their headlong rush to reach the gold mines. It would compare favorably with Mormon trains, except it was organized by families, rather than companies, and was not as tightly controlled. It numbered about forty-five men, twenty-five women, mostly young mothers, and approximately forty children under eighteen, divided evenly between girls and boys. The party's family makeup makes it reasonable to conclude most were going to California to make new homes there. We know this was the case with the Bakers, George and Manerva, and their four children; John M. Jones and his wife and two children; and the widow Cynthia Tackitt and her six youngsters.

The leaders of this company were both mature family men who had been tested by frontier life and proved trustworthy. From what we know about

---

4   Malinda Thurston, Deposition in support of H.R. 1450 and H.R. 3945, October 15, 1877, Record Group 123, Indian Depredation Claim 8479, Thurston vs. the United States and the Ute Indians, and Deposition, Malinda Thurston, Joel Scott, Frederick Arnold, and Andrew Wolf, May 2, 1911, Thurston vs. the United States and the Ute Indians, Indian Depredation Claim 8479, RG 123, National Archives.

them, we can assume they understood their responsibility for the welfare of over sixty women and children in their care, roughly half of the company.

Forty-five-year-old Alexander Fancher was a farmer and stockman. He was tall and slender, known as a man of uncommon common sense. Fancher was suited to lead because he had made the journey at least once before. In 1850, he and his brother, John, had driven cattle from Arkansas to Salt Lake, then south along the Wasatch Range to meet the Spanish Trail near Cedar City and follow this early trade route, via Las Vegas Springs, to Los Angeles and San Diego. This trip, he brought along his wife, Eliza, nine children, and two cousins. Since he was taking his family, I think he aimed to live there and serve a growing demand for beef.

John T. Baker's reason to go, on the other hand, was business. Unlike his son, George, the fifty-two-year-old stockman went to make a fast sale of "138 head of fine stock-cattle," said his wife, Mary, who stayed home.[5] Baker knew about California from another of his sons, John H. Baker, who had lived there from 1852 to 1854.[6] If he liked it, he intended to return with his family and settle there.

As their company moved south from Great Salt Lake, Fancher might have marveled at the difference in settlement from the first time he passed through, seven years before. Houses and fields now filled Salt Lake Valley almost to the Jordan River narrows. In Utah Valley, largely empty in 1850, a string of closely spaced settlements, whose borders enclosed available water and land resources, reached to the south end of Utah Lake. Seven years before, a large herd would have caused little friction. Now it did.

At Corn Creek, near present Fillmore, they met Apostle Smith, returning from southern Utah, escorting ten or so Southern Paiute and Pahvant chiefs to Salt Lake for a meeting with Brigham Young. Also in Smith's party was Jacob Hamblin, who described the company in 1859 as "ordinary frontier 'homespun' people."[7] Ordinary and homespun they may have been; foolish they were not. At spotting Smith and Indians traveling north together, they became alarmed.

---

5   Papers pertaining to the Territory of Utah, Records of the U.S. Senate, RG 46, National
     Archives.

6   Ibid.

7   "Special Report of the Mountain Meadow Massacre, by J.H. Carleton, Brevet Major,
     United States Army, Captain, First Dragoons," H. Exec. Doc. 605, (57-1), Serial 4377,
     2, 3.

To this point, halfway from Salt Lake to the Spanish Trail, they had traveled at less than eight miles a day. But from Corn Creek to their last resting place, they increased their rate of travel to about as fast as they could go with a large herd of cattle. Their actions showed they were trying to get away.

As they went, an independent-minded Mormon on his way home to southern Utah went with them for three days. John Hawley later recalled, "We discovered that they was pretty much all men of famileys and had quite a large drove of cattle all going to locate in California." He said the captain told him they had some trouble at Provo and Nephi over their cattle grazing on herd grounds, but that they intended to observe the laws of the territory.[8]

At both locations, the source of friction had to do with differing ideas about land possession. In Utah, land was divinely owned and communally managed. To the emigrants, the meadow they camped on was federal land: "Uncle Sam's grass."[9] To settlers, it was winter feed for their livestock. At Provo and Nephi, words were exchanged, but at both places Fancher and Baker backed away from conflict.

Jacob Forney, who replaced Brigham Young as superintendent of Utah's Indian affairs, described the company as "farmers." After investigating their behavior "toward the people of this territory in their journey through it," he told Washington that "they conducted themselves with propriety."[10] Verifying his conclusion were Senator Berry's description and the first Arkansas newspaper report of the massacre of the families from Carroll County. "If it be true," it said, "we have lost some of our best citizens."[11]

Not for eighteen months did anyone make an effort to identify seventeen surviving children from eight families and return them to relatives. Forney at last got around to it in March 1859. He found them, one party member said, "in a most wretched and deplorable condition."[12]

8   John Pierce Hawley, Autobiography, P13.F317, Library and Archives, Community of Christ, Independence, Mo.

9   Collected Statements on Mountain Meadows Massacre, MS2674, LDS Archives.

10   Jacob Forney to A. B. Greenwood, August 1859, Sen. Doc. 42 (36-1), 1860, 75.

11   "Extract from a Letter [from] Carroll Co.," Arkansas State Gazette and Democrat, February 18, 1858, 2/2.

12   James Lynch deposition, July 27, 1859, Sen. Doc. 42 (36-1), 1860, 81–85.

All were under seven years of age at the time their parents were killed and remembered little about it. Sarah Baker recalled the spreading red splotch on the front of her mother's calico dress, and Elizabeth Baker remembered their pretty eight-year-old sister with the long black hair being led away to be killed.

After their recovery, these little victims received the attention their condition required. Forney identified them as best he could and had clothes made for them. General Albert S. Johnston, commander of U.S. forces in Utah, ordered spring wagons and a dragoon escort for their return with a sergeant's wife to care for them. State senator William Mitchell, who lost two sons, a daughter, and infant grandson, met them at Fort Leavenworth and took them home to Arkansas.

Senator James Berry was seventeen years old the day Mitchell delivered the orphans to the Carroll County courthouse. "I saw them as they were lined up on the benches, and Col. Mitchell told the people whose children they were, at least, whose he thought they were," he said. "I have seen war along the lines of the Border States in all of its horrors, but no scene in my life was ever so impressed upon my mind, as the little children without means, with no human being to look to."[13]

Mary Baker, Captain John T. Baker's widow, spotted her son's daughters by their sunbonnets. One of them, Sarah Baker, later said, "I called all of the women I saw 'mother.' I guess I was still hoping to find my own mother," she said, "and every time I called a woman 'mother,' she would break out crying."[14]

Well, what can we learn of a positive nature from all this?

One lesson should be given in Washington today. The inflamed rhetoric that Utah leaders at all levels gave vent to during this period cannot be excused by past wrongs and an oncoming American army. Some no doubt dismissed it as just letting off steam, but others took it seriously. John Higbee, who gave the militia its murderous order, said years later, "There was with many a great reformation, with others a craze of fanaticism, stronger than we would be willing now to admit."[15]

---

13   U.S. Senator James H. Berry from Arkansas, *Congressional Record*, February 11, 1907.

14   Sallie [Sarah] Baker Mitchell, "The Mountain Meadows Massacre—An Episode on the Road to Zion," *The American Weekly*, August 25, 1940.

15   John Mount Higbee, Statement, June 15, 1896, MMM File, LDS Archives, Folder label, 1896, J. M. Higbee Trial.

The moral is plain. The duty of leadership bears the obligation to use language with moderation and self-discipline. This is especially true in the realm of religion, where belief and emotion are so closely tied.

You and I don't fill high leadership positions. But events near here 150 years ago show that we bear the same obligation they did, as shown by the stories of two men who were here on that awful day. Nephi Johnson was twenty-three years old when he led the killing of the women and children, including at least eighteen girls from ages seven to seventeen. Asked at John D. Lee's second trial why he had done it, he said, "I didn't think it was safe for me to object." When asked what he was afraid of, he pointed to Cedar City military leaders. In brief, he, like some others, was afraid *not* to do what he did.[16]

Sixty-one years later, as he lay dying, Johnson prayed in Indian tongues and sang. Suddenly he stared straight upward and howled, "Blood! *Blood!* BLOOD!" as if drowning in it, in a voice that made an onlooker's scalp crawl. He had led the Indian attack on the women and children and he was reliving the horror. And he was still afraid—afraid to die.[17]

As our forefathers knew, one of the Bible's most frequent injunctions has little to do with what we usually think of as moral conduct. It is: Don't be *afraid*. "Be strong and of good courage," the Lord told Joshua as he led the children of Israel across the Jordan River. "Fear not," said the angels to the shepherds on the night our Savior was born. "Be not afraid," the Lord told young Jeremiah.

One who wasn't afraid was John Hawley. He stood up in a meeting in Washington County and opposed his leaders' call to destroy the passing wagon train and murder its people. Later, warned his life was in danger, Hawley said he was as ready to die then as at any other time. Tell them, "I stand on the same ground I took yesterday," he said.[18]

How different this occasion might be if only a few more good men had stood up and opposed what was done that awful day. We can only wonder

---

16   Testimony of Nephi Johnson, Second Trial of John D. Lee, Lee Trial Transcripts, W. L. Cook Papers, Manuscript Division, Library of Congress.

17   Described by Juanita Brooks in *John Doyle Lee: Zealot, Pioneer Builder, Scapegoat* (Glendale, Calif.: Arthur H. Clark Co., 1972; reprinted, Logan: Utah State University Press, 1992; second printing, 1994), 15.

18   John Pierce Hawley, Autobiography, Library and Archives, Community of Christ.

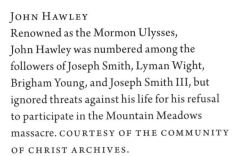

JOHN HAWLEY
Renowned as the Mormon Ulysses,
John Hawley was numbered among the
followers of Joseph Smith, Lyman Wight,
Brigham Young, and Joseph Smith III, but
ignored threats against his life for his refusal
to participate in the Mountain Meadows
massacre. COURTESY OF THE COMMUNITY
OF CHRIST ARCHIVES.

how often Nephi Johnson wished he had before he passed on. But that was then; this is now, as David McCullough said. And the present you and I live in requires that good men and women must stand together and possess the courage to defend the freedom we take for granted, including religious freedom. No matter what the cost. There is no room today for unrealistic barriers between us.

A good sign of such reconciliation was the memorial service eight years ago to rebury the bones of the victims uncovered during construction of the new monument. It was a deeply moving service. Reverently descendants carried the bones of their relatives in small handmade wooden arks to the monument near the rim of the Great Basin on the headwaters of the Santa Clara River. There they placed them in soil from Arkansas. As they did so, they were escorted by Boy Scouts from Mormon communities in southern Utah.

That service and our meeting tonight commemorate an event in which none of us was involved and all of us deeply regret. Let us reconcile and stand together to meet the threats our communities, states, nation, and churches face today. . . . And if a few more good men are needed, be not afraid. Remember John Hawley. And be there!

❧

David L. Bigler:
A Selected Bibliography

BOOKS, ARTICLES, AND AWARDS

Utah State Historical Society, Service Award for outstanding service to the Society and Utah History, 1992; Honorary Life Member, for distinguished service to the State and Society, 2004; Fellow, for distinguished service to Utah's history, 2010.

The Gold Discovery Journal of Azariah Smith. University of Utah Press, Salt Lake City, 1990; paperback edition, Utah State University Press, Logan, 1996.

Forgotten Kingdom: The Mormon Theocracy in the American West, 1847–1896. The Arthur H. Clark Co., Spokane, Wash., 1998; paperback edition, Utah State University Press, Logan, 1998. Best Book Award, Westerners International, 1999.

Army of Israel: Mormon Battalion Narratives, ed., with Will Bagley. The Arthur H. Clark Co., Spokane, Wash., 2000; paperback edition, Utah State University Press, Logan, 2000. Steven F. Christensen Award for Best Documentary on Mormon History, The Mormon History Association, 2001; and Amy Allen Price Military History Award, Board of the Utah State History.

A Winter with the Mormons: The 1852 Letters of Jotham Goodell. The Tanner Trust Fund, J. Willard Marriott Library, University of Utah, Salt Lake City, 2001.

Fort Limhi: The Mormon Adventure in Oregon Territory, 1855–1858. The Arthur H. Clark Co., Spokane, Wash., 2003; paperback edition, Utah State University Press, Logan, 2003.

Innocent Blood: Essential Narratives of the Mountain Meadows Massacre, ed. with Will Bagley. The Arthur H. Clark Co., Norman, Okla., 2008.

273

The Mormon Rebellion: America's First Civil War, 1857–1858, with Will Bagley. University of Oklahoma Press, Norman, Okla., 2011. Western Writers of America Spur for Best Western Nonfiction Historical; Reader's Award for Best Non-Fiction Book, *Salt Lake City Weekly*; Amy Allen Price Military History Award, Board of the Utah State History; and John Whitmer Historical Association Smith-Pettit Best Book in Latter Day Saint History.

"The Crisis at Fort Limhi, 1858," *Utah Historical Quarterly* Spring 1967.

"'O Wickedness, Where is Thy Boundary': The 1850 California Gold Rush Diary of George Shepard." Edited with Donald Buck and Merrill J. Mattes, *Overland Journal*, Winter 1992.

"Mormon Missionaries, the Utah War, and the 1858 Bannock Raid on Fort Limhi," *Montana The Magazine of Western History*, Autumn 2003.

"Garland Hurt, The American Friend of the Utahs," *Utah Historical Quarterly*, Spring 1994. Winner, the Dale L. Morgan Award, Board of the Utah State Historical Society, for best scholarly article of the year.

"Terror on the Trail: The Massacre at Mountain Meadows," *Spanish Traces*, Old Spanish Trail Assoc., Winter 2006.

"'Seeing the Elephant' in Utah: The Gold Rush and the Mormon Kingdom," *Western Windows: Studies on the America West,* ed. by Peter H. DeLafosse, Vol. 1, Utah Westerners, Salt Lake City, 2006.

"The Aiken Party Executions and the Utah War, 1857–1858," *Western Historical Quarterly*, Winter 2007.

"A Lion in the Path: Genesis of the Utah War, 1857–1858," *Utah Historical Quarterly*, Winter 2008. Nick Yengich Memorial Editors' Choice Award, Utah Board of State History, 2009.

BOOK REVIEWS

"Chief Joseph Country: Land of the Nez Perce," by Bill Gulick; Caxton Printers, Ltd.; *Salt Lake Tribune*, March 21, 1982.

"Mormon Thunder: A Documentary History of Jedediah Morgan Grant," by Gene A. Sessions; University of Illinois Press, 1982; *Salt Lake Tribune*, September 12, 1982.

"Orrin Porter Rockwell, Man of God, Son of Thunder," by Harold Schindler; Second Edition, Revised; University of Utah Press, 1983; *Salt Lake Tribune*, February 20, 1983.

"Landscape Turned Red: The Battle of Antietam," by Stephen W. Sears; Ticknor & Fields, New Haven and New York, 1983; *Salt Lake Tribune*, January 8, 1984.

"The 1838 Mormon War in Missouri," by Stephen LeSueur; University of Missouri Press, 1987; *Salt Lake Tribune*, August 23, 1987.

"National Parks, The American Experience," by Alfred Runter; University of Nebraska Press, Second Edition, Revised, 1987; *Overland Journal* 5:2 (Summer 1987).

"New Views of Mormon History, Essays in Honor of Leonard J. Arrington," edited by Davis Bitton and Maureen Ursenbach Beecher; University of Utah Press, 1987; *Salt Lake Tribune*, December 6, 1987.

"Judah P. Benjamin, The Jewish Confederate," by Eli N. Evans; The Free Press; *Salt Lake Tribune*, February 7, 1988.

"Establishing Zion, The Mormon Church in the American West, 1847–1869," by Eugene E. Campbell; Signature Books, 1988; *Salt Lake Tribune*, September 25, 1988.

"Juanita Brooks, Mormon Woman Historian," by Levi S. Peterson; University of Utah Press, 1988; *Salt Lake Tribune*, November 20, 1988.

"An Abundant Life: The Memoirs of Hugh B. Brown," edited by Edwin B. Firmage; Signature Books, 1988; *Salt Lake Tribune*, December 18, 1988.

"Zion in the Courts: A Legal History of the Church of Jesus Christ of Latter-day Saints, 1830–1900," by Edwin Brown Firmage and Richard Collin Mangrum; University of Illinois Press, 1988; *Salt Lake Tribune*, March 12, 1989.

"The City of the Saints," by Richard F. Burton, Foreword by Baker H. Morrow; reprinted by University Press of Colorado, 1990; *Overland Journal* Spring 1991.

"The Word of God: Essays on Mormon Scripture," edited by Dan Vogel; Signature Books, 1990; *Salt Lake Tribune*, November 11, 1990.

"Toward Understanding the New Testament," by Obert C. Tanner, Lewis M. Rogers, and Sterling M. McMurrin; Signature Books, 1990; *Salt Lake Tribune*, January 27, 1991.

"Glory Hunter: A Biography of Patrick Edward Connor," by Brigham D. Madsen, University of Utah Press, 1990; *Salt Lake Tribune*, March 3, 1991.

"Excavations of the Donner-Reed Wagons," by Bruce R. Hawkins and David B. Madsen; University of Utah Press, 1990; *Utah Historical Quarterly* 58:2 (Spring 1990).

"The Essential Parley P. Pratt" with Foreword by Peter L. Crawley; Signature Books, 1990, *Dialogue: A Journal of Mormon Thought* 24:3 (Fall 1991).

"Things in Heaven and Earth: The Life and Times of Wilford Woodruff, A Mormon Prophet," by Thomas G. Alexander; Signature Books, 1991; *Salt Lake Tribune*, February 16, 1992.

"Crossing the Plains: New and fascinating accounts of the hardships, controversies and courage experienced and chronicled by the 1847 pioneers on the Mormon Trail," by Harold Schindler, comp. and ed.; *The Salt Lake Tribune*, April 5–July 24, 1997; *Utah Historical Quarterly*, 66:3 (Summer 1998).

"Henry William Bigler: Soldier, Gold Miner, Missionary, Chronicler, 1815–1900," M. Guy Bishop; Utah State University Press, 1998; *Journal of Mormon History* (Fall 1999).

"The Texas Republic and the Mormon Kingdom of God," by Michael Scott Van Wagenen; Texas A&M University Press, 2002; *Western Historical Quarterly* 34:2 (Summer 2003).

"Utah Historians and the Reconstruction of Western History," by Gary Topping; University of Oklahoma Press, 2003; *Overland Journal*, Winter 2003–2004.

"Devils Will Reign: How Nevada Began," by Sally Zanjani; University of Nevada Press, 2006; *Utah Historical Quarterly* 75:1 (Winter 2007).

"The Mormon Vanguard Brigade of 1847," Ronald O. Barney, ed.; Utah State University Press, 2005; *Journal of Mormon History* 32:2 (Summer 2006).

"Reminiscences of Early Utah with Reply to Certain Statements by O. F. Whitney," by Robert N. Baskin; Signature Books Classics, reprint edition, with foreword by Brigham D. Madsen. 2006; *Journal of Mormon History* 33:3 (Fall 2007).

"Guarding the Overland Trails: The Eleventh Ohio Cavalry in the Civil War," by Robert Huhn Jones; The Arthur H. Clark Co., 2005; *Overland Journal*, Spring 2008.

"Massacre at Mountain Meadows," by Ronald W. Walker, Richard E. Turley, Jr., Oxford, 2008; *Western Historical Quarterly*, Autumn 2009.

Index

Pages with portraits of people or images
of places appear in *italic* type.
These topics appear under general headings:
American Indian nations, forts, trails and cutoffs, and rivers

Designed and set in Arno
by
Ariane C. Smith
Capital A Publications, Spokane, Washington

Printed on #60 Glatfelter Natural Offset
Limited to an edition of 1,000 copies

✣

ON THE FRONT ENDLEAF

"Utah, And the Overland Routes to it, from the Missouri River.
Published with 'Route from Liverpool to G.S.L. Valley'."
Liverpool, England: Franklin D. Richards, 1855.
COURTESY OF SPECIAL COLLECTIONS,
J. WILLARD MARRIOTT LIBRARY.

ON THE BACK ENDLEAF

Henry T. Williams. "A New Trans-Continental Map
of the Pacific R.R. and Routes of Overland Travel to Colorado,
Nebraska, the Black Hills, Utah, Idaho, Nevada, Montana, California
and the Pacific Coast." New York: American Photo-Litho. Co.,
1877. COURTESY OF THE DAVID RUMSEY
HISTORICAL MAP COLLECTION.